BARBY'S
Adventures with Tim

Two motorhoming newbies let loose in Europe!

Barbara Millington

Grosvenor House
Publishing Limited

This book is published by
Grosvenor House Publishing Ltd
Link House
140 The Broadway, Tolworth, Surrey, KT6 7HT.
www.grosvenorhousepublishing.co.uk

A CIP record for this book
is available from the British Library

ISBN 978-1-80381-218-2

Foreword

When Barbara handed me the draft of her first book I could sense a degree of trepidation in her approach. She needn't have worried, from the very first chapter I was drawn into the familiar subject matter by the informative and often humorous style of writing. Barbara manages to bring to life both the fascinating and mundane aspects of her travels in a truly captivating manner so that the reader can almost live the adventures and scrapes alongside her.

Tim Kent

Tim Kent, June 2022

Preface

Don't be confused! This book is neither about the fashion doll with a similar name to mine (who, of course, was named after me!) nor the Belgian cartoon reporter Tintin, though after one particular French haircut, Tim bore an uncanny resemblance! It's a chance to take a sideways look at the ups and downs of motorhoming and laugh with us – and at us – through mishaps and triumphs as we embarked on our first motorhome adventures around Europe.

Tim and I met in later life through singing, both of us having been involved in music throughout our lives, so it seemed like a wonderful idea, when we retired, to buy a motorhome and travel around Europe (while we still had the health and motivation), singing where possible, and indulging our other shared loves of history, language, good food, wine and lots of fun (plus occasional artistic opportunities for me).

Whilst on our first trip we had some wonderful and exciting adventures and I'd promised to share our experiences with friends and family via a blog: in itself a learning experience for me. Although the process of researching and putting together a record of our travels was something of a labour of love at times (especially when internet connections were playing up!), it was a very enjoyable pastime and enriched our knowledge of many of the locations we visited. The historical and background information regarding the places we visited is as accurate as I could make it, having mostly been gathered from the sites themselves or leaflets provided locally, with, occasionally, a little help from Google. In Spain our trusty Lonely Planet book (Ham, A., Davies, S., Gleeson, B., Isalska, A., Noble, I., Noble, J., Sainsbury, B., St Louis, R., (2016) *Lonely Planet's Best of Spain,* 1st edn, Lonely Planet Global Limited) came in very useful.

The blog gradually attracted a number of readers, many of whom encouraged my literary pursuits and eventually I took the decision to make it into a book; 'pretty much done', I thought, 'just a bit of editing to do'! Oh, how wrong I was!

Since then, actually making the blog into a book has been a journey all on its own! I was overwhelmed by the amount of advice on-line and at times became quite despondent about the chances of the book ever becoming a reality. It seemed that every time I felt I'd taken a step nearer to publication, I discovered more editing that was required: checking for inconsistencies, repetition, formatting, layout, grammar and punctuation, inserting and labelling photographs, the list seemed endless and, of course, everything seemed to take much longer than I imagined. There were times when I almost gave up and had to step away from the task for a while, but stubbornly didn't give in, although I definitely perfected the art of procrastination! In addition, I wanted to paint my own cover image (for completion, you understand) but, not being a cartoonist, had to look at, and try out, various different ideas.

However, you now have before you the proof that I finally got there! I do hope that you'll enjoy having a chuckle at our expense, whilst enjoying a virtual trip of Europe. Maybe you'll be inspired to experience motorhoming for yourselves (and hopefully not be put off it for life!), or perhaps encouraged to venture into Europe and drive on the 'wrong' (or perhaps I should say 'right') side of the road!

I'd like to thank Tim, with whom I've had so many wonderful adventures, for his support and patience as I've agonised over every decision, Gwynneth for her invaluable help with proof-reading, and all of those people who faithfully followed the blog and provided encouragement. (Blogs from later adventures are available at: https://2shadesineurope.wordpress.com filled with many more exciting learning experiences!)

Table of Contents

Introduction

As Tim and I were both almost complete camping novices and also fairly newly-together, our decision to buy a motorhome came after much deliberation and research. Some of our family and friends were amused to speculate that spending several weeks in such close proximity would test our relationship! (Cynical lot!)

However, we set off on our first trip and, despite lots of 'rookie' errors and weather and road conditions that could have been kinder at times, maintained our enthusiasm even when faced with disappointments, difficulties and bits of the van dropping off here and there! Surviving steep-sided mountain passes, and narrowly avoiding low bridges, inflatable arches and supermarket barriers became just part of a normal day as we motored along, occasionally stopping to savour an amazing moment.

The book's three main sections cover the first motorhome trips we made: our first major journey was to France, Spain and just over the border into Portugal; on the second trip we again visited France and Spain and spent more time in Portugal; for the third excursion we ventured through Germany and Switzerland to explore the treasures of Italy and Sicily, finally heading back to north eastern Spain for the last few weeks. Our trips were made pre-Brexit and pre-Covid, so there may have been a few changes since then, but I'm pretty sure, at the time of writing, that at least Pompeii and the Colosseum are still there!

There are details about campsites and local eateries that we used, and some fascinating historic background information about cities, famous buildings and Roman (and other) remains visited. There's also an Information section at the end that, if you read it, will arm you with heaps more information about vehicles and sites than we had at the start of our first adventure! In addition, I've added a table showing the location of the sites and aires we stayed on.

Most of all, I hope you'll enjoy reading about our travels. Off we go!

The Trial Run: Near Robin Hood's Bay, North Yorkshire – March

Having finally bought our motorhome (more detail in Information section) – hereinafter referred to as 'the van' – we decided to try it out at **The Flask Pub and Holiday Park** between Whitby and Robin Hood's Bay on the Yorkshire coast, where Tim had sung, as a teenager, with his band: 'Tim Kent and the James Brothers!' Not quite Back by Popular Demand after about 50 years! Friends Andy and Pam (seasoned campers, they'd probably just come to have a laugh at our inexperience!) joined us briefly on our first day for fish and chips in Robin Hood's Bay, a picturesque village, with cobbled lanes and fishermen's cottages crammed together near a secluded harbour once haunted by smugglers.

The scenery around there is stunning and, after our friends had set off for home, Tim and I embarked on what should have been a very pleasant five-mile walk back. Somehow or other we turned off the track at the wrong point and ended up on a 10-mile cross-country hike, that saw us stumbling over rough terrain and attempting some very dodgy manoeuvres as we endeavoured to find our way back on a pitch-black night, all the more worrying when both of our phones eventually ran out of battery! We began to wonder whether we'd make it back to the van and, at one point, his outside light having been activated as we walked past, a very puzzled householder kindly came out to inform us that if we kept going we'd very soon end up in the sea; now that would have been a shock!

Just our luck a major storm had also decided to visit that weekend, and the following night was spent rocking in the gale force wind and 'enjoying' the hammer of torrential rain on the roof! Thankfully, we survived the baptism of fire and the van gave us confidence in its resilience, in readiness for our planned trip to Spain a few weeks later.

The First Trip:
France, Spain and (just)
Portugal – April to August

Home to France – April

At last we arrived at the weekend we'd been anticipating for so long and set off (albeit considerably later than planned) to head south, making it to the Channel Tunnel crossing with seconds to spare.

The crossing was trouble-free and, having left a cold and rainy England, we arrived in...an equally cold and rainy France! It was after 8pm (French time) by the time we reached Le Mans and headed off, full of excitement and anticipation, for our first night on an 'aire' (see Information section). From the description (All the Aires of France, Vicarious Books), the one we had chosen looked lovely, close to a river and shaded by trees. Sadly lots of other campers had had the same idea and the place was full by the time we got there, so we followed the directions to the next one and ended up spending our first night in **Mezerey**; and it was a pretty 'mezereyble' car park on a wet and windy night, with only a lorry's trailer unit for company.

Spain at Last: France to Getaría and San Sebastian – April

The rain was still torrential as we left the next day, with a temperature of 6° and, being still a little wary of the van shower, experienced our first shower in a motorway service area; it was, in fact, very clean and well maintained. By 2pm we were an hour north of Bordeaux and the temperature had reached the dizzy heights of 16°.

We were looking forward to getting further south for some warm sunshine and made good progress, crossing the border into Spain later in the day. Tim was keen to visit Getaría, a place he had visited previously and, after a tortuous tour of the town trying to find parking places for a 7.5m van, we finally managed to get one on the harbour front that seemed okay. At the Mayflower restaurant nearby, we were lucky enough to secure a table overlooking the harbour, so that we could keep an eye on our pride and joy (the van, of course!), whilst enjoying a delicious meal of Merluza à la Parilla; *merluza* is 'hake' and *parilla* literally translates as 'grill', but this was more like an outside fire, with a grid. That way of cooking fish is a speciality in that area; Tim considers it to be some of the best fish he's tasted in the world and he's tasted quite a lot!

Unfortunately, no overnight stays were allowed in Getaría, so we had to head back to an aire in San Sebastian. (More information about San Sebastian in later sections.) I had put in the postcode for the aire we'd chosen, but it seemed our satnav 'friend' had other ideas and took us up a **very** steep, winding, single shale track, that came to an abrupt end, with no sign of the desired aire. It was very dark by then and, as Tim amazingly managed to turn the van around in the tiniest of spaces, skidding on the gravel road, perilously close to a sheer drop at the side, the smell of burning rubber emanating from the tyres reminded me that, just before we'd left home, I'd noticed the herbs in the rack had spelt out MORT (Mint, Oregano, Rosemary and Thyme) and hoped it wasn't a portent of doom. Thankfully we survived (otherwise this would be a very short book!) and made it to the desired **Area de Bereo** by around 10.30pm, somehow squeezing the van into a space hardly big enough for a sardine.

On investigation it transpired that, although co-ordinates were given against the aire in the information I had, I hadn't read to the bottom of the paragraph, where it stated: "...actual co-ordinates are ..." now, why on earth didn't they put the 'actual' co-ordinates at the top? Answers on a postcard please!

Cáceres, Seville and (briefly) Portugal – May

We managed a decent night's sleep, then breakfasted on some of Tim's mum's home-made marmalade, with proper coffee (using our nifty little filter cone). A mammoth trip of 663kms followed to our next stop in **Cáceres**, arriving late afternoon.

At last the temperature had reached a comfortable 20° and we arrived just in time, before the aire totally filled up for the night, the last van to arrive being a disgruntled Frenchman, who (unreasonably, we thought) was complaining that there wasn't enough room. Everyone (except us) then proceeded to get out all of their specialist cleaning equipment and set about washing and polishing every inch of their vehicles, with gusto. Incidentally, you might be interested to know that *gusto* comes originally from the Latin *gustus* meaning 'tasting, flavour, sense of taste', which is the source of French *goût* and Spanish and Italian *gusto*. In this sense it has evolved to mean 'a taste for life' and from there to describe vigorous activities. The man with the biggest van spent over an hour polishing and caressing his prized possession. Meanwhile, Tim and I sloped off in search of the restorative effects of a local bar in the beautiful old town, where there was a wonderful atmosphere as families gathered to watch entertainment in the plaza.

Figure 1 Dancing in Cáceres, Spain

After a much needed beer we decided to eat out and had an excellent meal of hors d'oeuvres, fillet steak, chips and roasted vegetables with a glass of wine, followed by a glass of brandy each and a coffee for Tim, all for the magnificent total of €34! Our evening was nicely rounded off with a chat with two Dutch couples sitting at an adjacent table (who spoke extremely good English).

The following morning, whilst topping up the fresh water in the van, I inadvertently started winding in the water hose before turning the tap off and had an impromptu shower (yet another lesson learned)! After we had finally dried out the interior of the cab and my clothes and hair (!) we set off for Seville, stopping only for a quick lunch and arrived by around 2.30pm at the **Area de Autocaravanas de Sevilla**, near the river: a large tarmac area, with a reasonable amount of room between vans and accommodating around 75. It had all the basic facilities, 'basic' being the operative word, but with the particular benefit of being a locked and monitored compound. A less attractive feature was that it was adjacent to a very busy industrial vehicle unit and although Wi-Fi was available it was necessary to sit in a rather smelly and unpleasant reception area to access it. We were very pleased to get the last electric point, then cycled over to the local Aldi for supplies (home from home!). A celebratory bottle of champagne helped us to relax thoroughly into the evening whilst chatting to our camping neighbours, Colin and Sue. Seeing their van's Spanish registration we'd greeted them with *Hola* (Spanish for 'hi'), but quickly learned that they had moved from the UK to Spain's east coast some years earlier.

The champagne had clearly had the desired effect of relaxing us, to the point that we overslept the next morning! Consequently, it was a little later than planned that we walked into the centre of Seville, around a mile and a half along the side of the river.

Figure 2 Flamenco Dancers in Seville, Spain

Seville is a beautiful city full of character, and we sat with coffee near one of the big fountains watching some flamenco dancers then wandered around the main centre before heading back to the van. Our new friends, Colin and Sue, invited us over for drinks and nibbles, which ended up being our main meal of the day.

Seville is – allegedly – the third most cycle-friendly city in Europe but we were a little wary of leaving our bikes in the city centre, having heard that some fellow campers had had theirs stolen the previous day. Thankfully we found a cycle shop and bought an even more robust lock than we already had, so felt a bit safer when we locked them up in the city centre and, sizzling in 30°+, cooled down with a beer in the plaza.

We felt that we couldn't go to Seville and not visit the wonderful Cathedral, although it did involve queuing in the sun for quite some time; oh the suffering we endure on our travels! The cathedral is apparently the third largest in Christendom (so large that it was impossible to fit it into one photo) and is an amazing building, with an ostentatious interior that defies description! It took us around two hours to look around and then climb the 35 flights to the top of the tower for a panoramic view of the city.

Figure 3 Seville Cathedral from the tower

Gluttons for punishment, we then joined another queue to go into the Alcázar (derived from the Arabic word for a castle or palace), which was very peaceful and extremely beautiful in different ways, with many Muslim influences in the decor, huge expanses of delightful gardens with fascinating water features and numerous nooks and crannies to explore.

Figure 4 Alcazar, Seville, Spain

Having been on our feet for about five hours by then, we were relieved to relax at a little tapas bar close to the cathedral while we watched beautifully-dressed people arrive, some on foot, others in cars, taxis and numerous variations of horse-drawn carriages, to attend a wedding in the cathedral. The sound of music then drew us to the main route through the city, where a procession of decorated floats was followed by a band and accompanied by flowers thrown from the windows above! Such a wonderful, vibrant atmosphere, it was lovely to be a part of it.

Figure 5 Procession in Seville, Spain

Our final visit of the day was a guided tour of the magnificent bull ring, learning about its history and exploring the areas behind the scenes, before cycling back along the river.

As it was only around 1½ hours away, it seemed like a good idea to 'pop' over the border to Portugal for at least one night. Hah! It seemed that most of the population of Seville had made the same decision and our journey took about twice as long as we'd anticipated. We arrived at the lovely resort of **Manta Rota**, just over the border, but were really disappointed to find that the aire, that accommodated 100 vans (or units, as they are sometimes called) was completely full. Whilst pausing by the entrance, considering what to do, the 'commandante' of the site came out and told us in no uncertain terms that we couldn't stay there (well, our knowledge of Portuguese was pretty much nil, but her body language and vocal tone didn't leave us in much doubt!). We left, dejectedly, but then realised that just across the way there were around 50 vans parked on a car park, so we joined them.

After a walk around the pretty little seaside resort, we had dinner al fresco, whilst enjoying the sound of the sea on the gorgeous beach around 50 metres away; then, feeling very relaxed, we went for a walk and ended up sitting on the deserted beach, enjoying a beautiful, romantic sunset. Suddenly, Tim shouted, "Don't look Barbara!", but it was too late, I'd already spotted the lone – very well toned – naturist making a dash for the waves about 100 metres away! I was ready to join him, but Tim restrained me and I settled for a discreet photo as a memento.

Figure 6 On the beach at Manta Rota

Back in Spain: First Stop Casares – May

A lack of toilet emptying facilities on the car park at Manta Rota influenced our decision to return to Spain, rather than stay another night. By late afternoon we'd arrived at a very small aire (**Area de Casares**), adjacent to the Tourist Information Office, just on the edge of Casares (not the same place that we stayed at two nights ago, this village is just north of Málaga on the Costa del Sol) and went for a walk into the very pretty *pueblo blanco* (Spanish for 'white village or town'), nestled in the mountains. That area of Andalusia, particularly around

Málaga, is famous for its attractive whitewashed towns and large villages.

Figure 7 Casares, Spain

Being in a rather exposed position, we were rocked to sleep at night due to the (external!) wind. After a morning exploring the village again, we purchased a leaflet of local walks from the Tourist Information Office and chose one that claimed to be low-moderate difficulty, with an estimated time of three hours and which, it claimed, could be done on horseback, bicycle or on foot; thankfully we chose the latter (well, we hadn't brought the horses with us!). We were struggling to find the starting point for the walk, so went back to ask the Tourist Information lady, who very patiently (not!) pointed out to us that the first waymarker was actually directly opposite our van door (oops!), so off we went.

I must say that one of the major challenges was simply spotting the waymarkers. I know, you're probably thinking, "Well, they couldn't even see the one right in front of them" but, in the main, they were just green and white splodges of paint randomly applied to trees, stones, fences, posts etc, at varying heights, many of them quite faded and often non-existent! In addition, the map and directions were, to put it mildly, very rudimentary.

Nonetheless, we were enjoying the walk and just getting nicely into our stride when we came upon a large German Shepherd dog, lying right in our path; so, heeding the well-known saying 'let sleeping dogs lie', we tried a detour, only to be put off course by another large (and loose) dog whose barking set off about another dozen in the area. With griffon vultures circling overhead, we decided it would be safer to try yet another detour by road, adding approximately a mile to the walk, but better safe than sorry. Unfortunately, we then had inordinate difficulty getting back on track and, indeed, staying on track due to the random placing of the waymarkers! However we were making reasonable progress, whilst enjoying stunning views of the Rock of Gibraltar and the coast of North Africa.

We finally reached the foot of the valley with the village above us and, despite the cool mountain breeze, we were really looking forward to a refreshing drink, but first we had to find the path. After numerous fruitless attempts we armed ourselves with bamboo canes and beat down five-foot high thistles so that we could scramble down the bank and across a dry river bed to make our ascent up the very steep and craggy cliff side. I can't imagine how anyone would have got bikes through that! After around 4½ hours walking in total, the cool drink was very welcome and we treated ourselves to some steak from the local butcher, which was later washed down with an excellent bottle of vino produced at Tim's brother's vineyard in the south of France.

Ronda and the Pileta Caves – May

We'd checked into a very nice campsite (**El Sur**) for the night so, once parked up, we free-wheeled downhill the two miles or so into the amazing little town of Ronda; perched at the top of enormous cliffs; the last Islamic stronghold on the Iberian Peninsula.

Figure 8 Cliffs in Ronda, Spain

The Arab Baths, situated at the foot of the cliffs, close to what would have formerly been the gates of the city, are fascinating; dating back to around the 13th century, they are extremely well preserved, with reception area and hot and cold rooms.

At the top of a tower was the site of a wheel that would have operated a pulley system to bring water up from the river and then along the aqueduct to the baths.

Figure 9 Arab Baths, Ronda, Spain

We also descended around 80 metres (or approx 226 steps!) to visit the excellent 14th century 'Secret Mine' below the Palace of the Moorish King (which, sadly, was in dire need of restoration). The mine is believed to have been constructed as a hiding place during the wars but, unfortunately for its inhabitants, their idea was thwarted as their attackers cut off the water supply, forcing them to surrender.

Our visit to Ronda finished with a visit to the bull ring, which is, in fact, even bigger than the one in Seville, with two tiers of seating, and we were fascinated to look around behind the scenes; the photo shows the rope and pulley system to open the doors and release the bulls into the ring.

Figure 10 Ronda's Bull Ring, Spain

Figure 11 Stalls in Bull Ring, Ronda, Spain

We then, of course, had to make a supreme effort to cycle (or mostly walk, to be honest!) uphill all the way back to our campsite!

The Pileta Caves, which were discovered in 1905 by a local farmer when searching for bat droppings as fertiliser for his land, were only around five miles away. Our journey there the following day was a 'white knuckle' ride of tortuous narrow and winding mountain roads (luckily, we only met a few vehicles en route, as the sheer drop of several thousand feet was very intimidating). There were then a couple of hundred steps up to the entrance and ticket office, so we weren't keen on climbing them too many times, but thankfully we managed to get tickets for the next visit, that took us around 800 metres inside (about 20% of the total area of caves).

Most of the chambers we passed through were around 12-15 metres high, but some were as high as 30 metres and the formations within them were amazing. However, the most astonishing feature of the Pileta Caves is that remains found there, in particular a number of cave drawings, are at least 32000 years old! Some of the drawings were remarkably clear: horses, goats, bulls and (especially interesting as the caves are many miles from the sea) fish and seals. It was quite humbling to walk in the footsteps of mankind from so long ago. Understandably, no photographs were allowed inside.

Estepona – May

After a quick visit to Carrefour – and a rather too close shave with the overhead gantry – we made ourselves at home at **Camping Parque Tropical** near Estepona, then realised we had forgotten one essential item for our evening meal: potatoes! Having seen an Aldi not far away, we decided to cycle there, but the path, on the inside of the crash barrier of a busy dual carriageway, with its associated debris and hazards, took me more than a little out of my comfort zone! I was very glad to get back in one piece!

Having had quite a busy few days (I'm sure your heart bleeds for us!), we spent a day relaxing in the sun and another day having lunch with some friends, who had, coincidentally, arranged a long weekend in Puerta de la Duquesa, about 12 miles away from where we were staying. Later that evening, after a walk along the nearby beach, we spent a very pleasant evening with our campsite neighbours from Belgium, who shared a good two thirds of a bottle of brandy with us. The ten yards between their van and ours seemed strangely longer on the way back than it had earlier!

The following two days definitely confirmed that the rain in Spain does not stay mainly on the plain! We were glad to have done our three loads of washing earlier, although I'd had a bit of a panic on returning to the laundry to empty two concurrent wash loads, only to find that the electricity had gone off, leaving both loads wallowing miserably. Thankfully, everything was eventually retrieved unharmed and dried on our nifty rotary drier during the better weather.

Having decided to take advantage of the excellent pool on site, we were puzzled to find the door to the pool area locked, although it was after the advertised opening time. When we asked at reception, the attendant commented: "You must be English, the Spanish would never swim in this weather" but it was a heated indoor pool!!! Anyway, at least the rain gave us a chance for more relaxing, with a brief evening walk along the beach again in a break between showers.

Granada – May

The rain continued to follow us and, as we left Estepona, passing the resorts of Marbella and Málaga, we ran into one of the most horrendous rainstorms imaginable. We were glad to arrive safely at our next campsite, **Fuente del Lobo**, near Granada, but had to sit outside it for an hour, until reception opened. Once we had been admitted through the large and rather unwelcoming gate we found that we (and a very friendly but seemingly wild dog) pretty much had the run of the place; the person on reception was mostly absent, there was no promised shop or café and the pitches were quite overgrown and unkempt.

Figure 12 Granada and Sierra Nevada Mountains, Spain

We had actually booked this campsite in advance, thinking that, as it was only a few kilometres out of Granada, we could cycle there. Hah! We hadn't reckoned on the fact that it was nestled in the Sierra Nevada mountains and there was no way we were going to attempt a cycle ride on those narrow mountain roads! Unfortunately, the only alternative was to drive the van along them, which was not too easy either and, although we were very pleased to find a large parking area for motorhomes at the Alhambra Palace, it was a very expensive one! We figured it was worth it to be able to visit the Alhambra, so we happily walked down to the ticket office, where there was a long queue. After around 45 minutes, an announcement was made that there were no more tickets available for the afternoon; although rather disappointed, we decided to take the time to explore Granada. Unfortunately the clouds thickened and the rain began around the same time, which did tend to take the pleasure out of our afternoon, especially as I had on open sandals and neither of us was wearing very warm clothes.

We had some tapas at a nice little restaurant and had a look around Granada and some of the free areas of the Alhambra before making our way back to the campsite for the evening, again entirely alone. A very helpful young man at the Tourist Information Office had advised us that to be sure of tickets for the Alhambra Palace we would need to be in the queue for around 6.30am, so we decided to set our alarm for 5.00am, as the Alhambra was one place I was particularly looking forward to visiting.

5.00am came around very quickly and it was still dark, so negotiating the mountain roads seemed even more treacherous. We arrived at the Alhambra at exactly 6.30; thankfully it wasn't raining, but the dashboard temperature in the van said 5° as we set off to stand in the queue, wearing as many warm clothes as we could muster. We were around 40th in the queue, even at that time, and the day seemed to be dawning with a clear sky as we waited, shivering, and chatted to a couple from Argentina who were behind us in the queue. As time progressed we learned that only 156 tickets for the Palace were available for the day. We then discovered that, hidden from our view and with no visible sign, there was another, similar queue, where payment was credit card only (ours was cash only) and that was also included in the 156. However, we decided that as we were 40th in the main queue we should stay put and we would be fine.

At 8.00am the ticket office finally opened and the large screen above the door clearly stated 156 tickets for the Palace. As we gradually edged forward we were astonished that many of the individuals at the front of the queue were buying multiples of tickets that they appeared to then be taking away, perhaps to sell on? The figures on the screen over the door were dropping dramatically and then, with just four people in front of us, went to zero and the announcement came that no tickets remained for the Palace, just for the gardens and less well-preserved buildings. I cannot begin to tell you how utterly disappointed we were as we bought our tickets for the gardens and went through the turnstile, but our frustration and anger increased when, a few minutes later, our new Argentinian friends joined us, only to tell us that they had managed to get the full ticket for the Palace!! We complained to the office staff and went with them to the front of the queue again, where the board was now showing one ticket remaining but they refused to make any allowances, saying only that sometimes tickets were returned or miscalculations were made. I have to say that, as well as still shivering for about another hour after our long, cold wait, my frustration about the shambolic organization of the ticket sales lasted for some time. (Handy tip: Buy tickets for the Alhambra well in advance of your visit!)

Figure 13 Alhambra Palace Gardens, Granada, Spain

After walking around the gardens and 'permitted areas' of the Alhambra, we left and wandered around the streets of Granada. Thankfully, at least, the day, although cloudy, was a little better than yesterday so we were able to sit and take in the fabulous view.

Figure 14 Alhambra, Granada, Spain

The Arab area of the town was well worth a visit, with its fascinating streets full of colourful stalls and shops. I was thrilled to find that they have such things as *teterías* (*té* is Spanish for 'tea' and a *tetería* is a 'tea-shop'), as well as cafeterías, so we eventually went in to one and tried some of their spiced tea and *dulces* ('sweet pastries'). Incidentally, we had also seen quite a few *ferreterías*, but as we didn't fancy a ferret we hadn't gone in.

Finally we visited Granada's huge cathedral, completely different in style from that in Seville, but nonetheless very impressive. Apparently, it was started in the early 16th century and took over 180 years to build, but is still not finished; only one of its planned 80-metre towers was ever started and even that remains half-finished! They certainly don't rush things here! The word *mañana* (literally 'tomorrow') comes to mind!!

The rain had returned and we gradually made our way back up the steep hill to the van, paid the almost €30 parking fee for the 12 hours and returned to our very unwelcoming and unkempt campsite in the mountains. I checked my phone's pedometer and found that we'd walked over 11 miles during the day, no wonder we were worn out!

Cartagena – May

We couldn't face the prospect of being disappointed at the Alhambra again, so, vowing to return on a future trip, we decided to leave Granada (and, we hoped, the rain!) and checked out of the most expensive and least pleasant site we'd experienced so far. During our journey to Cartagena, we actually saw some blue sky and sunshine and a temperature of over 20° for the first time for over a week. Finally we arrived at an exceptionally clean and welcoming aire (**Area Autocaravanas Cartagena**), not far from the centre of Cartagena, which was less than half the price of our last site in Granada.

The sun was shining and, after a nice relaxed morning, we walked the kilometre or so to the bus stop and caught the bus into Cartagena. After stopping for a cool beer part way along the main route to the port, we reached the Tourist Information Office just as the clock was striking 2pm, when the doors shut until 5pm; the customary Spanish *siesta* can be frustrating! We had, however, already heard that there is a huge Roman amphitheatre in Cartagena, so we went into the adjoining museum and from there to the amphitheatre itself: an awe-inspiring place, built in the 1st century BC, which has been amazingly well preserved considering that, or perhaps because, less than 20 years ago, it seemed no-one knew of its existence!

Figure 15 Amphitheatre, Cartagena, Spain

How can you lose something that big you may ask! Well, a whole town's worth of houses and shops and a huge Church, had been built over it many years ago, even using the capitals and sections from Corinthian columns as building materials! But at last we got the chance to appear on stage in Spain!

Figure 16 Amphitheatre, Cartagena, Spain

From the amphitheatre we continued wandering through the city and were constantly amazed at the amount of excavation sites and Roman (and later) ruins. After sampling a *Café Asiático* (a local speciality and, it seemed, just a good excuse for the Spanish to add lots of alcohol and sugar to their coffee), we ventured uphill and passed a fairly complete bull ring, though in serious need of TLC, whilst visiting one of the three castles guarding the city from marauding armies. From the very interesting video we saw, we learned that their armies were regularly defeated, and the fortunes of Cartagena have fluctuated considerably over the last three thousand years!

As the clouds were beginning to reduce the heat of the sun somewhat, we decided to head back for the bus, but on our way we were drawn into a ferretaria and came out with....a salad bowl, no ferrets to be seen! (The name comes from the Latin *ferrum* – 'iron' – and, of course, refers to a hardware store.)

The sun was shining again the following day, so we made our way back into Cartagena and this time headed for the Roman Forum and baths area, an exceptionally well-presented exhibit that included a section of Roman road and some original murals.

Cartagena seemed to be trying very hard to re-invent itself after a depression; there were innumerable half-demolished buildings and many slum areas, but there were also some beautiful Baroque-style buildings and, of course, its impressive Roman past, which was clearly in the process of being excavated at various points around the city.

We bought some supplies at the little supermarket down the road and ate our meal al fresco, enjoying the evening sunshine.

Benidorm (via Villajoyosa) – May

As we approached Benidorm, Tim suggested that we go via Villajoyosa, a very pretty resort, whose history as a town dates back to the 6th century, although the town as it is known today was founded in 1293. Throughout the centuries, Villajoyosa (literally 'joyful town') has traded in olive oil, cereals, wine and shipbuilding, but today is most famous for its chocolate, the most well-known being Valor chocolate, that can be found in most shops and supermarkets throughout Spain.

We drove down to the one-way, single track road along the sea front where there seemed to be a fiesta of some kind taking place, so it was quite busy, with stalls on the beach and lots of people milling around. Suddenly we were faced with an inflatable arch across the road that was about the height of the van (!) and was slightly offset so that we could not quite approach it straight on. We had no option but to go for it and almost removed it from its moorings as it clung to the roof for a short distance, oops! The policeman on duty was not at all amused but we pointed out that we had no choice! A large delivery van was following us, but had stopped to make a delivery, so I'm not sure whether the inflatable arch survived the rest of the day!

After escaping from there unscathed but traumatised, we drove up to the mountain village of Sella – where Tim had stayed on a previous occasion – to calm down. The mountains there are quite spectacular and *bancales* ('terracing', enabling the steep slopes to be farmed) have been created high on the mountain sides since the early 8th century, when much of the Iberian Peninsula was governed by Muslims who had come over from North Africa.

The clouds were gathering again and we were beginning to wonder whether the rain really was following us. We called in at Maria's restaurant where we had a traditional Spanish meal of salchichons (sausages to you!), salad, dried and soaked broad beans (don't ask, but quite tasty) and then proper traditional paella made with chicken and rabbit, delicious! After leaving Maria's we called at the local bar in the village's *Plaza Mayor* ('main square'), where we arranged with Toni, the proprietor, the details for our first proposed forthcoming gig, under our stage name of 'Two Shades of Grey' (referring to the colour of our hair of course!).

Having stocked up with essentials at Carrefour we arrived at **Camping Benidorm** fairly late in the evening, got pitched up and put away our purchases: wine, beer, brandy, hmm seems to be a theme there. We were struggling with suitable places to store the wine and brandy and had to resort to putting the reds under the bed!

Thankfully the rain had passed us by without lingering, so we had a brief walk before settling down for the evening.

The next day dawned bright and sunny at last! We caught the bus from directly opposite the campsite into Benidorm and walked along the very busy Playa Levante, then caught the tram into Villajoyosa where it was much quieter; the fiesta and the inflatable arch had gone; who knows whether it had survived the day intact? We enjoyed some delicious designer tapas in the Taverna Valenciana El Pòsit – a little restaurant overlooking the beach – washed down with a rather copious amount of wine, then staggered across the road and relaxed on the beach in wall to wall sunshine and 28° for a couple of hours, bliss! We even managed a little paddle in the sea before making our way back towards Benidorm, where we met up with my son-in-law's parents, John and Christine, who lived nearby at that time. It was really nice to have a chat and a few drinks with them before getting the bus back to our campsite.

By now three weeks had passed since we left the UK and we'd travelled almost 3000 miles. We had, of course, become fluent Spanish speakers (ha ha!), well, as long as we didn't have to ask for anything too tricky, or understand the reply!

Amazingly more blue sky and sunshine greeted us the next day and we made use of the train to Villajoyosa again. This time we had one of the nicest pizzas we've ever had for our lunch (at Sole Mare Pizza) and then made it just across the road for another attempt at an (almost) all-over tan on the gorgeous beach there. Our peace was shattered by a couple of teenage girls keen to ensure that everyone on the beach could hear them, especially a teenage boy close by who was treated to a very sensuous demonstration of the application of sun-tan lotion.

In the evening we sat outside the van for our cup of tea, listening to the chirruping of the cicadas and the distant call of bingo numbers late into the night.

Calpé – May

As we left Benidorm we called in again at Sella and had a short walk down to an old mill, believed to date back to Moorish times, where we picked some oranges and lemons from the trees on our way, delicious.

Our next campsite – **Camping La Merced** – at Calpé, around 30 miles north of Benidorm, was much quieter than the last campsite and we soon felt very much at home.

Figure 17 Playa de Fosse in Calpé, Spain

The site was only around 5-10 minutes' walk from the fabulous Playa de Fosse close to Calpé's famous Peñón de Ifach rock (*Peñón* is Spanish for 'crag' or 'rocky outcrop') and, what's more, only about three minutes' walk from Aldi! Tim, however, found out to his cost that our campsite is a particular favourite of mosquitoes.

Having dealt with two loads of clothes before lunch, we collapsed, exhausted, on the beach in the afternoon, until some workmen had the effrontery to make a noise while we were trying to relax! Then a couple with two very small children sat about two metres away from us; a lovely family, but much too close for comfort! Our ability to attract noisy neighbours was clear!

After a sizzling night (!) Tim was forced to acknowledge that he shouldn't have fallen asleep in the sun without first applying sun cream, but he bravely tackled the cycle path from very close to the campsite, that took us right into the town centre.

After parking the bikes, we negotiated the 'tourist trail' of 'gift' shops and peddlers, without purchasing a single fake watch or handbag. We did, though, buy some detailed maps and, over a glass of wine and a coffee, planned our proposed trip into the mountains next week.

Figure 18 Calpé, Spain

A husband and wife duo singing to backing tracks was our evening entertainment at a nearby hotel and we picked up a few ideas, both good and bad! They were very slick at their routine, but, of course, when singing to holidaymakers, it's possible to continually do the same 'set', as the audience is constantly changing.

The following morning, we cycled to the promenade close to the Playa de Fosse and had a traditional Spanish breakfast: orange juice, coffee and *tostados* ('toasted baguettes') with pulped fresh tomato and olive oil: delicious and all for €2.50 each!

Our afternoon rehearsal in the campsite bar was to an audience of two small, rather fractious children and their mum, who, at least, appreciated us as a distraction if nothing else. We felt that we sounded at least as good as the couple we'd seen last night; maybe not quite as 'slick', but at least we hadn't lost whatever 'mojo' we'd had!

The couple of hours' relaxation on the beach was soon forgotten when, just after getting back to the van, we realised we'd forgotten to get vegetables for our evening meal; I went back to the supermarket while Tim put the chicken in the oven but on my way back I met him returning to the supermarket, as the potatoes had gone rotten! Just to complicate things further, the roasting bags had wedged themselves behind the drawer and I spent an hour or more trying to remove them with various implements and much frustration. We ended up eating at about 10pm! So much for relaxing!

Our morning plans also went a bit awry; whilst enjoying our al fresco breakfast, the time somehow got itself round to 10.30am, now, how did that happen? We'd been told that the bus to the tram station left just outside the campsite at 11.00am, so had to get ourselves quickly into gear, only to then discover that buses are less frequent on a Sunday (we'd lost track of the days!); we ended up walking into town and getting a taxi to the station – oh well!

After that, our journey went smoothly (we should have relished those rare moments!); the change of tram at Benidorm was seamless and we caught the bus to join my son-in-law's parents for a drink on the balcony of their apartment, with a beautiful view of the Mediterranean coastline.

After a pleasant meal in Benidorm's old town overlooking the sea, we said our goodbyes; our next meeting with them would be in the UK in September for our joint grandson's christening. Tim and I made our way back to the station, arriving in plenty of time for our 6.18pm tram back, so we got out our books and read for a little while. We were suddenly aware that a tram had arrived at the opposite platform, but going in our direction. Dashing across the tracks we made it to the door...just as the tram pulled out. We couldn't understand how we could have been at the wrong side, but then realised that that station is actually a passing point on what is otherwise a single-track line, so trams only use the platform we were waiting on when there is another tram coming the other way at the same time! I'm sure the tram driver and the two teenage boys on the platform thought it was very funny.... we were less amused as, although there was another tram to Benidorm in half an hour, we had missed our connection back to Calpé and the next one meant a wait of 1½ hours!

Fortunately it was a balmy evening, with a beautiful warm breeze, so we tried to be positive and made the most of our unexpected sojourn on Benidorm station, then, again, with a coffee, at Calpé as we then had a half hour wait for the bus back to the campsite. The bus eventually arrived...and then drove off, empty! We looked again at the timetable and realised the 9.10pm bus only ran in July and August! By then, a good hour's walk back to the campsite was not something either of us relished (especially not in my new shoes!), so we phoned the taxi company (thankfully we'd taken a business card in the morning) and eventually arrived back at about 10.00pm, a journey of four hours! Nothing is simple is it? Maybe we should plan a little more!

After an exhausting morning cleaning and washing we bravely forced ourselves to have another cycle ride after lunch, this time around Calpé's iconic rock that stands at 332m high. It is a popular challenge for climbers and notices warn that they must begin their climb before 10.00am as otherwise the sun becomes too hot by the time they reach the top. Again, the cycle path is excellent and it was a very peaceful and interesting ride, with beautiful views across the bay and we continued along the promenade towards town and rewarded ourselves with a couple of cool drinks whilst we sat and watched the world go by.

We had noticed, during our trip so far, that the ex-pat community is huge, in that part of Spain particularly; huge in both senses of the word: no six-packs, but lots of large barrels! We do wonder whether the lifestyle there has something to do with that too; after all, on a hot day, what could be nicer than a long cool beer or wine? (Suggestions please!) We had seen some people having a Baileys with ice for breakfast recently, which seemed a bit extreme, although I can't deny that we've occasionally had a celebratory Bucks Fizz at breakfast time, only when appropriate, naturally!

Our musings were interrupted by the excitable young women at the adjacent table (how do we keep finding these noisy people?) who were discussing the merits of tattoos, interspersed with that frequently over-used and entirely unnecessary adjective that begins with 'f'. We had to smile when one of them declared that she'd had her trimmed pubic hair dyed green and a tattoo above it saying 'keep off the grass'!

Tim cycled for a haircut the next morning – thereafter to be known as 'Sean' ☺ – and after lunch we had another rehearsal in preparation for our 'gig' at Toni's bar in Sella on Friday evening. As we set off for our hard-earned siesta on the beach, we chatted briefly to our neighbour, who mentioned he was having chicken and chips for tea. Well, that was it, our planned quiche and salad just didn't cut it with Tim any more, so the evening saw us at the little restaurant across the road, tucking into chicken and chips. As an added bonus, though, we managed to get ourselves another gig for Sunday evening at the restaurant.

So the quiche became breakfast.....then Tim discovered that the first bus from outside our campsite didn't leave until 10.00am (we weren't having much luck with the buses were we?). In the end, he sprinted down (well that's what he told me) to the stop at the Mercadona (one of the most popular Spanish supermarkets) for the earlier bus into town, to pick up our Peugeot 207 hire car, then off we went on some amazing winding roads, with the most spectacular views across the mountains and row upon row of bancales. That particular area is used by many sports people, both for training (the 'Sky' team trained there in 2014 and we saw one dedicated guy on two skateboards using ski poles to propel himself uphill!) and for fun (we spotted a trailer of bikes at the top of the Sierra Aitana, that people then hire for the joy of freewheeling the 36kms downhill to near Villajoyosa); I'm not so sure I'd find it fun on those steep, winding roads, even if it is downhill all the way!

We discovered the Trestellador restaurant, hidden away in the mountains at Benimantell and, in temperatures reaching 31°, shared a delicious paella on the beautiful terrace there, whilst taking in the fabulous views over the mountains to the sea in the very far distance. Later, after a stroll to walk off our meal, we visited Guadalest, where the castle, built in the 11th century by Muslims, is astonishingly ... well... 'perched' upon a rock, with the only, small, entrance through the rock face! The beautiful clear blue sky allowed us some exceptional views.

Figure 19 Spain – Guadalest Castle (centre) on the rock!

After breakfast the next day we paddled in the sea at the beautiful little cove at Benitaxell, followed by a cool (though expensive) drink, before we set off into the mountains again, this time on a different route but with similar splendid mountain scenery, blind corners, hairpin bends and steep, narrow roads. Our hire car was very comfortable and Tim considered it to be quite good to handle, though he remarked that it was so devoid of power 'it wouldn't pull the skin off a rice pudding' (as his mum and granddad would have said!)

We explored some of the little villages on the way, with tiny streets almost impossible to get through without catching the walls, even just in our small car! After becoming disorientated in one of these tiny villages, Tim's *almost* unerring (he would say 'legendary') sense of direction sadly let us down and we ended up going around 20kms out of our way! Hah! After that, we decided to ask Ms Satnav to make sure we didn't go too far off our route again. I have to say that, apart from some instances when she had led us (literally!) up blind alleys, we were pretty impressed with the Tom-Tom's ability to take us to, for example, the nearest Aldi, or to a campsite when our only information was its name!

As the day wore on, we kept a look out for somewhere to eat and eventually, in desperation, we decided to stop at an uninspiring small pool bar in Facheca. However, we were pleasantly surprised by the quality of the home-made tapas: salad, *croquetas de cerdo* ('pork croquettes'), calamari, cheese and delicious bread and oils that went down very well with a pleasant glass of red wine. Incidentally, it's worth mentioning that even the tiniest of villages seems to have a well maintained, good-sized, but little used municipal swimming pool; they seem to be closed for most of the year, only opening in July and August.

Our next stop was Agres, a small village located on the northern slope of the Sierra Mariola, at 723 metres above sea level. From the last houses of the village, the road climbs a steep, tree-lined hillside to the Sanctuary of the Mare de Déu del

Castell (a Convent) that was built in the 15th century on the site of a Moorish castle. It was a beautiful evening and we enjoyed a peaceful walk through the cypress trees surrounding the convent.

On our way back through the village, we refreshed ourselves at the drinking-water fountain in the centre of the village, and were very pleased to manage conversations with a few Spanish ladies (who spoke no English)! One of them very proudly showed us her house, explaining that it had three floors and spanned the two streets we were looking at. In this area, though, Valencian Spanish is used alongside Castillian Spanish, which is a bit confusing for us, valiantly trying to get to grips with the language; some of the words are similar, eg *playa/platja* ('beach'), *agua/aigua* ('water'), and *calle/carrer* ('street'), but others are very different. Of course, many people who go to Spain get by very well without learning the language, but knowing a little has been very useful, especially during our trips to some of the more remote villages.

It was getting quite late as we set off back to the campsite and we wanted to get to the supermarket before it closed, so Tim put in some practice for the Monte Carlo rally!

The next morning, we took another small road, with more amazing views and, as always in the mountains, rows and rows of bancales; some well-maintained and some sadly neglected. Whilst having a drink at a lovely little bar in Piños, overlooking the valley and Calpé, we chatted to a couple of Scotsmen on a walking holiday, before continuing our meandering journey around the picturesque mountain roads.

Several very interesting little restaurants were dotted around, quite randomly it seemed and, after a brief visit to Jalón (*Xaló* in Valencian), famous for its ancient wells, we decided to take a chance on the Verd i Vent at Masserof. From the outside it was rustic, to say the least, but inside, well, even more so, but such a lovely atmosphere and the food was delicious. We had five excellent courses with wine, coffee and, of course, some water, all for €20 each. The afternoon was made even more pleasant by some Spanish singers who came in to entertain.

Our evening gig accelerated our return to the campsite and, with the car packed with our equipment, we made it in good time to Toni's bar in Sella, around 45 minutes' drive away. I have to say it wasn't the largest audience we've ever had, but those who were there were very appreciative and complimentary and we left with Toni asking when we could go back again!

After returning the hire car the following morning, we walked back through the town and along the promenade and stopped for another €2.50 Spanish breakfast before finding a place on the beach, the busiest we've seen it during our stay, it was Saturday though and another very hot day.

Tim decided it was much too hot to cook, so, once we'd freshened up, we cycled back into Calpé for a meal, a less exciting experience than yesterday's, but nonetheless a reasonable meal and a rather wobbly cycle ride back after half a bottle of wine and a limoncello! (...and Tim blamed his bag for unbalancing him, ha ha!)

Another beautiful day dawned and after an al fresco breakfast we were looking forward to relaxing on the beach again. But it wasn't to be; within what seemed like a few minutes (I just lost track of the time!) a strong, gusty wind blew up, completely sand-blasting and thoroughly exfoliating us, we were definitely rust-free! I reckon you would have paid a fortune for that treatment in a salon! With the fine layer of sand stuck to the sun cream on my skin, I think I could have struck a match on my arm quite easily! Sadly, the wind didn't seem like it would be easing any time soon, so we, along with most of the others on the beach, decided to leave.

Later on, de-sanded, we took all the equipment across the road to Piazza Di Spagna for our evening gig and were really pleased that our campsite neighbours and their friends (who lived locally) came to support us. It was a busy evening and our gig went really well; most of the customers were Spanish, French or German, so it was great to have them singing along with us and enjoying the music. Afterwards, we were treated to quite an array of drinks from customers who wanted to show their appreciation. We even got a bit of beer money in our hat!

It was a beautiful, balmy evening again and we sat outside chatting until quite late but we'd forgotten to put on insect repellent and Tim was attacked yet again. He needed another tube of antihistamine cream; luckily we were getting quite good at asking for it (*crema antihistamínica*) in Spanish!

Dénia – May-June

After another al fresco breakfast the van got a good clean and, in the lovely sunshine, our washing was dry by 12 noon, just as well, as we had to be off the site by then and, once we'd stocked up at Aldi (other retailers are available, but such good value!), we drove the 25 miles or so to **Los Patos** (literally 'the ducks') campsite at Dénia.

The site seemed a very friendly and pleasant place and we soon settled in. For the first time we actually put up our awning (we'd either not needed it, or, on aires, had not been allowed to have an awning up, though some people do).

A bit of investigation of our surroundings revealed that we were about 50 metres from the most beautiful beach that seemed to stretch for miles. We were, of course, faced with another massive decision: should we turn left or right, oh the angst! After some deep discussion, we decided to turn left and had a wonderful leisurely walk along the water's edge, with the tide lapping up over our feet as we walked.

Figure 20 Beach at Denia, Spain

Lots of kite surfers (I wonder what the correct collective noun is: maybe a 'breeze'?) created a colourful sight, but the sheer exertion was too much for us, so we had a long rest on the beach to recover from our exhausting walk, before making it back to the campsite for our evening meal.

Dénia is a very pleasant, interesting, town and, having decided to visit, we expected to be able to cycle there in a few minutes. It seemed we were further away than we'd realised and our journey took us around 50 minutes; well we were heading into the wind (that's my excuse), but it was a distance of about seven to eight miles, thankfully along an excellent cycle path that ran parallel to the beach all the way.

We were quite triumphant on finding the Tourist Information Office quite quickly and thrilled that it was open! In many places the office seems to be tucked away in some back street and by the time you've found it you've already managed to discover many of the tourist attractions in that area, or it's shut for a protracted lunch break! Whilst perusing some of the literature, we noticed on the local map that there was a naturist beach nearby, and were surprised to note that it appeared to have a panoramic viewpoint just above it! Very good for the voyeurs and/or exhibitionists I suppose!

One thing that the helpful tourist information person hadn't mentioned was the large castle at Dénia (!), so we went for a look around; I think Tim just wanted to get a good vantage point so that we could spot the nearest Mercadona or Aldi! The castle has sections dating back to Roman and Muslim times and in the 14th century King Jaime II insisted that the inhabitants of the city live within the castle walls. It remained as the city centre until the 18th century, after which it was owned privately and the terraced embankments within it (the ubiquitous *bancales*) were used for raisin cultivation until the last century when it was returned to public use.

From one of the castle towers we could not only see a Mercadona, but the church and its beautiful tiled dome, similar to the domes that adorn many churches in Spain. Alongside it was what we later learned is a Jacaranda tree with vivid lilac coloured flowers that seem to stand out almost as if they had been painted! The trees are quite prevalent in Spain and really do provide a beautiful splash of colour.

Figure 21 Church, Denia, Spain (with Jacaranda tree)

Dénia also has a number of pretty little plazas and we sat and had a coffee and a sandwich overlooking one of them. The main street – Calle Marqués de Campo – is lined with beautiful maples that we learned had been planted in the last century thanks to a bequest from the sisters of the aforementioned 'raisin cultivator', to provide shade for the townspeople.

After leaving the castle we called at the Mercadona (spotted from the castle) and loaded our rucksacks with supplies. As we'd bought some frozen and chilled foods we cycled back with a little more determination and, thanks to the following wind, made it in around 40 minutes, with frozen food still intact!

After a quick shower and change we were picked up at the campsite by a former colleague of Tim's, Rob and his wife, Penny, who live in Dénia. They took us to the Hero restaurant, not far away, where we had a delicious al fresco meal and a chat before returning to the campsite for around 10.30pm.

I figured it was time I had an artistic moment, so, the following day, we went for a walk down to the beach, armed with relevant equipment. The wind was quite blustery again, so we positioned ourselves along a wall edge, but, unfortunately, the easel seemed to have lost a vital part somewhere along the way. Gallantly, Tim went back to look for it but by the time he returned (without the required wing-nut despite having done an extensive search) I'd managed to balance the painting pad and almost finish my pastel of the beach looking north towards Oliva, where more kite surfers were in action. Meanwhile, we both managed to get thoroughly sand-blasted again; it's amazing where the sand gets to!

Figure 22 Pastel sketch nr Oliva, Spain

In the evening our attempts to cook some steak (of a kind) on a disposable barbecue were not as successful as we'd have liked! Fortunately, we both like our steaks fairly rare; Tim vowed never to use another disposable barbecue, but I have to say the steaks, with frozen chips, carefully carried back on our bikes yesterday, were very good.

Tim was inconsolable at breakfast, next morning, when he finished his mum's home-made marmalade, whatever were we going to do! However, he settled down with a 'Lidl' help, after a three-mile round-trip cycle ride to the small town of El Verger, where we also discovered a Chinese hardware store that was filled with loads of things we hadn't realised we desperately needed.

Rob and Penny picked us up later and took us back to their beautiful villa, where we enjoyed their company and some delicious food, whilst sitting by the terrace pool, with the most wonderful views over the bay, before we were returned to the campsite, replete and relaxed, later in the evening.

A few days of washing (it's notable here that the only washing machines are in the ladies' toilet & shower blocks, which seems a bit sexist; I wonder how any men-only groups are supposed to get their washing done!), cycling, reading, sketching, swimming and walking along the beach ensued. We also discovered a campervan workshop and store, so arranged with them to carry out a few minor repairs before we left Dénia.

Our new friends, Colin and Sue (who we'd met on the aire in Seville at the end of April, do pay attention!), joined us at the site and we enjoyed the evening hog roast meal, with entertainment by a Cuban/Latin singer, who was very good with his bongos! Our evening continued sitting outside the vans, sharing bottles of wine and brandy, well into the evening and they told us of some of their many motorhoming adventures over the years and the thriving social scene at their comparatively new home-town of Moraira.

We were very reluctant to leave that haven of sun, sand and serenity. I think it was safe to say that we'd, finally, both begun to relax!

The van was duly left at the excellent campervan workshop and accessory shop by the road in El Verger, while we had a cycle ride of around 12kms through the town and down to the beach, then back to the workshop for just after 12 noon.

The repair men had made a fantastic job of repairing our damaged fly screen door and a dodgy back light, but hadn't been able to repair the broken door handle. As we got back into the van, we noticed a pool of water on the floor and realised that we'd forgotten to switch the gas on for the fridge, so it hadn't been running for a couple of hours and in temperatures approaching 30° that's not a good idea, eek!

Valencia – June

As we were driving along the main road out of Dénia towards Valencia, I was amazed to see lots of – what might politely be described as – 'ladies of the....day', on the roadside, plying their trade. Tim had mentioned there were some on the way in to Dénia (better-looking he said!), but I'd been busy map reading at the time and hadn't seen them.

The rest of the journey was uneventful, we managed to avoid Piles – thought it was for the best – and arrived at **Valencia Camper Park** at Bétera by late afternoon. It was a large, very pleasant aire with an outdoor swimming pool so we enjoyed a lovely refreshing swim before tea.

We realised in the evening that the electricity was tripping at the switch but despite trying all sorts of things we couldn't seem to resolve it and were worried that maybe there was some kind of electrical fault in the van. Unaccountably, our Dutch neighbour was adamant that the fault was with our wiring!

In the morning, we caught the train from close to the aire into Valencia, about 30 minutes away, then, after perusing the map, set off for the centre of the city, the third largest city in Spain after Madrid and Barcelona. The signage generally is in Valencian here (of course!) and, as mentioned, slightly different from the Castillian Spanish that we've been trying to learn.

After walking for around 15 minutes, we turned around and re-traced our steps, this time heading the **correct** way into the centre of Valencia, hey ho! In the large plaza outside the cathedral and City Hall we noticed a car with the word 'Bombers' written on the side of it; they don't mess about here! (Actually firemen are called *Bomberos* in Castillian Spanish, but in Valencian Spanish they are indeed *Bombers*.) With considerable difficulty (again!) we finally found the Tourist Information Office and bought tickets for the tourist bus around the city. First of all, though, we visited Valencia Cathedral, another beautiful religious building, built between the 13th and 15th centuries, adorned with endless paintings and sculptures.

However, the cathedral in Valencia also houses what it claims to be the Holy Grail, the cup that Jesus is said to have used at the last supper. I understand that there are many claims regarding the whereabouts of the true Holy Grail, a disproportionate amount of which seem to believe it to be in Spain, but who am I to judge? So, here is a picture of the Valencian Holy Grail.

Figure 23 The Holy Grail? Valencia Cathedral, Spain

Behind the cathedral, just in case there wasn't enough space in there to worship, there is a magnificent basilica, with a beautiful dome covered in frescoes, pictured below:

Figure 24 Valencia Basilica, Spain

We then took the tourist bus around the historically significant areas of the city. Valencia was founded as a Roman colony in 138 BC and was later under the rule of the Muslims. It is situated on the banks of the Túria River, on the east coast of the Iberian Peninsula. One particularly interesting feature is that the Túria used to flow through the centre of the city but in 1957 a huge flood devastated parts of the city and the Spanish government subsequently decided to re-route it. The entire former course of the river has now been made into a park area.

When we returned to the main plaza, we decided to have a break and found a lovely little restaurant called the 'Mar Cuatro' (I think they could '4-sea' our arrival, ha ha!) where we had a wonderful lunch.

We continued on the tourist bus for the rest of its journey to the port – the fifth busiest in Europe – where we disembarked and ambled along the astonishingly wide beach, stopping, on our way, to watch people doing fantastic sand sculptures.

Back in the city centre, we had hoped to be able to go inside the Central Market, which is a very grand building, but sadly it was closed when we went and as time was moving on we decided to catch the train back to our aire; it's worth mentioning that it was around 7pm as we headed towards the station and it was still 31° in the city centre!

As we arrived at our platform, there was a train waiting so we, along with another couple, headed for the doors but they were locked! We were gutted, as the next train was about another half an hour and we were quite worn out by then; I know, you feel for us don't you?! Luckily, a few moments later we noticed someone actually get on and we dashed to the doors again and boarded, the driver must have taken pity on us, thank goodness! We arrived back for about 8.30pm, to find that the electricity had tripped again at some time during the day; the Dutch woman continued to blame our wiring but an English couple loaned us their cable to see if the same thing happened and it did. In the end we moved the van to a plot adjacent to the English couple and plugged into the electric point there (secretly just to get away from the annoying Dutch woman!), then sat and chatted to our new neighbours.

Super sleuth Tim discovered that, because the electricity supply was only five amps at this site, it had been cutting out because it couldn't cope with the fridge and the water heater if they were both on together, another valuable lesson learned! (See the Information section at the end of the book for more guidance regarding electricity supplies.)

Tarragona – June

We arrived at our new campsite, **Las Palmeras**, in Tarragona, at around 5.30pm. It was a huge campsite, nestled at the edge of a beautiful beach, along which we had a stroll before our evening meal. We noticed here, as at many of the campsites we've visited, that the site is almost full of caravans, but hardly any of them are occupied. We presumed that more people arrive as the season progresses and have been told that around Christmas time it is difficult to find a place anywhere.

Unfortunately during the night we were bothered firstly by goods trains about every 10-15 minutes on the track that ran very close by the campsite and then by a mosquito that seemed to have managed to infiltrate our defences. Consequently we had a late breakfast – croissants and coffee – before setting off for a walk through the pine forest adjacent to the campsite.

It was a lovely woodland walk along the coast and we passed a number of little sheltered coves, with lovely beaches, some of them clearly popular with naturists, which must definitely cut down on the washing! We headed for Torre De Mor, the next village along and treated ourselves to a nice cool drink by the beach, then chose one of the aforementioned coves to spend a few hours reading, sketching and generally relaxing, before heading back for our al fresco evening meal.

Figure 25 Pastel sketch near Tarragona, Spain

Tarragona is in Catalonia, the richest region in Spain, which was attempting to become independent from the rest of Spain; it has its own language, again in some ways similar to, but often very different from Castillian Spanish. Indeed, there are quite a lot of French influences in the language, presumably because this was previously the French-owned area of Aragon.

Figure 26 Roman Street in Tarragona, Spain

The bus from just outside the campsite was very convenient and, armed with helpful advice from the Tourist Information Office, we were soon able to explore the city, steeped in history. Our first visit was to the Rambla Nova, where we discovered (well, I think someone had spotted it before us) the remains of a Roman basilica and street. On the way there, we also noticed another tiled market hall (Mercat Central) similar to the one in Valencia. This one was in the process of being repaired, so a temporary one was in use and we popped in to have a look at the stalls, before meandering through the city to an extremely large and well preserved section of the Roman wall that had once surrounded the entire city. The walls here were built in the 3rd century BC and are (allegedly) the oldest Roman walls outside of

Italy. Unfortunately there was little shade there, and with temperatures in the 30s we were glad of a cool drink in the shade of one of those lovely Jacaranda trees in the Roman Pallol Square.

We walked along some more of the quaint streets and came across the cathedral, which is, again, quite an impressive building, built in the 12th century. Close by, in the medieval market place, we found a lovely little restaurant, called Gallo Moron; the waitress was definitely not moronic and was pleased to explain to us that the name of the restaurant translates to 'Black Cock', which elicited a smile. Later research indicated that it refers to the 'legend of the rooster' dating back to the 16th century, from the area of Morón de la Frontera, now the province of Seville.

Fully replete, we wandered along to the Roman tower, with fabulous views over the city from its ramparts and then, for us the pièce de resistance in Tarragona, the Circ Roma, which is, in fact, the remains of a Roman Chariot racing arena.

Figure 27 Underground passages at Circ Roma, Tarragona, Spain

Figure 28 Tunnels with seating area above, Tarragona, Spain

We were absolutely awe-struck by the underground passages that would have been below the seating area of the arena, and we could see some of the tunnels where charioteers would have gathered before entering. The charioteers were, apparently, slaves, but many grew to be exceptionally famous and became part of teams.

The rivalry between the teams was similar to that, for example, between Liverpool United and Everton, with wildly fanatical supporters (derived from the Latin *fanaticus*, originally meaning 'belonging to the temple', which evolved to mean overly-zealous behaviour, now usually shortened to 'fans', of course). Entry for the crowds was free and there would be places to eat and drink within the arena; the events were sponsored by very rich men looking for advancement or others in high positions.

Some of the seating was still visible in places, as well as part of the arena itself. It was an incredible place and there is clearly a lot of work still in progress, as they uncover more sections.

Figure 29 Roman Amphitheatre, Tarragona, Spain

Finally, we visited the amphitheatre, which was also pretty spectacular, situated at the edge of the beach and with many original sections and seating. It was built in the 2nd century BC and the centre of the arena there had, over the years, been variously: a basilica dedicated to some poor souls who had been martyred in the arena of the amphitheatre; a church; a convent; a prison; and finally, during the 20th century, parts of it were restored to their former glory.

We were pretty exhausted by this time, having walked a total of seven miles during the day, so caught the bus back to our campsite. On the way back we noticed the sign 'Taller Mecanic' and wondered whether he deals with the really big vehicles! (*taller* actually means 'workshop'☺). Quite a few young families had arrived during the day, so the site was much busier than when we'd left and it was good to see them enjoying all the facilities of the campsite: swimming pools, tennis courts, play areas, etc.

We headed into Tarragona on the bus again the next day and walked further along the Rambla Nova, catching a second bus (thanks to the helpful advice from the Tourist Information girl yesterday) that took us to the absolutely amazing Roman Aqueduct. It is also known as *Pont del Diable* ('Devil's Bridge'), apparently because, when it was first built, a strong wind destroyed it; the builders are said to have made a deal with the devil, who agreed to re-build the bridge on condition that he had the soul of the first person who crossed it!

Figure 30 Pont del Diable near Tarragona, Spain

The bridge (along with other Roman sites in Tarragona) is listed as a UNESCO World Heritage Site and was built in the 1st century AD to transport water into the city of Tarraco as it was then known. It is 27 metres (89 ft) high and 249 metres (817 ft) long, including the ends, where it tapers into the hillside and is composed of two levels of arches: the upper section has 25 arches and the lower one has 11. Apparently all arches have the same diameter of 20 Roman feet (5.9m) and the distance between the pillars is 26 Roman feet (7.95m).

We spent a little time there, walking beneath and along the top of the aqueduct, before heading back into the city and along the Rambla Nova (*Rambla* originally meant 'broad street' or 'built on a dry river-bed'), where we spotted this rather astonishing bronze sculpture of a human tower. Apparently creating increasingly higher and more dangerous human towers is quite a tradition in Catalonia and Valencia, and Tarragona was the location of the first human tower that was not, as had previously been the case, simply the finale of a traditional dance.

Figure 31 Rambla Nova, Tarragona, Spain

The Rambla was busy with a food and wine fair that was rather tempting, but as it was, by then, well into the afternoon, we decided we should head for one of the lovely plazas and have something a little more substantial. However, we found that the plazas were full of (the previously referred to) football fans who were supporting a local team playing in a regional final against Pamplona later that day and were – you might say – rather lively.

We eventually chose a slightly quieter restaurant, but the waiter was somewhat off-hand and the table we were shown to was in full sun. After hanging around for about 10 minutes without receiving any further attention, we were getting rather hot under the collar and left, returning to the Gallo Moron where we had eaten yesterday and where the waitresses were extremely pleasant.

On our way back through the old part of the city, we noticed this amusing mural on the gable end of a house, close to another section of the chariot racing arena.

Figure 32 Frescoes in Tarragona, Spain

We arrived back to a positively bustling evening, with people everywhere. I guess that the season was getting underway and, of course, many families would just be there for the weekend; there must have been well over a thousand people on the site. An England football match was being televised in the bar, so Tim went along to watch it, reporting later that he'd been in the company of only two other English people, plus one Irish man and three Russians, while over 80 people dined in the al fresco area outside! We have only met one other English couple during our few days here; most people seem to be Spanish families spending their weekend at the coast.

As mentioned previously, as well as a number of vans coming and going, there are lots of caravans that clearly don't move very often, if at all! We've been astonished at the set-ups: caravans with huge awnings attached to extra awnings, with external fridge freezers, barbecues and 'kitchen tents' and many with separate eating and sitting areas. We noticed one of the little kitchen tents had a 'for sale' sign on it and were musing as to what the circumstances might be; maybe chef has decided that if s/he's on holiday s/he won't be cooking!

The next morning we decided to have another lovely walk in the pine forest adjacent to the campsite, then chose a different cove for a couple of hours' relaxing in the sun. I did a bit more sketching and we both read for a while, before heading back. We'd got some meat out of the freezer for tea before we left in the morning, but had felt that if we left it out altogether, the weather was so hot that we might have returned to find the meat unusable, so we had put it in the fridge. Of course, it hadn't thawed very much at all, so we just had to try out the restaurant on the campsite, oh the sacrifices we make! It was a lovely evening and we sat at a table overlooking the beach and both enjoyed a delicious confit of duck.

When we returned to the van, we decided to do a bit of practice for our next concert in the south of France and we gathered a small crowd of people, some of whom came up to us and said how much they were enjoying listening, phew! We were a bit worried that, next morning, the campsite was again virtually empty and hoped that we hadn't been responsible for everyone's decisions to leave!

Barcelona – June

We packed up the van and called at the Mercadona not far away. Some of these supermarket car parks are clearly not designed for motorhomes! On the way out, I got out to scan our receipt bar code in order to raise the barrier and to check that we weren't in danger of hitting the 'conveniently' placed overhead gantry! As Tim edged forward, the barrier came down between the back of the van and our bikes on the carrier! I was panicking in case it had seriously damaged the van, the bikes or the barrier. Fortunately the barrier's sensor raised it again, but not without leaving a rather nasty scar on the back of the van!

We then made the relatively short trip to the **El Garrofer** campsite at Sitges, just south of Barcelona, the details of which we'd got from our ACSI book and which we thought looked nice because it was close to the beach as well as having good access into Barcelona. I have to say that the ACSI book is well worth buying (despite the odd errors/inconsistencies that we've encountered), it cost about €16 and includes a card that allows a fairly generous discount at participating campsites throughout Europe (including the UK); we saved around €20 a night at this site alone.

We found a nice spot under the pine trees then, after unpacking and a quick lunch, we thought we'd have a look at the beach nearby and went to the gate at the back of the campsite, that was clearly marked on our map 'access to beach'. We were astonished to find, when we got to it, that it is only open on a weekend! Feeling somewhat disgruntled, we asked how to get to the beach and ended up walking about a mile along the edge of a busy road and down through some houses before finally reaching the very long sandy beaches of Sitges, where we spent the afternoon. When we got back, we found that most of the needles from the aforementioned pine trees had deposited themselves on our table, chairs, mats and every other available surface!

The electricity supply there was four amps, so, bearing in mind our previous experience (we were 4-warned!) we didn't turn on the water heater, to avoid the supply cutting out. We were becoming a little concerned in case we ran out of gas, as we hadn't realised that there are so many different gas fittings and sizes; the aperture for gas on our motorhome would only take a 6-7kg canister and most of the canisters on sale were much bigger. We had bought the appropriate fittings for canisters in Spain, but didn't know if they would fit French canisters! We just hoped we didn't run out mid-meal one evening!

The next morning we caught the bus from just outside the campsite into Barcelona. It was almost an hour's journey, on a luxury coach for only €4 each, which we thought was very good value. During the journey we chatted to a couple who were also staying at the site, and Tim mentioned that he'd spent most of his working life in hospitality and catering. Later in the conversation, it came up that one of our favourite little kitchen appliances was an egg-boiler that cooks our eggs to perfection every time. I'm afraid I couldn't stop laughing when the man leaned over and said, dryly, "You mean to tell me that you've spent over thirty years in the catering industry and you can't boil an egg!"

Amazingly, we found the Tourist Information in a little portable cabin on the Plaza de Catalunya, close to where the bus had stopped. We bought a card that gave us entry to three attractions of our choice (it was possible to buy a card for four or five attractions) and our first visit was to La Pedrera (pictured), one of the houses that the architect Antoni Gaudí had designed; this one, for the Mila family, was completed in 1912. There was a long queue but we had been told at the Tourist Information Office that our card allowed us to skip the line, so we went to the head of the queue, only to be told that we had to go back to the end and wait. We were not too happy about that and when Tim pointed out the relevant statement on the information we'd received with the card, they grudgingly let us in.

Figure 33 La Pedrera, Barcelona, Spain

La Pedrera is an amazing house, the exterior is very curvaceous and we learned that Gaudí based many of his designs on the soft lines of nature. Furniture was designed to fit the curves of the user; for example chairs with soft lines and comfortable arm rests and door knobs made literally by moulding the shape of a hand grip. On the rooftop, the chimneys are in various curious shapes:

Figure 34 Chimneys at La Pedrera, Barcelona, Spain

Gaudí felt that there was no need for practical items to conform to rigid designs and some are covered in ceramic mosaics (another trademark of his). There was even a bedroom with an en suite, something very few families would have had in 1912!

Two floors of La Pedrera were later made into apartments that are still occupied today. I must say that Gaudí's constructions are quite spectacular and very much ahead of their time.

We headed next for the Sagrada Família, with a quick lunch stop on the way. Many people mistakenly think of this magnificent building as Barcelona's cathedral; it is, in fact, a basilica. Interestingly, in Roman times *basilica* was used to describe a public building used for courts and other official functions, usually located in a town centre, opposite a temple; later churches were built using that same, now traditional, design and architecturally or historically significant ones can only be designated as a basilica by the Pope.

This particular basilica is a must on a visit to Barcelona; it was designed by a fairly young Gaudí in around 1880 (he was born in 1852) after the original architect had resigned. He worked on the building of it for over 40 years and died, as a result of a tram accident, at the age of 74, having seen relatively little of his design come to fruition. Many of his plans were destroyed during the Spanish civil war, but enough remained for the construction of this astonishing building to re-start in the mid-20th century, solely through private funding and fundraising. It is a project that was still ongoing and we were told that they hoped to finish it in 10 years' time. (We made a note to ourselves to return – circumstances permitting – to see it then.)

Tim and I had visited the Sagrada Família before, but it changes considerably as progress is made; the roof was finally added in 2010 and, at the time of this visit, it had been recently consecrated by the Pope (though services were not held in the main section as yet, just in the crypt). Our visit was again part of the 'deal' which, for this one, included a 1½ hour tour with the services of an excellent guide.

The north doorway is something to behold, but as we entered the building the only word was 'wow'! Gaudí's use of light and space has created an ethereal feel and the stained glass windows allow the area to be bathed in beautiful soft natural light, constantly changing as the sun moves around the building.

Figure 35 North doorway, Sagrada Familia, Barcelona, Spain

Figure 36 Sagrada Família, Barcelona, Spain

The south doorway had been finished more recently and Gaudí's request was that individual sculptors and designers should put their own 'stamp' on their work. Thus, the statues at that side are of a more modern design which, I have to say, was less to my taste personally.

The east door was eventually to become the main door, but at the time of our visit there was a four-five metre drop immediately outside it, the eventual intention being that there would be a ramp or steps (good job too, otherwise going out that way would be something of a 'fall from grace'!), but some local residences needed to be demolished in order to achieve that particular aim!

After leaving there, we used our travel card, very kindly donated by Colin and Sue, to get to Parc Güell and made our way up an enormous hill, to the Park, a large area of which was, again, designed by Gaudí. Unfortunately, by the time we realised that we needed tickets to get into the main area (and made our way to the other gate to purchase them as there had been no information about it anywhere else) it was too late for us to enter.

Figure 37 Parc Güell, Barcelona, Spain

We did, however, see quite a lot of the area around it before we caught the bus back to the Plaza de Catalunya that arrived at 7.58pm, and ran the 200 yards or so to the stop for our 8.00pm bus back to the campsite, making it just by a whisker!

On our next trip into Barcelona we went down Las Ramblas, paying a visit to the market (mercat) there; we really enjoyed comparing the mercats.....

Figure 38 Barcelona Market, Spain

... and some of the stalls were beautifully merchandised. We saw some sheep's heads (with the eyes still in, to see you through the week!) but Tim resisted the temptation to ask if the assistant had a sheep's head as we thought she might be offended! (The old ones are still sometimes the best ☺)

We then walked down Las Ramblas to the port, which was a lovely relaxing place with some absolutely huge yachts as well as other, much more modest ones. After stopping for a coffee on our way back along Las Ramblas, I thought for a moment that Tim had suddenly developed an interest in horticulture, but I was wrong....some of the stalls were displaying an array of seed packets claiming to produce some rather rude-looking plants! (I can't take him anywhere!)

Figure 39 Interesting seed packets, Las Ramblas, Barcelona, Spain

We wandered cautiously through the many little side streets (I should mention that, although we weren't affected, we know of quite a few people who have had items stolen around the Ramblas area) and came across the cathedral. Unfortunately, we couldn't go in (Tim was showing too much leg!), so we had a few tapas in one of the little plazas, then made our way to one of the offices for Julia Travel (the provider of our attractions card) and set off for our trip to Montserrat. This involved a trip of an hour on a coach, up into the magnificent mountain range, then a short trip on a mountain-hugging train to the Sanctuary at Montserrat, another claimant to the Holy Grail.

The basilica there is beautiful and very tranquil and is built on the site of former chapels, records of which go back to the 9th century, when a model of a black virgin and child (there is some controversy regarding the reasons for its colour) – believed to have been carved in Jerusalem by St Luke – was discovered in a cave nearby. The virgin holds a ball (similar to a sceptre), that is considered to be exceptionally sacred and, for hundreds of years, people have made pilgrimages to touch it. The queue, when we visited, snaked around the basilica, so we just looked from afar.

Figure 40 Montserrat Basilica, near Barcelona, Spain

The boys' choir there is internationally famous and sings at two daily services; unfortunately the timing of our tour meant that we weren't able to hear it for ourselves.

The surrounding mountains take some very unusual shapes (*Montserrat* literally means 'serrated mountains') and it's possible to take the funicular railway to the top, but we didn't have time to do that, although we did enjoy the amazing views that we had.

Part of our trip did, however, involve visiting the museum and tasting some of the excellent liqueurs that they produce at the Sanctuary.

The coach dropped us back into Barcelona just in time for our 8.00pm bus back to the campsite.

After hanging out a load of washing next morning, we decided to try and find a closer beach so cycled around a mile or more, eventually arriving at the back of the campsite (to where the gate would have given us access!); it was about another mile from there to a rather exposed beach (in more ways than one!) We sat for a while, but Tim was keen to get back for the afternoon football match, so we made our way back to the van, only to find that a 'friendly' pigeon had left an unwelcome message on Tim's shirts and undies on the line (and his pigeon mates had covered the van). Otherwise we had a quiet afternoon (well, apart from Tim's shrieks of joy as England scored!).

We had been told by an English couple we had chatted to on the bus that it was Gay Pride weekend, which explained why there were more single people and same sex couples around us than usual. We did ponder on the fact that a gay men's dog was getting very friendly with a lesbian couple's dog but weren't sure whether the dogs were the same sex as each other too!

It was a lovely evening again and we sat up until late; well, I was writing my blog and was concerned that our 10 hours (for €9) of Wi-Fi might run out before I got it published, but I made it with about half an hour to spare!

Finally, at almost midnight, we were just about to settle down for the night, when Tim remembered that the chemical toilet needed emptying! He decided to do it right then (knowing that we'd need it during the night!), but he was gone for ages and I was beginning to get concerned. He finally returned safely, but hadn't been able to find the toilet emptying point despite having asked several fellow campers (of various nationalities) and even a couple of staff members, none of whom had been able to put him on the right track; eventually, he'd emptied it in an ordinary toilet. Incidentally, we also noticed a sign on the toilet block saying 'No Pipas' which, bearing in mind that in Spain the letter 'i' is pronounced 'ee', was quite reassuring! (We think it must have meant electronic cigarettes?)

Bay of Roses – June

We were up bright and early the next morning, despite Tim's late night meanderings. I was half expecting to see notices warning people to be on the lookout for a strange man wearing a dressing gown and black rubber gloves, who'd been roaming around the campsite at midnight.

After breakfast we set about cleaning all the pigeon mess from the van and removing all the pine needles that seemed to have covered or filled every imaginable surface and orifice and some unimaginable ones too.

Then, avoiding El Prat and, later, Tossa, we headed for Girona, which on-line had looked quite an interesting city. As we travelled further north, the sky was distinctly gloomier and the temperature was hovering around 20-23° (I know, I bet you're heartbroken for us!). We checked out the only campsite that was close to Girona, but it was very much off the beaten track and definitely not on a bus route into the city, so we headed for another site close to the town of Roses, calling in at a handy Mercadona (without barriers) for a few supplies on the way. This time, the campsite was full, so, beginning to feel a bit dejected, we headed for **Aquarius Camping** at Sant Pere Pescador, a few miles south of Roses. This one had plenty of room (450 spaces altogether), so we settled in and went for a look around.

The campsite was excellent and the facilities very well laid out and exceptionally clean, a huge improvement on the last site and for the same price (with our ACSI discount)! It was German-owned and everyone we saw on our first day was either German or Dutch. In addition, the signs were now in Catalan Spanish (not

Castillian, the one we know best), German, Dutch and English, so it felt a bit like we'd left Spain already! We're both fascinated by language and most words have some similarities with at least one other European language, but we noticed that (as well as many other words I'm sure) the word for 'dogs' is completely different in at least six languages that we've come across (including English): Perros (Castillian Spanish), Gossos (Catalan Spanish), Hunds (German), Cani (Italian) and Chiens (French).

The site was at the edge of a wide sandy beach (the Bay of Roses) that stretches for miles in either direction but unfortunately we didn't get time to enjoy it then as the skies were blackening and we could hear the rumble of thunder not far away, so headed back to the van, thankfully getting back just before the heavens opened. We had a mild panic when the TV/DVD player wouldn't work then realised we hadn't yet switched on the internal power supply, still learning!

The rain abated so we sat outside for our delicious meal of lamb leg steaks with potatoes and peas and some fresh rosemary from the campsite's herb garden that visitors are invited to use. What a lovely idea!

Sadly, the rain had returned during the night and continued on and off the following day, so we had a lazy day until, in the early evening, the sun came out and we were able to have some Spanish sausage al fresco! We thought we'd take advantage of the pleasant evening (though still chilly: mid-teens temperature, which, to us, now hardened sun worshippers, felt like around zero) and have a walk. As we did so, we could hear live music in the distance, so we followed the sound and ended up at a campsite nearby, where two men were singing; the music was enthusiastic, rather than good, but we got a drink and sat and listened for a while.

Eventually, we decided we'd better get back, as it was getting dark, so we headed back in the direction of the entrance we'd used, only to find that the 8ft high gate (with intimidating spikes) was padlocked, as were all the others we came across as we walked with some trepidation around the site perimeter. We like a lock-in, but this wasn't really the kind we fancied and we were beginning to wonder whether we'd be interrogated as to why we wanted to leave this site, or, indeed to enter our own!

We frantically followed the high and imposing perimeter fence, searching for a way out; it was beginning to look like we might have to curl up in a corner somewhere (just out of reach of the searchlights?!) and wait until morning. Finally, after a much longer and more traumatic walk than we'd envisaged, we were very relieved to find the guarded main entrance. We almost expected to have to provide ID and have our bags checked as we walked through, then, in the dark by now, made our way back to our own campsite!

A few Spanish families had arrived on the site during the day and we finally met an English lady as we made our way back to the van. Just to round off the day, Tim accidentally mistook a tube of haemorrhoid cream for his toothpaste and had to eat half a pack of sweets to take the taste away (well, that's what he told me!).

It was a much brighter day that dawned, though quite windy, so we ate our traditional English breakfast (a Sunday treat) inside, hoping that it would fortify us for our planned bike ride. We then set off on one of the cycle tracks shown on our map, in the general direction of 'some Roman ruins' that the reception staff had casually mentioned in passing, around 10-12kms away.

We were amazed, on reaching the site, to find that it covered a huge area that included a Greek city and port founded around the 6th century BC and called Emporion (which in Greek means 'market'; more mercats to compare!). In the 2nd century BC the Romans arrived and eventually set up a city at Empúries, just up the hill, which, approximately 100 years later, merged with the Greek city to form a single city named Municipium Emporiae. However, as Girona, Barcelona and Tarragona gradually became more important, Emporiae became less so and in the late 3rd century AD the whole area was abandoned and lay undiscovered until 1908. Excavations have continued since then and currently around 25% of the site has been excavated.

The whole area was exceptionally well presented, firstly with a short film explaining the history, then with an audio guide and map that gave details of each important section. Finally, there was a museum with some of the artefacts discovered, which included many personal and practical items, as well as axe heads from the original bronze age settlement on this site.

The Greek city included part of a Temple and Forum that had been erected as examples of how they would have looked at the time; there were also some excellent examples of drains, water storage pits and water filters, an original section of wall, an Atrium, Agora (market place) and the mosaic floor of a banquet hall (by the way, I learned that *symposium* is Greek for 'banquet').

Figure 41 Municipium Emporiae nr Bay of Roses, Spain

In the Roman city, there were the remains of some very large houses with exceptionally well-preserved beautiful mosaic floors, a public baths and gymnasium, a Temple, a huge Forum and basilica as well as many shops and the Roman external wall of the city, along with the remains of an amphitheatre. Trust Tim to find the phallic symbol on the city wall!

Figure 42 Municipium Emporiae nr Bay of Roses, Spain

It took us around four hours to have a good look around and, despite the strong wind, the temperature was in the high 20s, so we were glad of a cool drink in a beach bar, after which we found a nice, sheltered, spot on the beach at Sant Martí de Empúries and spent two hours or so there, before cycling back. The wind, by then, had increased to what felt like gale force as it was head-on all the way back. As we passed some of the beaches, we were, again, sandblasted, no rust on us!

As it was Father's Day, Tim felt he deserved a meal out, so we went to the restaurant on the campsite and had steak and chips that were 'ok'; the steak was a bit tough and overcooked, but they were good chips!

Having decided to move on the following day, we found that we could only reverse out in one direction so had to drive around the edge of the site to get to the exit. We were just about to turn left to get to the service point in order to empty our waste water, when we saw a car and caravan heading towards us, so Tim kindly reversed a couple of feet to let them through and we hit a low brick corner post just hard enough to smash one of the lights and make a rather nasty hole in the back corner of the van, aaaaagh! Why do they put things like that on campsites: not large enough to be seen, but enough to cause damage? We need answers please! Tim was so distraught he decided not to bother emptying the waste water, but made a hasty and distressed retreat.

Feeling thoroughly fed up, we called in at the Carrefour in Figueres, only to find, when we came out, that somehow I'd accidentally left the tap on and completely emptied the water tank (via the sink thank goodness!) that we'd filled prior to leaving and caused the waste water tank to overflow all over the car park; not a good day, it seemed!

France: Cap d'Agde – June

We were very sad to leave Spain but across the border into France we reached our next campsite, **Mer et Soleil** (sea and sun) at Cap D'Agde on the coast, just above Perpignan, around 2.30pm. Tim had some tricky manoeuvring to do in order to fill up with fresh water again (oops!), before finally parking the van. Then we realised that we had lost the handle from our boot door (it broke off a few weeks ago and we have been managing by turning it in the lock, then storing it, but we must have left it in position – probably at Carrefour – and it had dropped out en route!). We fervently hoped that those were our three misfortunes for the day! It does seem that something breaks or needs repairing in the van on a regular basis and we gather, from chatting to other travellers, that it's not just us!!

After a cup of tea and a quick reconnoitre of the campsite, we cycled to the port (about 3kms). It was a beautiful afternoon (around 28°) and, while Tim had a beer, I had Sex on the Beach; very nice! We then cycled back and Tim cooked one of his many specialities – Carbonara – before he went to the bar to watch the England football match. Meanwhile, I went for a shower and nearly had my skin ripped off, it was such a force!

Thankfully England at least drew their match but Tim had had inordinate difficulty watching it at the campsite: the animation team were busy miming to pop tunes, using the big screen, so he had to go into the tiny TV room on the terrace. The television wasn't switched on and the remote had no batteries, but when he tried to get someone to help him, or to provide new batteries, he received the typical 'Gallic shrug' in return. He eventually managed to figure out how to get it to work manually (desperation is a strong motivator) and watched the match in the company of an Irish man (not the same one that was watching the match near Tarragona!), another person of indeterminate nationality and, later, a Swedish man with his 15 year-old daughter.

The next day we went for a swim in the pool on site. It was really lovely: a good-sized pool for swimming, plus lots of other smaller ones with slides etc for the children (and another 'relaxation area' that we were clearly not paying enough to be allowed into).

The Mer et Soleil site had kindly provided a 'helpful' booklet when we arrived, that showed a good plan of the site. However, it failed to provide various essential pieces of information, that we gradually learned through trial and error: first of all, of course, we'd had to search for the appropriate tap to fill up the van; only two of the five toilet/shower blocks shown were in use (the others presumably were reserved for the high season); there was only one place to deposit rubbish, which wasn't marked on the map; and (I finally learned after carrying my basket of washing around for about half an hour between washing area, van and reception!) the washing machines cost €6 for a load and would only take €1 or €2 coins.

Having finally completed our tasks, we cycled into the port area again, where we had seen, yesterday, some notices advertising a Music Festival that was to take place in the late afternoon today.

It was a beautiful afternoon, so we strolled around the port area, where there were some quite large fish swimming in the magnificent marina!

Figure 43 Marina, Cap D'Agde, France

We tucked into a delicious ice cream sundae and a coffee while we listened to one of the groups practising in readiness for later, then came across a very good Abba tribute band practising on one of the big stages.

Near to the marina we listened to three different choirs: a children's choir, a ladies' choir and a mixed one. They did a good job, but it made us realise how good the choirs we sang in were and also reminded us of the importance of standing still (or all moving in the same direction if we are moving!) and of paying attention to the beginnings and endings of words and phrases!

We really wished we could have brought our singing gear into town and done some busking ourselves; there have been a few opportunities, during our trip, for busking, but we haven't been able to get the speaker & microphones to the location. The motorhome is great, but it's not easy to manoeuvre into town/city centres!

It was a bit disappointing that all of the main acts were due to start at the same time – 8.30pm – which meant we had quite a bit of time to kill before then and wanted to leave around 9pm, as we had a 25 minutes or so bike-ride back and didn't want to be cycling in the dark, so we were pleased to find an excellent jazz band just off the main marina, who started at 8.00pm.

We enjoyed listening to them for about 40 minutes, before heading back to the marina, where there were a few small groups and individuals – of varying quality – singing in bars. As we headed back towards our bikes we passed the main stage at 8.50pm, but 'Abba' had still not appeared; we had been looking forward to seeing how they would transform themselves, but will never know, as we decided we'd have to cycle back to our campsite.

We were in for a treat, however, as an act called Electric were singing on the stage there and they were excellent: a male/female duo, supported by a brilliant musician. Their act included some very good choreography and we stayed there for an hour or so, in awe of their energy and talent (they were quite a bit younger than us!!). We have noticed that in Europe it seems to be expected that performances should last around two to three hours without a break, unlike in the UK, where the norm is two 45-minute sets with a break in-between.

We spent the following day on the beach, before heading back in the late afternoon, with the expectation of a bit of singing at the advertised karaoke evening, only to find that they were showing the Belgium football match on the big screen, hey ho!

Around Montagnac – June

Leaving Cap D'Agde, we drove through Sète, on the coast, but couldn't find anywhere to park, so, heading for our next destination, turned off the main road and were travelling very slowly along, admiring the countryside, when suddenly a fire engine sounded its siren immediately behind us! We obviously let it pass and then, around the next bend had to stop as the fire engine had joined a couple of others blocking our road ahead, while they dealt with quite a large fire in a small wooded area at the side of the road.

It became apparent that we weren't going anywhere in a hurry and there wasn't an alternative route without going miles out of our way, so we pulled in and made ourselves some lunch while we waited. Another three fire engines came past to bolster the ranks and we were able to observe their valiant fire-quenching efforts.

Finally, after about 45 minutes or so, the fire was suitably dampened and we continued our journey, passing a number of vineyards, and finally reaching the beautiful Domaine Saint Hilaire – the 175-acre, award winning vineyard, belonging to Tim's brother at that time (it no longer does) – where we were to spend the next few days. The Domaine is believed to have been in use since Roman times and produced up to 200,000 bottles per year at the time of our visit.

We were made very welcome by everyone and, after some nervous moments getting the motorhome through a narrow gate at a perilous angle, we had a good look around.

The splendid 18th century house was built by Baron Saint Hilaire, who fought with Napoleon at the beginning of the 19th century; an art deco wing was added in the 1930s. The grounds were very peaceful and serene and we ate our evening meal al fresco on the terrace, overlooking the swimming pool.

The following morning, we awoke to find that Britain had voted to leave the EU, provoking much discussion with our fellow guests over a wonderful breakfast on the terrace again. Tim then made an excellent job of the stressful task of reversing the van through the aforementioned gates so that we could have a look around the towns nearby. After I'd mopped his brow, we visited

Mèze, a pretty little town with some nice squares, a lovely marina and a small sandy beach. We particularly wanted to visit the Tourist Information Office as our friends Andy, Pam, Diane and Jimmy were due to join us for a week and we were keen to find out as much as we could about the area in readiness. After asking for directions, we finally reached its door as the church clock was striking 12 noon, when – guess what – the door was firmly shut on us!

Next we drove through Marseillan, a few miles south of Mèze, but, again, found it difficult to park our van, so we drove on to a fabulous, typically French (well it should be of course!) little restaurant alongside the canal, not far from Agde, that one of the people at Domaine Saint Hilaire had recommended. We had a gorgeous meal: for starters, I had moules (mussels, which, along with oysters, are a speciality around here; there are lots of oyster beds just to the east of Mèze) and Tim had soupe de poisson (fish soup), with croûtons, aïoli and grated Emmental. We then both had a meal of Colin! (hake), served with rice and French beans, with a creamy sauce. Finally, for dessert, Tim had chocolate mousse and I had îles flottantes (that literally translates as 'floating islands', and consists of meringues floating in a custard sauce) all of which were delicious. We, of course, washed it all down with a house wine and then I was offered a liqueur to finish (Tim declined as he had some serious driving to do!). We did, however (entirely in French!), manage to negotiate ourselves a gig for next week.

We were really looking forward to welcoming our friends the following day, so planned to spend the rest of the day relaxing around the vineyard. However, we were told about a festival in Montagnac, the nearest village and decided to cycle the 5kms (mostly uphill) in the evening to investigate. There was a lovely, friendly atmosphere, with lots of families sitting around eating and drinking together and little children racing around and having fun.

We'd obviously missed the local entertainment, but we saw the 'headline' act, that consisted of six people, playing guitars, drums and a violin and singing; they were, essentially, a rock band, and did some songs that we hadn't heard before, plus some slow versions of better-known songs, such as Hotel California. It was a very pleasant evening and, as we'd remembered to fit our bike lights before leaving, we left it until gone 10.00pm before we set off back, by which time it was more or less dark.

As we were leaving Montagnac, I spotted a large snake (around two to three feet long) on the road; it was dead, but it still unnerved me a little. A little further along Tim had to stop to adjust his lights, only to find that a swarm (well, at least three or four!) of very large beetle-like insects started crawling up his leg – it was like a scene from 'Indiana Jones' – then, as we were cycling along we were being bombarded by flying insects. After that, we kept our mouths shut, so as not to swallow any and concentrated on pedalling back as quickly as we could; fortunately it was mostly downhill!

The following day, we sat on the terrace, by the pool, for a 'simple' one-course breakfast (not the three-course variety we'd had yesterday), idly watching the wasps taking turns to glide along the water as it swished out of the pool and then fly up and do it again! Naturally, we needed to conserve our energy in readiness for our friends' arrival and being lazy in such a wonderful setting is very easy. I sat and did a bit of painting, then cooled off in the pool, while Tim spent a good 20 minutes doing research into the influence of large waves on wasps.

Our friends arrived later in the afternoon and it was lovely to meet up with them all again. We enjoyed a fabulous al fresco meal, courtesy of Chef Tim and chatted late into the evening.

Figure 44 At the Domaine with, L to R: Pam, Andy, Diane, Jimmy, me and Tim

Another wonderful Michelin quality three-course breakfast set us up for the following day and we drove (our friends had thoughtfully hired a seven-seater car so that we could all travel together) to the nearby town of Mèze and had a look around the market there, enjoying the beautiful weather, around 30° again. We were fascinated to note that in many places there are hooks on the outside of doors and pondered on what their purpose might be...

A late lunch in one of the little restaurants near the marina was suggested...but after the big meal last night and such a large breakfast? Our arms didn't take too much twisting (the diet starts later!) and Tim and I both had a huge pan of delicious mussels! From our table we had a fabulous view of the marina and were curious to see that there was a tiered seating area and boats with what appeared to be ladders at the back; what could they be for? Another mystery.

Afterwards we returned to the Domaine and all had a splash in the pool before managing to force down a buffet tea. We heard screams later on and were worried about Diane in the kitchen, but it was just the insect zapper doing its job and causing her some alarm!

Next morning, we all piled into the car and headed for Loupian, a very charming little town not far away, famous for its historic streets and, particularly, for the remains of a Roman Villa. However, having found that the Villa was not open until 1.30pm, we had a walk around, enjoying the tranquility of the little streets in the walled town.

In the afternoon we managed to gain entry to the remains of the Roman Villa and were shown through to the area by a French guide, speaking in English to us. A very modern building covered the remains, with walkways so that we could see some of the beautiful tiling from above. We sat patiently, while the guide proceeded to explain (in French) the different rooms and the ceramic tiling to the group of French people who had come in at the same time as us, anticipating that he would explain to us in English next, but after about 10 minutes or more, we realised that our turn was not going to come! We were very put out and felt the need for some (childish?!) retaliation, eventually managing to organise ourselves and follow the written guidance notes and plan in a structured way, doing our own English commentary (Tim practised his 'foghorn' voice whilst we were close to the other group, in protest), so that we made the best of our visit. It did seem unfair that the French people were treated to a guided tour of around 30 minutes and we didn't pay any less! We did point out to them the injustice of this but, guess what, another Gallic shrug was all we got in reply. It was a shame, as the mosaics and remains were very interesting, but it did spoil the experience a little.

After leaving Loupian, we made our way to Bouzigues, on the coast of the Étang de Thau, one of the many natural harbours that occur on the north-east coast of Spain and in southern France. We decided to visit the museum there, which gave a history of oyster and mussel farming, for which that area is famous but we weren't sure where the museum was. Andy's astute accountancy skills had come to the fore earlier, when he challenged the waiter in an ice-cream shop, who'd tried to charge us for eight ice creams instead of six; however, we weren't as impressed with his orienteering skills as he followed his phone's satnav, leading us via numerous back streets in an attempt to reach the Oyster museum. Several people told us different directions as we walked around in ever-decreasing circles, we even noticed a car driving up and down the road, presumably to keep an eye on these crazy English people out in the midday sun (around 30°C). It turned out that if we'd just turned left out of the ice-cream shop we'd have been there within a couple of minutes. By the time we arrived we'd been en route for about 25 minutes and were very thirsty and extremely grateful for the free bottle of water from the lovely lady at the museum. Anyway, the museum was very interesting and we learned some fascinating facts. We also discovered that the hooks on the outside of doors are to hang rubbish bags!

Finally, we went back to Mèze and this time tried La Sanboulou restaurant in the marina, where we had a gorgeous meal of (for me anyway) three tapas for starters, then a beautifully cooked fish dish, followed by a Crêpe Suzette all for €15.50. The staff were very pleasant and friendly, helping to make it a really enjoyable meal, as well as being extremely good value.

England's defeat in the football was not greeted with joy, made worse for Tim by the fact that he'd made two €10 bets that they would win; it was not a happy night! William Hill (other betting companies are available) will not be inviting him to work for them in the near future! (Not that he's looking for a job!)

Thankfully, a good night's sleep made things seem a little better and, while Tim, Jimmy, Andy and Pam went off on a shopping expedition, Diane and I put the world to rights from our sun loungers. Jimmy returned triumphant as he'd managed to persuade the others to buy at least five kilos of tomatoes to last him for a day (we've never seen someone eat so many tomatoes at one meal!) and Tim (cheese monster!) was delighted to have secured enough cheese to last him a while (again approaching the 5kg mark).

After a bit of practising for our gig the following night, we had a quiet afternoon just chilling out around the pool followed by a lovely barbecue in the evening and more singing.

The 'boys' headed off the following morning into Montagnac to try and get a haircut for Tim. Unfortunately the hairdresser couldn't fit him in that morning, but by the time he'd found out, the others had gone off for a coffee. They eventually rescued him, wandering the streets looking lost and forlorn!

Later, we were given a very interesting tour of the vineyard, followed, of course, by a wine tasting and another lazy afternoon, with a dip in the pool, before squeezing into the car, along with speakers, boxes, music stands, etc and heading for the very rustic Guingette d'Asterix restaurant that Tim and I had visited last week.

There was a bit of confusion about where we should set up, as there was another duo who were also playing that evening, but we eventually got sorted out and then sat down to a gorgeous meal: goat's cheese salad, fish and an extremely alcoholic banana dish for me! Our music went down very well with all the people there, in fact, so well that the other duo seemed to be anxious that we were never going to finish!

We were thrilled when the charmingly eccentric owners of the restaurant discounted our bill and gave us a bottle of champagne to finish off the evening!

Andy and Pam had been so looking forward to having a new air conditioning unit in their bedroom (having spent a few steamy nights so far), but we learned, the following morning, that, after turning it on and settling down for a cool night, they'd had a shock when water gushed down the wall, fortunately just missing them but hitting their bedhead! They, of course, reported it and the plumber was summoned for urgent repairs! (I must point out that the room they were in was not, at that time, available to paying guests, a number of rooms were in the process of restoration.)

The boys went back to Montagnac for Tim's hair appointment. He certainly got his money's worth and wasn't likely to need it doing again for quite a few weeks, although he didn't get the ear, nose and eyebrow trim that he'd received in Calpé a few weeks previously!

We then headed for the Abbaye de Valmagne, one of the most ancient vineyards in the Languedoc region (by the way *Languedoc* actually means 'the language of Occitanie', Occitanie being the old region here, and some of the road signs are written in both French and Occitanie). We had a look around the herb garden before having an excellent al fresco meal at the restaurant there, in a beautiful, tranquil setting. All the food was locally produced and beautifully presented, adorned with various edible flower petals and herbs, providing some unusual but really wonderful flavours.

After our lunch had settled we went for a look around the Abbey, founded in 1139. It is most unusual to find an Abbey of that age so intact, but apparently the monks inhabited it for a relatively short period, after which the area around it became a vineyard (that continues to this day) and the Abbey was used to store huge barrels of wine, that are still in situ, a most unusual sight in a Gothic cathedral! As a result, the Abbey was not destroyed as so many others were. The Tuscany gardens were beautiful, as were the cloisters and chapter house with ribbed vaulting.

Figure 45 Abbaye de Valmagne, Languedoc, France

In the evening we sat outside at the Domaine and enjoyed a few nibbles and, of course, more wine! The insects clearly found Andy very tasty and unfortunately, despite his best attempts at protection and deterrent, they succeeded in attacking him.

The plumber had duly attended yesterday and had carefully adjusted Andy and Pam's air conditioning unit, ensuring that this time during the night, the gushing water actually landed on them; well at least it cooled Andy's insect-bites!

We had our final delicious three-course breakfast prepared by the delightful housekeeper, then set off for St Guilhem le Désert, around 50 minutes' drive away, considered to be one of the most beautiful villages in France and close to the quite spectacular Gorges de l'Hérault. As we began meandering through the picturesque streets of the ancient village we could certainly see how it had gained its reputation; there were some beautiful old buildings, with many features dating back to Roman times. The

Camino de Santiago (the Way of St. James) also runs through this village: a large network of ancient pilgrim routes stretching across Europe and coming together at the tomb of St. James (Santiago in Spanish) in Santiago de Compostella in north-west Spain.

Figure 46 St Guilhem le Désert, France

We explored the winding alleyways and cobbled streets and then were astonished to round a corner and find the beautiful Abbey de Gellone, dating back to the 11th century. With temperatures soaring into the 30s again, we enjoyed a pleasant drink in the square before entering the Abbey: a much simpler, but no less beautiful interior than some we have seen on our travels (although the organ was quite remarkable!) and with interesting cloisters and gardens.

From the Abbey we could see what appeared to be the ruins of a former residence at the very top of a huge rock; we couldn't imagine why would anyone want to live in such a perilous position?! We later refreshed ourselves in another quaint little café then found a lovely area of wild flowers close to the waterfall that falls just below the Abbey, rounding off our enchanting visit.

Figure 47 St Guilhem le Désert, France

We couldn't believe the week had gone so fast, but our friends were due to leave the next day, so we decided to have our final meal at La Sanboulou restaurant in Mèze's marina, where the food and the staff had been so lovely a few nights earlier.

As we got there, we realised that some event was taking place in the marina so went for a closer look. There were lots of people in the seating area and a jazz band was playing, whilst, in the marina, two of the mysterious boats with ladders contained teams and were being used for jousting matches, with one person from each team standing at the top of the ladder with a long pole aimed at the person from the opposing team as they rowed towards each other, each trying to topple the other jouster! It really was a delight to behold and there was a wonderful atmosphere in the marina as the spectators in the seats lining the port cheered them on and whooped with joy when someone was 'stabbed' and fell in the water. We were able to watch some of the excitement, whilst we ate another excellent meal, provided by really pleasant staff and, of course, in the company of our good friends.

Figure 48 Jousting boats at Mèze, France

We got back in time for the Wales vs Belgium football match, where we all sat down and relaxed to finish off our lovely week together and help Wales celebrate their win against Belgium, who, Tim told me, were the number one ranked FIFA team in the world.

We were sad to say goodbye to our friends as they left the following morning, but wished them well for the concert in which Andy and Diane were due to sing, within about an hour of their expected arrival in England!

Carcassonne and Lourdes – July

We decided we would leave Domaine Saint Hilaire too, planning to be back there for a family party later in the month. So, after packing up the van, we drove to **Camping de la Cité** at Carcassonne: a very pleasant site by the side of a canal, with a nice pool and all the necessary amenities easily accessible. We were a little puzzled, however, by the strange arrangement of sanitation facilities: there was a shower and washing facilities area for women, a shower and washing facilities area for men and an area that contained toilets for both men and women but showers for women only. As usual in France though, no-one seemed concerned by any of the signage.

I have to say that some of the speed bumps in both Spain and France have been particularly vicious and yet again, as on almost every other journey, our clothes (complete with hangers) had bounced off the rail and lay in a crumpled heap at the bottom of the wardrobe. So much for my fastidious ironing last week, ha ha!

Sadly, the temperature had dropped somewhat from the dizzy heights of mid 30s over the last few days, so we sat inside for our evening meal.

The next morning was much brighter and we walked the short distance along the canal to the medieval city of Carcassonne and what a wonderful place it is! From the outside it looks just like a 'fairytale' castle – I could imagine Rapunzel letting her hair down from one of the towers – and after we'd climbed the steep steps up to the Aude Gate (Aude being the river it overlooks), we went inside to explore.

It really is an extraordinary place, the best preserved medieval city in Europe (*probably...*); excavations have shown that a settlement existed there as long ago as 600 BC and the city as it is now has evolved over a period of 2500 years. An exterior wall, flanked by towers, was built in the 3rd century AD; the castle and Romanesque cathedral were built in the 12th century; and an outer rampart was built in the 13th century, when the inner one was also restored, making the city impregnable. However, in the 17th century, the area of Roussillon in which the city is situated was united with France, meaning that Carcassonne was no longer on the border of France and Spain and consequently, being of no further use as a frontier post, was left to deteriorate until restoration was undertaken in the 19th century.

We really enjoyed looking around the castle and walking around the ramparts, with fabulous views over the 'new' city, before investigating the Gothic cathedral within the city.

Figure 49 Castle at Carcassonne, France

Within the walls, there are lots of shops, hotels and restaurants and we decided to have a crêpe in one of the squares. Unfortunately the waitress was rather unpleasant, as, indeed, was the crêpe, so not the best food experience, but there was no way it was going to spoil our day.

After eventually leaving the medieval city, we walked down and across the nine-arch bridge to the 'new' town and then up to the Canal du Midi.

The town itself had been built in the 13th century when the inhabitants of the old city were exiled, but, apart from one or two of the buildings, it rather lacked charm. I nearly became very flushed when I almost got locked in an automatic (self-cleaning) toilet in one of the squares! I had hesitated in the doorway and it started to close ready to start the cleaning process; luckily Tim came to my rescue and dragged the door open again! He decided to give that particular convenience a miss, but after we'd walked back along the canal to the campsite (doing a bit of keep fit along the way!), he wished he'd availed himself of the previous facility, as all the toilet blocks were closed for cleaning at the same time!!

The temperature had been a very pleasant mid 20s, so we sat outside for our evening meal and walked down to the bar later. Tim was hoping to watch the Iceland vs France football match, but by the time we got there France were leading 2-0, so he decided there was no fun in watching the rest.

As we packed up to leave the next morning, Tim realised that he'd ended up with the Sky remote from Domaine Saint Hilaire in his lap top bag, the same place my 'missing' watch had ended up a few weeks earlier! I was beginning to think he had jackdaw tendencies!

It was a beautiful cloudless sky as we headed for Lourdes, a couple of hours' drive away. As we approached the campsite Tim quipped that Lourdes is the spiritual home of cricket and almost immediately the skies began to darken and the temperature was dropping....oops! By the time we'd got set up it was thundering and the storm got underway and continued for most of the night. I did wonder whether it was divine retribution!

The campsite (**D'Arrouach**) was a small, but very picturesque, campsite at the foot of the Pyrenees, very clean and well equipped (another one from the ACSI book, which saved us around €6 per night). It even boasted a sauna and 'conviviality suite' and had a small shop providing basic requirements, including fresh bread.

After our evening meal, we noticed greasy dribbles on the floor and were desperately sad to find that our trusty M & S (other outlets are available) aluminium tray (from a distant 'Dine in for two' meal) had developed a hole! We'd had good use from two of them, plus two of the plastic dessert glasses from the same meal; what good value that had been!....This is not just food...

We walked into Lourdes the next day, which had dawned much cloudier and cooler than we'd been used to. It felt quite strange having to wear a jacket for the first time since we'd left Granada! We were informed by the campsite receptionist that we should turn right out of the campsite and it was a 2kms walk. However, she had omitted to point out that there are two exits from the campsite; we, of course, went out the way that we had come in the previous day and found that we had taken a rather large detour, so ended up walking around 4kms into Lourdes, trust us!

The spire of a basilica was visible as we approached via a park area and past rows of lighted candles to the Grotto of Massabielle, which is where someone called Bernadette is alleged to have seen numerous apparitions of Mary, the Lady of Lourdes, in 1858, leading to the building of the basilica at Lourdes and its becoming a place of pilgrimage.

Figure 50 Basilica Superior, Lourdes, France

As we rounded the corner from there though, we saw the Rosary Basilica in all its glory and realised the spire we had seen was from the Basilica Superior above! It was humbling to see a huge crowd of people with various disabilities, who had clearly come on their own personal pilgrimage to this beautiful place, grouping for a photograph on the steps of the basilica.

Figure 51 Rosary Basilica, Lourdes, France

The doorway and surrounding decorated recesses of the Rosary Basilica were, themselves, quite magnificent, but we were both stunned by the spectacular interior, completed in 1901, that seats 1500 people. We have, of course, visited a number of beautiful cathedrals and basilicas on our travels, but somehow we felt that this one was very different in its beauty. There was a mass taking place as we entered, so we sat and observed the remainder of the service which, although not in our language, was very spiritual.

Afterwards we were able to look more closely at the magnificent dome and decorated chapels. We then went up the stairs to the basilica above, built in 1871, which had a much more traditional interior and a beautiful crypt, built in 1866.

The town of Lourdes, especially in comparison to the glory of the basilica, seemed surprisingly rather run down. We noticed the Hôtel La Solitude close to the basilica, but it looked a bit lonely and I bet they only have single rooms, ha ha!

After a light lunch (that, for me, included a delicious tarte tatin) and a coffee, we made our way back – the correct route this time – and sat out in what had become a much more pleasant day by then. As we sat reading and enjoying the evening sunshine, we could hear the goat's bells tinkling as they roamed the hills, that were, of course, alive with the sound of music ☺

After leaving Lourdes we stopped at a supermarket and were thrilled to see that they had some gas canisters at their fuel station that were the correct size for our van; we had been looking for a long time, but everything had been the wrong size! The woman at the gas kiosk gave us a price, but then we realised that the fitting was different from ours, so decided we'd check first whether the supermarket had the correct fitting adaptor. They had, so we waited patiently at the till, whilst the check-out girl chatted happily with the customers in front, whom she clearly knew, showing no concern for the lengthening queue of customers – fuming – behind. Eventually we were served and Tim went back to the kiosk to buy the gas bottle, only to find that it had closed for two hours until 3pm! We were then told we couldn't have a refund for the fitting, only a credit note, not much use to us as we were unlikely to pass by there again. The manager was called but said we'd have to wait outside her office while she verified the price that we'd been quoted for the gas bottle. After hanging around outside her office for a good ten minutes, Tim became increasingly impatient and eventually knocked and entered, only to find her casually eating her lunch! Some strong words were exchanged (mostly in French) and, in the end, we got both the fitting and the gas bottle at a bit of a discount! Nothing is ever straightforward is it?

Spain: San Sebastian – July

After paying all the French road tolls and receiving a very frosty reception at one of the manned ones, when we offered a €20 note for our payment, we finally got to San Sebastian later in the afternoon. We had decided to return as we had a little extra time on our hands, and also felt that we hadn't done it justice on our previous brief visit about 10 weeks ago, when (if you're paying attention) you may recall Ms Satnav had taken us up a steep, no through road, nearly ending our holiday before it had begun! However, San Sebastian had more treats in store for us, and locating the site on this occasion was again – wouldn't you know – not without problems, as the ACSI book's coordinates took us about two miles short of our destination and gave the wrong name for the campsite: it was actually **Camping Igelda**, which was not mentioned in the book! We then had to do a bit of shuffling around and ended up having to remove the bikes and fold up the bike rack in order to fit ourselves into our allotted *parcela* (pitch) before we could finally relax (oh it's such a hard life). We were beginning to wonder what San Sebastian had against us!

There was a bus stop just outside the campsite, where we caught a bus into San Sebastian and astonishingly found the Tourist Information Office straight away! San Sebastian is called Donostia in the regional Basque language, which, apparently, is the only language in the world that appears to have so many words that bear no relation to other languages. Out of interest, I've listed just a few everyday words below in English, Spanish, French and Basque as examples:

English	Spanish	French	Basque
Food	Comida	Aliments	Janari
Table	Mesa	Table	Mahaia
Chair	Silla	Chaise	Aulkia
Door	Puerta	Porte	Ate
Restaurant	Restaurante	Restaurant	Jatetxea

English	Spanish	French	Basque
To Walk	Caminar	Marcher	Ibili
House	Casa	Maison	Etxea
Road	Camino	Route	Errepidea
Lunch	Almuerzo	Déjeuner	Bazkari
Station	Estación	Gare	Geltoki

After a coffee in one of the plazas, where we had a look at the map and information, we set off to look for a particular street (mentioned in our information booklet), but couldn't find it on the map so we asked a Spanish man who very kindly looked it up on his phone: its name on the map was in Basque but was in Castillian Spanish in the booklet and was quite a different word altogether, no wonder we couldn't find it!

San Sebastian was founded in 1180 and became a fortified town due to its proximity to France and strategic war time location. It narrowly survived the plague in the 16th century, and numerous sieges, until in 1719 it fell into French hands and was then 'liberated' by Anglo-Portuguese soldiers, who burnt the town down in 1813, some liberation! Consequently the old town was built almost from scratch at that time and at the end of the 19th century began to develop into the tourist destination it is today. When we were there San Sebastian had the honour of being the European City of Culture. It is a lovely city, with a huge sandy beach and wide streets lined with trees.

There are, as in many large cities, quite a few beggars. However, we have noticed some subtle differences between these beggars and those in England: they don't generally have dogs; they wear reasonably good clothes; they have mobile phones; and they seem mostly quite well-fed! I feel I should point out that we raise a lot of money for charities so don't generally hand money directly to beggars

Figure 52 Square in San Sebastian, Spain

After wandering around the harbour, lined with restaurants, we visited the very attractive old town with lots of bars and shops, and a Rococó style church tucked away at the end of a street. We also came across the square shown in the photo, which had, in the past, been used for bullfighting. The balconies would have been used as viewing areas (they are numbered, above the windows on the left). Later, we discovered a little gem of a restaurant, La Fabrica (meaning 'The Factory', which is what it used to be), where we had an excellent three-course meal: an amuse bouche to start, then fish soup with lots of succulent pieces of fish for me, while Tim had a risotto; we both had duck breast, beautifully cooked and presented; finally I had a baked cheesecake and Tim had triple layered chocolate, again beautifully prepared. Service was excellent and the price of €26 included wine, water and bread which we thought seemed pretty good value for such a lovely meal. Just as we left, we bumped into our campsite neighbours for the second time, this time in the harbour area where they had eaten at one of the little fish restaurants.

Even after that lovely meal, I still had to drag Tim away from a specialist cheese shop we passed! And, as we walked along the promenade (*with an independent air,* of course) we met our neighbours yet again, amazing in such a large city!

I have to say that we were impressed with the public conveniences in San Sebastian (and we have reached an age where we tend to spend a lot of our time looking for them!). Unlike many other cities in Spain, there were plenty of very clean and free public conveniences! Perhaps we should be writing a guide to foreign loos!

We awoke – well, I did, Tim had been kept awake most of the night it seemed – to the torrential rain, so took our time over breakfast and decided not to do some of the washing that was now piling up. By mid-day, the rain had slowed to a drizzle so we headed into San Sebastian and, as yesterday, our timing was perfect, the bus was waiting and set off just after we'd boarded.

As it was not the best of days we decided to head up to the monument at the top of the iconic Mount Urgull, at the east end of the large bay. It was a fairly steep climb and the temperature was also rising, so we very soon removed our kagoules. We were very pleasantly surprised when we reached the top to find there was much more to see than the Sacred Heart monument, the only place from which the city's three beaches are visible. La Mota Castle, constructed in the 12th century, is also situated on Mount Urgull and has been a major defence in the city's history. Many of the cannons are still in place and we found lots of turrets and stairways to explore.

The history exhibition in the museum that now forms part of the castle was very impressive; much of it was in Spanish (we were becoming a little better at translating the written texts) but some of the audiovisual displays had English subtitles and it was very interesting to hear the locals' descriptions of early 20th century customs; apparently only the rich would bathe (in beach wear covering most of their bodies, as in Victorian England) and they would each have their own lifeguard who accompanied them into the sea (in full uniform!) and would pass them a cloak as they emerged from the sea, to preserve their modesty on the way to their beach huts.

After our descent from Mount Urgull, we visited the Basilica Santa Maria, a Baroque style church, built in the second half of the 18th century on the site of a Roman church from around the 12th century, destroyed during previous conflicts. This church is a beautiful and very traditional place of worship, with amongst others, a relief of Saint Barbara (looks just like me!). We then meandered through the town in what had become a pleasantly warm afternoon. One of the (seemingly very well fed) beggars was hassling us for money so Tim said to him, in Spanish, "You are not hungry"; he laughed and didn't bother us any more.

We, however, were starving! We hadn't eaten since our late breakfast (although we had been tempted by the delicious arrays of tapas in the mid-afternoon), so by about 5.30pm we were in a dilemma what to do, as restaurants in Spain don't open until 8.00pm. In the end, we decided to buy some *merluza* ('hake', a very generous portion for €4.75) and a bottle of Txakoli (the local wine, for €8.50). Tim cooked a gorgeous meal when we got back to the van and poured the Txakoli into our glasses from a height, as is customary here, in order to provide a sparkle to it (and, by the time we'd finished the bottle, to us too!).

Figure 53 Tapas bar, San Sebastian, Spain

It was another cloudy start to the following day, but we finally got a load of washing done and set off to San Sebastian again, wondering whether the washing would be wetter when we returned, as thunderstorms were forecast.

We alighted from the bus at the Funicular railway (cable-operated railway, from the Latin *funis*, meaning 'rope'), opened in 1912 and, it seems, still using the original carriages.

Figure 54 Funicular Railway, San Sebastian, Spain

The railway took us to the top of Mount Igeldo, the highest of San Sebastian's coastal mountains, at the west end of the bay, where there is a wonderful old-fashioned fun park and it was so nice to see young families enjoying themselves on the roller coaster (that travels around the very edge of the cliff), the little waterway, slides etc. There is also an old lighthouse, built in 1778, now used as a museum, with the most famous panoramic view of San Sebastian.

Figure 55 View over San Sebastian, Spain

The sun had come out as we looked around the park and enjoyed a drink on the balcony overlooking the beautiful bay and we decided to walk down the hill and along the promenade. Promenading is a very popular pastime with older Spanish people and we saw a number of well-dressed couples, walking arm-in-arm, particularly in the late afternoon/early evening.

Figure 56 Puppeteers, San Sebastian, Spain

After stopping to watch some excellent street puppeteers, we walked across the famous Puente de Zurriola (*Puente* means 'bridge') to the surfing beach where all the young people gather. We thought that perhaps walking across the bridge might endow us with youth, but no such luck, so we walked back and joyfully chanced across an Aldi in the centre of town, very well concealed within a shopping mall. We again stocked up with meat for our evening meal and made our way back, and the washing was dry!

We have, incidentally, learned that, as well as being a most attractive and friendly city, San Sebastian boasts the largest concentration of Michelin starred restaurants in Europe: three with three stars, one with two stars and five with one star!

Yet another very miserable, drizzly day dawned, so we decided to just relax and read. We had thought we'd like to go to the new outdoor pool on the campsite, which had only just opened yesterday, but it was much too cold and gloomy. I must say this campsite was very well kept and scrupulously clean, but it was also the most expensive we'd stayed at so far, although we were, of course, by then in high season, so fees had increased. We'd noticed there were lots of Australians on the site and wondered whether they had come for the surf in San Sebastian, which is, apparently, usually excellent.

In the evening we walked to the restaurant close by (about half a mile) with our neighbours, Sue and Dave, from Dorset, with whom we spent a very enjoyable evening, over a couple of platters of tapas and wine.

The drizzle had turned to persistent rain overnight and we had forgotten to put our table and chairs away, so Tim had the unhappy task of packing lots of very wet things into the boot.

France: Toulouse (almost!), Narbonne, Agde, Villeneuve-lès-Béziers and back to Montagnac – August

Our plans had been to travel across the border to the west coast of France, but on checking, we found that we would only be heading to more rain, forecast for the next few days. The better weather seemed to be in the south east of France so we decided to head back in that direction.

On a random stop at a service area on the motorway, we were amazed to find it housed a very good exhibition about the Camino de Santiago (the Way of St. James), the route that went through the beautiful village of St Guilhem le Désert (the one we visited with our friends at the end of June; do try and keep up!).

We eventually arrived at **Le Rupe** campsite, on the outskirts of Toulouse, another pleasant, spacious campsite, although not as spotlessly clean as our previous stay had been and were interested to find that we were parked next to an old campervan (1993 we were to discover), registered in Huddersfield. We later spoke to its occupants: an elderly New Zealand couple, who had lived in England for a few years, at which time they had purchased the van. When they returned to live in New Zealand, they had left the van with a friend and since then flew to the UK every year, when the winter started in New Zealand, picked up the van and travelled down to the south of France. They explained that they always spend quite a few weeks in Marseillan Plage, which, you will of course recall, was where Tim, Andy and I sang at the Guinguette d'Asterix restaurant.

Neither of us had slept well due to torrential rain and almost continuous thunder and lightning during the night, which hadn't abated in the morning, but our woes seemed insignificant when we saw that the shower block was crammed full of people 'camping' in there, having been flooded out of their tents!

Consequently, we sadly abandoned any thoughts of travelling into Toulouse and decided to head for the sun (we hoped) on the east coast, arriving at **La Nautique** campsite, on the edge of the Étang de Bages, just south of Narbonne, in mid-afternoon. It was a little overcast and windy, but at least much warmer. We were very impressed to find that every pitch had its own en suite shower/toilet!

We walked down to the bar area in the evening, where a singer/guitarist was performing, but didn't stay long and had an early night to catch up on the missing zzzzz's from last night. A much better day dawned, though still windy, so we cycled the 5kms or so into Narbonne. Most of the ride was on a fairly busy road, but we cycled the last mile into Narbonne along the banks of the Canal de la Robine, which was very pleasant; houses and shops are built on the Merchants' bridge (along which ran the Via Domitia – see next paragraph – the route that joined Italy to Spain in the 2nd century BC and originally ran through the centre of the town) over the canal.

In the main Town Hall Square there is the very impressive Archbishop's Palace (apparently, France's second most important group of archbishopric monumental buildings after Avignon) that became the Town Hall and now houses a number of museums. In the centre of the square there is an enhanced section of the Via Domitia, uncovered in 1997.

Figure 57 Via Domitia, Narbonne, France

The city of Narbonne was founded in 118 BC, the oldest Roman colony outside of Italy and our next visit was to the Horreum: an amazing series of subterranean galleries (5m below ground level), that are believed to have served as a public warehouse in the 1st century BC. Discovered in 1838, but used as storage areas by members of the public until their historical significance was appreciated in the mid-20th century, they have been very well preserved and there is still a considerable area to be excavated.

Figure 58 Subterranean galleries, Narbonne, France

We ambled through the narrow streets in Narbonne; there were some very pleasant little areas, but also quite a few places that seemed to be sadly in disrepair. After a stop for refreshments, we visited the Cathedral of Saint Just and Saint Pasteur, built in the 13th century and situated adjacent to the Archbishop's Palace. It is the highest Gothic cathedral in the south of France, at 40 metres, but the cloisters were apparently never finished. However, there is now considerable restoration work being carried out in the cloisters and on many of the chapels within the cathedral.

We stopped for a rest in the Palace gardens; I do keep complaining that some seats are a bit high for my feet to comfortably reach the ground, but this was ridiculous! Maybe I shouldn't have had that last drink!

Figure 59 Narbonne, France

On the cycle ride back, there were some quite strong cross winds, making it a fairly strenuous ride, so we felt we'd earned our meal of roast duck with cherry sauce, mmm!

Bastille Day celebrations at the campsite consisted of a foam party in the pool, that looked to be great fun, but we only watched from the bar, before going down to the edge of the *étang* (lake) just after 10.30pm, to watch a firework display across the water.

The following day we saw a huge fire in the distance, attended by lots of emergency vehicles as well as some small planes dropping water to try and extinguish what was clearly a major blaze, the smoke from it was literally blocking out the sun in the afternoon. We later found out that it was a forest fire that was threatening to engulf nearby properties and hoped it hadn't been caused by the previous night's firework displays.

Now, most sites have a departure time of 12 noon, occasionally 11.00am, so getting off this one by 10.00am seemed a bit early; however, we made it in time and, after stocking up on supplies at Carrefour, headed for our next port of call: **La Pepiniere** campsite, near Agde.

You may recall that we stayed at the Cap d'Agde a few weeks ago; this was another very pleasant site but closer to the city of Agde and adjacent to the Herault River. For the first time for quite a while, the temperature was well into the 20s, so, after settling in, we cycled the couple of kilometres to the beach at the Grau d'Agde (a fishing port), along a very good cycle path by the riverside. We had a nice relaxing afternoon on the beach, I did a bit of sketching and we enjoyed some people-watching.

The next day, we cycled approximately 5kms or so the opposite way along the river bank, into the old town of Agde. Agde is the 3rd oldest Roman settlement in France, founded in 525 BC (just after Béziers (575 BC) and Marseilles (600 BC)), so we were hoping to see some history. Sadly, we were disappointed, as the only ancient relics (besides us) were statues found in the river in the second half of the 20th century and a few very small artefacts. The centre piece of Agde's medieval past is a cathedral, built of volcanic rock that looked very similar to breeze blocks, so not the most attractive of buildings and unfortunately the doors were locked so we didn't find out whether the interior was any more interesting.

We followed a route from one of the maps we'd been given, which took us along some of the old streets of Agde and along the river's edge, where we saw this board outside one of the restaurants. We were being hassled by the owners to eat there, so didn't stop to find out what the French side of the board said, but even if we'd been hungry, the English translation, 'Goat Dung', was just not tempting! We have smiled a few times at the attempts of some restaurants to translate their menus into English, but this one really beat the lot!

Figure 60 Interesting menu! Agde, France

Some of the areas that we walked through were very run down – even slum-like – but we came across a couple of areas that had been brightened up with frescoed scenes on the walls of buildings, much cheaper than restoring them!

We visited an interesting museum of local history, which included some information about the water jousting that we'd seen in Mèze in early July. Apparently, it is practised principally in France, but also in Switzerland and Germany, the rules varying slightly between regions and countries. Evidence of rather more adversarial water jousting has, in fact, been found on bas-reliefs dating as far back as ancient Egypt (almost 3000 years BC). The competitive sport of jousting, of the type that we saw, was, it seems, certainly practised in ancient Greece and Rome, with evidence that it may have originated at the time of the foundation of Massilia, the Greek colony founded around 600 BC that was later to become the French city of Marseilles.

We enjoyed an evening meal of Toulouse sausages (purchased at Carrefour, about as close to Toulouse as we were going to get on this trip!) then got ready for our evening gig at the campsite bar. The audience initially consisted of a few people dining, but very soon our campsite neighbours – a family of five – came along and were quickly joined by quite a few other groups of people. By the time we reached the end of our set (an hour later) we were being asked for several encores and had clearly made a few more fans, even if none of them knew what we were singing about! (This site seemed to be completely full of French people; we hadn't spoken to another English person since we left San Sebastian and had begun speaking 'Spranglish' to each other.)

In the morning we were left in no doubt as to the name for a 'cap' in French as we heard the family next door (in a tent, so we couldn't help overhearing!), trying to get ready for their day out and the poor, harassed mum saying to the youngest boy, about four years old, "Je cherche ta casquette, ou est elle?" (I'm looking for your cap, where is it?) and many other similar, desperate, 'cap searching' pleas. We didn't discover whether they found it or not, but, after what seemed like ages, they did eventually go out.

Tim and I cycled back to the beach, this time venturing a little further along the sea front (there are 15 beaches to choose from around Agde!) and I did a bit more sketching, while Tim read.

Figure 61 Pastel sketch, Agde, France

We then walked along the water's edge for a while, enjoying watching all the families having fun and later I indulged myself in a Blue Lagoon, while Tim had Sex on the Beach, which, he said, was a little disappointing, hey ho!

As I stepped from the shower in the evening, I stumbled over the step and twisted my foot; it was very painful and evoked memories of my two broken limbs after a stumble at the end of our holiday in Crete, almost two years previously. I was feeling very sorry for myself in the evening, I can tell you, but was well looked after by Nurse Tim.

Thankfully, having taken some painkillers I slept reasonably well but still couldn't put too much weight on my foot in the morning, so we felt the best thing was to have a couple of lazy days and hope that some relaxation would improve it enough to be able to do something soon.

After a couple of days' rest, my foot was feeling a little better as we packed up the van before setting off on our travels again.

We had a salutary lesson in checking prices, though, when we learned that the cost of this stay had been €30 per night, not €13; the lady on reception said it had been a mistake in translation (and we had not been given anything in writing, which is unusual). We did wonder whether they had deliberately misled us, as the original lady had taken our ACSI card, saying that we would be eligible for a discount, even though it was high season. (Not the most we'd paid though, San Sebastian still held that honour.)

We stopped at a motorway services to fill up with water (the service area at the last campsite had been a bit tricky to get into). The ladies' toilets were closed for cleaning (in the middle of the day!) and ladies were being directed to the men's toilets, which wasn't a particularly pleasant experience when I went. However, when Tim went later, he told me that a Muslim lady had joined the queue in the men's toilets and was being ordered, in no uncertain terms, by a (presumably Muslim) man in the toilet area to leave. He was wagging his finger at her in a very angry way and saying that she should not be in there, but the poor woman was not allowed in the ladies' toilets! They were speaking in English and I think the man was quite surprised when Tim interjected, saying, "Where is she supposed to go, in the car park?!" at which the man threw his hands up and then proceeded to ignore her (and Tim).

We arrived later in the afternoon at **Les Berges du Canal** campsite at Villeneuve lès Béziers: a really nice, quite small campsite, on the edge of the Canal du Midi and, after settling in, went for a walk along the canal and into the very pretty town centre.

On our way back we met an English couple (the first since San Sebastian, apart from the Muslim couple on the motorway services!) and, after our meal of moules frites, we went and joined them (Lee and Dorothy) at their caravan for some evening drinks and conversation.

The next day was beautiful, so we set off on our bikes along the Canal du Midi into the town of Béziers, about six miles or so. It was a lovely ride – mostly in the shade, thankfully – on really good cycle paths, making it very enjoyable and relaxing.

Figure 62 Canal du Midi near Béziers, France

The canal was constructed in the 17th century, in order to connect the Atlantic to the Mediterranean and it has been an important factor in the success of the Languedoc wine industry. At 241kms, it is the longest artificial waterway in France.

At one point, the canal crosses over the Orb river by means of an aqueduct – the *Pont Canal* (literally 'Canal Bridge') – the biggest of its kind in France.

Figure 63 Aqueduct over the Orb River near Béziers, France

The temperature was causing us to seek some refreshment and we came across a lovely little restaurant (Les Comediens, no joke!), where we decided to partake of their lunch menu offer. It was a lovely atmosphere – typically French and full of seemingly local French workers and groups of friends – and very reasonable (about €36 for two three-course meals, a carafe of wine, water and coffees).

Suitably refreshed, we cycled across the *Pont Vieux* ('Old Bridge'), a Romanesque structure, with 19 arches, measuring 260 metres long and with a width of 5 metres, which crosses the Orb River. The bridge dates from the twelfth century and was originally the only way to get to Toulouse. However, it eventually became too narrow and has now been replaced by – guess what – the New Bridge! They're very creative with their bridge names don't you think? (There are in fact now five bridges within about half a mile along the river.)

Figure 64 The Old Bridge near Béziers, France

We then made our way a little further along the canal, hoping to at least see a little of the famous Neuf Ecluses de Fonseranes: a nine-rise lock, that is the third most popular tourist attraction in the region, after Carcassonne (that we visited recently) and the Pont du Gard near Nîmes (whose delights still awaited!). We had been forewarned that the lock was being renovated and, sadly, weren't able to get more than a glimpse of just one of the locks in the midst of workmen and machines. By the time we'd cycled back along the canal we were both beginning to feel like we were melting, so we went for a cooling splash in the very pleasant campsite swimming pool and then treated ourselves to an ice-cream (pure indulgence, I know!).

The next day was my birthday and, coincidentally, the anniversary of Béziers being conquered and burned and its population massacred in 1209, hmmm, better not celebrate in Béziers today!

After opening my two cards (he couldn't decide!) and present from Tim (a leather handbag that can also be worn as a stylish rucksack, purchased in San Sebastian), I was treated to my favourite breakfast of smoked salmon and scrambled eggs. In the afternoon we visited Tim's brother and his wife (Nick and Lisa) and family who were holidaying at the Domaine Saint Hilaire (where we stayed with our friends at the end of June), and Tim's mum and stepfather, who had just arrived to stay until after the family party next weekend. I was very honoured to have two birthday cakes and a second chorus of 'happy birthday' and some more cards and gifts.

Once back at the campsite, we got changed and walked into the town of Villeneuve lès Béziers to the Enfants Terribles ('Terrible Children', what a strange name for a restaurant!) fish restaurant, where we had a lovely meal: a starter of langoustines for me, scallops for Tim, then dorade (sea bream) for my main, rascasse (scorpionfish) for Tim's, followed by tarte tatin.

Another quiet day followed, relaxing in the sun and swimming in the large site pool, then, in the evening, having previously arranged it with the campsite owner, we set our gear up and entertained guests at the campsite bar. We were gradually honing our 'pop' set to appeal to the audience demographic through lessons learned at previous gigs and had a really fantastic evening. We were singing in the bar area and before very long, people who were dining across the small road – on the decking along the canal side – were literally 'dancing in the street' (hmmm, wonder if that would make a good title for a song?!); people on canal boats moored at the side and others stopped mid-canal were joining in and there were even some who'd been walking along the far side of the canal who were also dancing along with us.

We finished the evening feeling very euphoric and were treated to drinks on the house and also courtesy of a group of French people.

We slept well, feeling very pleased with ourselves!

The following morning, we cycled along the canal in the opposite direction from our previous trip. It was a very hot day and a refreshing following breeze made it a lovely 40-minute ride along the canal to Portiragnes Plage. We enjoyed a thirst-quenching drink at the nice quiet little beach bar, then wandered along to find ourselves a spot on the beach; it seemed to be 'bring your dog to the beach day', I'd never seen so many dogs! Presumably it must be one of the few beaches in the area where they're allowed. Anyway, they were all pretty well behaved so we had a nice couple of hours there.

We had drunk all the water we'd taken with us, so decided to have another drink at the bar; the DJ decided he should justify his existence and turned up the 'noise' with a tuneless heavy background beat, until we could hardly hear each other speak. Maybe we're getting old....

On the way back along the canal, the refreshing breeze seemed to have turned into a full, head-on gale, making it a very strenuous ride home, especially in the heat. By the time we got back I think we were both pretty dehydrated and drank gallons of water before we came round sufficiently to cook and eat our evening meal of roast chicken and salad; roasting the chicken did nothing to help cool the van down inside, but it was delicious.

That evening's site entertainment was line-dancing, which seems to be very popular with the French and they were certainly up for having a good time, I have to say.

The next morning, feeling drained in the heat, we had a lazy breakfast and did a bit of washing. I suggested we turn the ignition on to see what the temperature actually was and were amazed to see that it was 41°C! No wonder we were feeling lethargic.

We did manage a walk into the local village and had a drink in the bar there, then had a look in the 11th century church, not a small church for a village – it had three side chapels – where it was very pleasant and cool. Villeneuve lès Béziers has some medieval side streets and is quite a pretty village. We bought some fruit and juice and meandered back, then sat outside for our lamb meal (garnished with a bit of rosemary we'd picked from a pot in the village!), while the insects attacked us. Eventually we lit our lemon candle and sprayed ourselves with repellent that ended up taking the colour out of our tablecloth; we were hoping our skin wouldn't be similarly affected.

A large group of young people arrived and we were quite fascinated to see that, in the evening, they just put down a ground sheet and all slept in their sleeping bags on top of it, in the open air. That's confidence for you.

Having failed to achieve a great deal of movement yesterday, we decided to set off at 8.30am on our bikes along the canal to Béziers, before it got too hot, making our way to the centre of the city, where we enjoyed a lovely breakfast of fresh bread and croissants with orange juice and, for a change, hot chocolate.

We then went to visit the magnificent Cathédrale Saint Nazaire. The structure dates from the thirteenth century and was erected on the site of an earlier building that was destroyed during the massacre at Béziers in 1209. It was formerly the seat of the Bishopric of Béziers that was later merged into the Diocese of Montpellier. After climbing the almost 200 steps of a spiral staircase to get to the top of the bell tower, with a fantastic view over the city, we sat out in the cathedral garden admiring the view (secretly, just while we got our breath back!)

Figure 65 Cathédrale Saint Nazaire, Béziers, France

Some of the streets of Béziers had been festooned with umbrellas to keep shoppers and diners in the shade, what a lovely colourful idea! (I have since seen umbrellas used in the same way in the UK.)

As we passed a beauty parlour there was an almighty row taking place. We weren't quite sure what it was about, but there were definitely some serious fisticuffs; all we could see was a pile of men and women punching each other and doing a lot of shouting and screaming! Perhaps a husband was complaining that his wife's beauty treatment hadn't worked, or maybe she'd been refused entry as a hopeless case!!! We shall never know but kept a low profile, not wishing to end up getting involved and had another drink (it was hot!), before cycling back along the canal and eventually enjoying another refreshing swim.

We slept a little later than planned and were only just surfacing when we heard the morning's zumba class getting underway. I was feeling quite guilty at not having participated in any of the zumba/aquarobics activities provided at the campsite, but by the time I'd cleaned up in the sauna that our van's interior had become by late morning, I felt exonerated.

I must say that the site was very friendly, with regular entertainment as well an animation team providing lots of day-time activities for children. I was particularly impressed that they provide children's toilets and a parent/child shower area that included a low level children's shower alongside the normal adult sized one.

Our campsite friends, Lee and Dorothy, also came over again to say a final goodbye and we exchanged contact details then checked out of the campsite. We were delighted to find that the site owners had considerably reduced our bill as a thank you for our evening's entertainment.

Then it was back to Domaine Saint Hilaire to join Tim's family, now including all four of his nephews: Simon, Chris, Richard and James, and niece, Laura. We were made very welcome and the sound of the cicadas and the beautiful setting instantly made us feel more relaxed. Over lunch we presented

Nick with my painting of Domaine Saint Hilaire that I'd started when we were staying there at the end of June and finished during our stay near Narbonne.

Figure 66 Painting of Domaine Saint Hilaire, France

We'd managed to get it framed at a place near Béziers, thanks to advice from Tourist Information (which, incidentally, was actually on a canal boat) near our last campsite at Villeneuve lès Béziers. I'm pleased to say that Nick seemed very happy with it!

In the evening, Nick and his wife, Lisa, hosted a party for local business owners, so Tim and I enjoyed practising a little of our French (and even some Spanish) speaking to the guests and, of course, sampling the wines and tapas!

After breakfast the next day, Lisa very kindly took us to Sète, where we picked up a Fiat Panda hire car. We stopped for a drink by the canal then had a look around Sète: quite a nice little shopping area and a couple of large squares, one of which was holding an antique market.

I had been fancying a nice crêpe whilst we were France, so we made our choice from the list on display at a small café, only to be told that they weren't serving crêpes at that time! We tried another crêperie, with the same response, so we figured we weren't going to get a crêpe today and settled for a croque monsieur at a different café.

By then it was time to go to the airport to pick up Tim's son, Stuart, his wife, Claire and son, Nathan and take them back to the Domaine to complete the family set for the weekend. An afternoon of fun and frolics ensued in and out of the pool (Lila the dog kept out of the way, cooling off in her own pool!), followed by an al fresco family meal that lasted late into the evening.

In the photo below are, left to right:

Back row: Tim, me, Tim's mum Gwen, Nick, Lisa, Claire, Stuart
Middle row: Tim's stepdad Ian, Laura, Richard, Chris, Simon
Front row: Nathan, James

Figure 67 Family photo at the Domaine, France

Another beautiful day dawned and Nick took us all on a tour of the vineyard the following morning, that was extremely interesting (we did have a tour with our friends in June, but this time we were shown some different areas and, of course, the vineyard's activities were now gearing up for the forthcoming harvest). The fun and frolics continued and Tim and I both had a dip in the pool before lunch and later went, with Stuart, Claire and Nathan, to Marseillan, where (at last!) we had a delicious crêpe in one of the little cafés by the port, then watched another water jousting session that was great fun, though quite brutal!

In the evening, we joined the rest of Tim's family at the permanent fun fair at Cap D'Agde, where the younger members of the family enjoyed some of the more adventurous rides and games and we all joined in on the bumper cars before heading back very late in the evening.

We all had a lazy breakfast, then Tim and I, with Stuart, Claire and Nathan, had fun building sandcastles on the beach at Mèze, before re-joining the rest of the family back at the Domaine for some target practice in the woods around the house. It was the first time I'd ever fired an air rifle, so I was thrilled to hit the target (not, of course, the bull's eye but hey!) on at least two of my three shots.

Tim and I then visited the nearby site of an exposed section of the Via Domitia (we had seen another section of it recently in Narbonne). You will recall that the Via Domitia is one of the oldest Roman roads anywhere, linking Rome in Italy to Cádiz in Spain; it was part of an immense road network of more than 70,000 miles, built by the Romans in around 118 BC.

At around 7.00pm we all gathered for pre-dinner drinks then sat at the outside table for our evening meal: a rather late 'big' birthday celebration for Nick. Within minutes of the starter being served, the thickening clouds finally produced a downpour, so we all had to hastily retreat indoors; such a shame, but it certainly didn't put a damper on the proceedings. We had a wonderful evening, great food and, of course, fantastic wines to complement each course. We chatted and laughed late into the evening again before staggering to bed.

An early start, consequently, was quite an effort, but worth it as we had to say goodbye to family who were flying back to the UK in the morning. We then had a relaxing few hours before we had to take Stuart, Claire and Nathan to Montpellier airport for their flight back to the UK and, of course, more goodbyes.

Back at the Domaine, we did a quick turn-around, changing into our 'performance' clothes and packing the car up with the singing gear, then headed for restaurant L'Eau Sel in Mèze, whose proprietors, Manuela and Didier, we'd met last Wednesday evening at the Domaine's Open Evening. Neither of them spoke a word of English and, communicating in French/Spanish, we'd arranged to do a one-hour gig for them tonight. However, when we got there we realised that they had thought we'd agreed to come and showcase ourselves for a future gig, oops! Maybe our conversational French/Spanish wasn't as good as we thought! Anyway, we sang for an hour for the dozen or so diners and friends and it went down very well; they must have enjoyed it, as they asked us to return whenever we can!

We drove to Sète the next morning to return the four-wheel drive Fiat Panda – that we must say has been a very handy and accommodating little car – and Lisa drove us back to the Domaine to enjoy our last lazy afternoon there, followed by wine and nibbles and some interesting conversation.

Through France, Belgium and Luxembourg towards The Netherlands – August

After saying our farewells to Nick, Lisa and family, we got an early start. Having spent a few days in a very small left-hand-drive vehicle, Tim had to quickly get used to driving a large right-hand-drive vehicle again, but managed to extricate the van from the driveway safely. Then we were on our way again!

Our first port of call was the fabulous Pont du Gard, just north of Nîmes, which supplied the citizens with running water for five centuries. Built around the 1st century AD, it's the tallest Roman aqueduct in the world, with three levels, reaching 50 metres high and 360 metres long.

Figure 68 Pont du Gard, France

Luckily someone with foresight in the 18th century made some modifications to prevent deterioration, ensuring that it remains a most impressive structure. We were less impressed with the commercialisation of the whole area: a total of €18 entry fee and we were funnelled past a number of stores selling tourist mementoes etc, but definitely worth seeing.

We climbed steps to the top of the aqueduct where we got some very good views and realised that, at the other side of the river, people were able to walk along the old aqueduct. We thought that would be a great thing to do, so we made our way across the lower section of the bridge and up the steps at the other side, only to be told (at around mid-day) that entry to the museum and upper level of the aqueduct was now closed until 3.30pm! Needless to say we were disappointed but we didn't have time to wait, as we needed to move on.

After a brief call at Lidl we set off, in the hope of dancing *sur le pont d'Avignon*, but were disappointed yet again; sadly, although Avignon looked like a lovely and very interesting city, the powers-that-be clearly had no intention of allowing anyone in a motorhome to park anywhere. All the car parks we found had 2 or 2.5 metre barriers and there was no street parking that would accommodate us, so, after Tim had valiantly negotiated the narrow streets in ever decreasing circles, we made our departure, hoping that one day we'd return. (Note: we did return to this wonderful city a couple of years later and danced on the famous bridge.)

We headed north and ended up in a little town called Trevoux, north of Lyon, where we parked on a very pleasant aire, though without any of the amenities that our aires book had suggested (ie it was just a piece of land). It was a lovely evening so we sat outside for our evening meal then went for a walk by the river and were pleasantly surprised by the number of families picnicking, playing football or petanque (like bowls) or generally relaxing in the park. Eventually a musical trio started playing on a stage positioned on a boat at the water's edge and we sat and listened for a while. They were singing some quite bluesy songs, in English, to the French audience and had drawn quite a good crowd.

In the morning, we rather naughtily sneaked into the campsite across the road to use their facilities then continued our journey north through France. We were as keen as mustard to get to Dijon :), but managed to avoid Dole and steered clear of Nancy, reaching the city of Metz, not far south of the Luxembourg border in the late afternoon.

Founded around 1000 BC, Metz (known then as Divodorum) became one of the biggest and most prosperous towns in Roman

Gaul and eventually the capital of Austrasia. (No, it hadn't moved from Australia! The word is believed to be a reconstruction of *Oster-rike*, the Old Frankish name for 'Eastern Kingdom'). It was the intellectual centre of the Carolingian empire and was the starting point of the Gregorian chant (originally called the Messin Chant). The city's geographical location resulted in it alternating, for many years, between French and German 'ownership'.

The site we found – **Camping Municipal Metz** – was at the edge of the Moselle river and very close to the city, so we had a walk round the city centre, built on the confluence of the rivers Moselle and Seille and visited St Étienne Cathedral, which was built in the 13th century and, with its 42 metre-high vaults, is one of the highest Gothic cathedrals in Europe.

Figure 69 St Étienne Cathedral, Metz, France

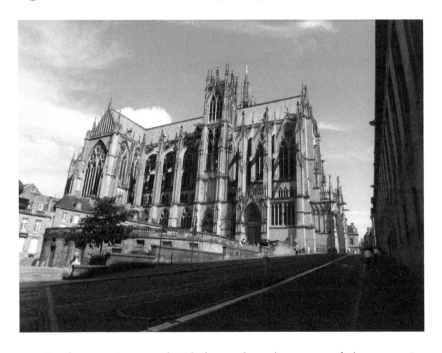

In the evening we decided to take advantage of the campsite take-away and had roast chicken and chips with a salad, that we ate al fresco.

We had considered staying two nights in Metz and exploring the city a little more, but when we woke it was pouring with rain (and the top temperature was forecast for 18°), so it seemed that the decision was made for us. We travelled through Luxembourg and then into Belgium and by the time we stopped at a motorway services (Aire d'Aische en Refail) I needed to avail myself of their facilities quite urgently, so Tim dropped me off at the doorway while he went to park the van. I rushed inside, only to find that there was a charge of 50 cents to use the toilet; I, of course, had not taken any money with me (like the Queen), so I then had to go and find Tim in the van. It's very difficult trying to run with your legs crossed.

We made ourselves a quick sandwich and got on our way. The sign at the exit wished us a 'good journey' in various different languages, the last being *Gute Fahrt*. I didn't think they would have heard!

The Netherlands: Amsterdam – August

As we travelled, we were discussing where to spend the night and eventually decided to carry on and do the 450kms or so to Amsterdam. We found a site there (**Amsterdam City Camping**), again with few facilities (only water and drainage) but situated directly across the water from Amsterdam's Central Station and after a little exploring (that involved having a quick look at a huge festival just getting underway for the evening on the old docklands area), we found that only a few minutes' walk away there was a free ferry to the station, right in the heart of Amsterdam.

Amsterdam has some huge multi-storey bike parks and the city is absolutely packed with bikes, on the move and also tied up to every possible anchor point.

Figure 70 Bike Park in Amsterdam, Netherlands

We had a walk around and visited the Sex Museum that sounds very saucy, but actually was rather boring – I know, I know – but it was almost all just faded sepia photos from the late 19th/ early 20th century of people being slightly cheeky with each other!

We didn't want anything too fancy for our evening meal and eventually decided on a small Tapas Bar & Grill with an offer of steak, chips and salad for €12.50 that we thought would do nicely. It wasn't packed, but service was very slow and we were beginning to wish we hadn't bothered, but when the food finally came it was absolutely delicious: a nice salad, good chips and as nice a steak as I've ever had: a thick piece of steak perfectly cooked and tender, mmm!

We managed to get the right night ferry back and, when we reached the other side, meandered through the huge festival (mainly because we took a wrong turn!), where there were at least a hundred different food stalls and music at full blast from several bands and discos. We eventually emerged from the festival area and passed some of the old docklands buildings on our walk back to the site, where we drifted off to sleep to the dulcet sounds of heavy rock music.

Most sites insist that you leave by mid-day on the day of departure, but at City Camping you are allowed to stay for 24 hours from the time you arrive, so, after breakfast we caught the ferry back to Amsterdam, this time taking the bikes with us and joined the merry throng of cyclists. Eventually, after securing the bikes to the only available tiny bit of railing we could find, we sat and had a coffee by one of the canals, at a little spot called Café-Bar Aen't Water, and it's a jolly good job it wasn't water at €11.40! We really enjoyed having some time in Amsterdam – it's such a vibrant city – and we were probably slightly high on cannabis anyway, the smell of it permeated every street! We almost tried a cannabis ice cream (which are widely available from street vendors and stores), but we had more travelling to do later in the day and thought we'd better stay safe.

Tim had a wonderful time challenging an assistant in a cheese shop to find him a tasty Dutch cheese but she did, to her credit and assured us that Edam is only really made ('made' backwards, of course☺) for the tourist market.

The Hague – August

Eventually, we caught the ferry back, packed up the van and drove around 35kms to Den Haag (The Hague) where my niece Carol, her partner, Erik and son, Damian, live. We had wondered about parking in the street near their house, but eventually drove to the Campsite **Stad Den Haag**, about 3kms away, where the proprietors were very friendly and we were able to park the van safely. Carol and Erik then took us back to their house and, after a cuppa and a quick change, we cycled to a local Italian restaurant for a lovely meal. We hadn't seen Carol and Erik for a long time and somehow it ended up being 2.00am before we got to bed!

After our late night (and first night in a 'real' bed since the end of June), I don't think it will come as any surprise that we were a bit late up! So, it was after a late breakfast that we set off on bikes to ride the 15kms or so to Delft. The cycle paths in Holland are amazing; we had been impressed generally with the provision for cycles in Spain and France, but I must say that Holland outstrips them all!

Delft is a very pretty little town, famous of course for its pottery, styled on imported Chinese porcelain from the 17th century. The artist Johannes Vermeer (best known for The Girl with the Pearl Earring) was born in Delft in 1632.

Figure 71 with Carol and Erik in Delft, Netherlands

The main square is vibrant, with stalls and musical entertainment of various kinds. We stopped at a little café in a smaller square for a drink and some Bitterballen – a typical Dutch meat-based snack, a bit like croquettes – that were delicious!

Figure 72 Tim eyeing up the Bitterballen! Delft, Netherlands

We then cycled along the very pretty canal side and the excellent cycle paths to Den Haag, the Netherlands seat of government. Although not the capital of the country (which is Amsterdam), it is the third largest city of the Netherlands after Amsterdam and Rotterdam and is one of the major cities hosting the United Nations. We walked through the grounds of the parliament buildings and stood at the point where many of the news reporters stand when filming their reports for TV.

Figure 73 Rotterdam's Parliament buildings, Netherlands

It was a beautiful afternoon, so we indulged in a sharing platter and a glass of wine, then, after a quick change back at Carol and Erik's house (a round trip of around 32kms altogether), headed to Scheveningen, close by, where we went to the Sui Sha Ya Japanese restaurant, specialising in Teppanyaki, for an amazing dining experience! Teppanyaki is a style of Japanese cuisine that uses an iron griddle to cook food; indeed the word *teppanyaki* is derived from *teppan* (iron plate) and *yaki* (grilled, broiled, or pan-fried). True to form, the food was prepared and cooked to perfection on the surface directly in front of us and we were treated to quite a theatrical spectacular, including the opportunity to catch (in our mouths) slices of omelette flicked by the chef! Tim and Erik both managed to catch at least one piece each; I caught one in my hair, but I don't think that counts!

After a fabulous meal, accompanied by a little liquid refreshment, we went for a walk along Scheveningen's promenade. Each year, from March to October, a long row of bars and restaurants is erected along the beach front, fitted out with comfortable settees, chairs and tables. The bars were all beautifully illuminated in the evening and many of the tables had, in their centre, a fire, giving the whole area a wonderfully relaxing feel. We stopped at one of the bars and made ourselves comfortable.

Figure 74 Scheveningen, Netherlands

After a little while, the waiter came and took our order and Tim and I both ordered a brandy. It seemed like ages before we got our drinks, but when they arrived, our brandy glasses were dirty, so we asked for clean ones. At least 10 minutes elapsed before the waiter returned with fresh glasses, but as soon as he put them down, he saw himself that they still were soiled so took them back again! Yet another 10-minute wait later, we finally got some clean glasses complete with brandy! No wonder they were not busy there but heaven knows how long we'd have had to wait if they had been! By the time we got back and chatted, it was approaching 2.00am again before we finally tumbled into bed!

Needless to say, another rather late breakfast was required, after which we drove to the beach north of Scheveningen and then went for a brisk walk amongst the dunes. We stopped off for a coffee on our way and had a look around the information centre there, that was very well laid out. Outside was a children's play area with a huge sand pit and a water system that enabled the children to fill up containers with water; they were absolutely loving it! We have noticed, on our travels, that provision for children is excellent in these countries.

After our coffee, we continued our walk to the beach; it was a pleasant, but very windy morning and not the warmest of days, and walking back up the deep sand to the dunes, with the wind blowing against us, was quite hard work!

After a quick welcome cuppa back at Carol and Erik's, Carol, Tim and I went to Rotterdam, home to Europe's largest port and the 10th largest in the world. We were treated to the sight of the cruise ship Rotterdam pulling out of the harbour, with all its accompanying water jets and horn blasts, then had a lovely walk around the centre of Rotterdam, known for its lively cultural life and maritime heritage, whose history (and name) goes back to 1270, when a dam was constructed in the river Rotte.

Rotterdam's city centre was almost completely destroyed during World War II, resulting in a varied architectural landscape (including sky-scrapers, most unusual in Holland) and we walked through the amazing new market hall (more markets to compare!) and past the weird cube houses and other quirky buildings. It is certainly a vibrant city and was voted 2015 European City of the Year and listed 8th in the Rough Guide's top 10 cities to visit.

Having covered around nine miles on our walks today, we arrived back just in time for delicious chicken fajitas that Erik had prepared for us while we were out and we were joined by their son, my great-nephew, Damian, who had just returned from a six-month working tour of Australia.

We spent the rest of the evening chatting and managed to make it to bed before midnight, which was good, as we had an early start the following day to say our goodbyes and drive the short distance of 35kms or so to our next and final port of call, Schiedam.

Schiedam to Home – August

Just as we arrived in **Schiedam**, we spotted a Lidl sign and just couldn't help ourselves, suddenly we'd turned down the street trying to find it! Alas, our quest was in vain, but luckily we found a very small parking area specifically designated for six vans and there was just one space left, so we quickly made it ours.

It was a very pleasant little spot, no amenities whatsoever, but right beside the canal and in sight of three of Holland's iconic windmills.

Figure 75 Aire at Schiedam, Netherlands

We had a very pleasant walk around the streets of Schiedam, well-known for its distilleries and malthouses and the production of *jenever* (gin), which was the town's main industry during the 18th and 19th centuries; in fact the word *Schiedam* has actually come to refer to the town's Holland Gin.

Later in the afternoon we went to call on an old friend of mine, who had recently moved to Schiedam, and spent the next couple of days chatting and catching up.

A violent thunderstorm and also coots squawking on the canal just beside our van disturbed us during the night, but not as much as when we returned to the van late on the final afternoon to find that (along with all the other motorhomes/vans) we had been given a parking ticket! It seemed that, although there was no indication on the sign, we were supposed to have paid for our two days' parking! After we'd calmed down, we spent the rest of the evening getting ready for our trip back tomorrow. (Incidentally, we objected to the fine when we got home and sent photos of the area and signage and didn't have to pay in the end: result!)

Finally, on the last leg of our grand European tour, we arrived at Rotterdam Europort, with about an hour and a half to spare before boarding. Consequently, our late afternoon meal was cooked and eaten as we waited at the front of our line in the queue for the ferry! (One of the joys of motorhoming!)

Once on board, we left our overnight bags in our cabin and sat in one of the lounges with a drink. Two different entertainers came on and we thought we could have done as well, if not better to be honest on a good day, but we were too tired to stay up for the main act and retired to our little bunk beds.

When we woke up it was raining and 14°, yup, back in the UK. It felt very strange to be back, but we were thankful to have returned safely, having travelled over 5000 miles through seven countries and survived 16 weeks in close proximity without murdering each other! I have to say we'd learned a lot about motorhoming (some of it the hard way), and the van had gained a few scars in the process, but we were already looking forward to our next trip.

We were brought firmly down to earth when we got home, discovering a problem with the water tank, causing water to gush out of the overflow all over the garden, then a problem with the gas. Fortunately, a handy handyman very kindly came and sorted things out quickly. Welcome home!

We then had to sort out how to fit in my son Stuart's wedding, my grandson Jake's christening, a Golden Wedding party, two 60th birthday parties, and how to accommodate my soon-to-be visiting daughter Helen, her husband Andy and their three children, from Australia.

The Second Trip:
France, Spain, Portugal –
March to June

I'm pleased to report that all of the planned celebrations went smoothly! The photos show my three children: Helen, Stuart and Kate at the christening, and my three grandchildren, Hannah, Ruby and Jake (respectively, 6, 4 and 1) after the wedding.

Figure 76 Helen, Stuart & Kate

Figure 77 Hannah, Ruby & Jake

The van had been very useful as a spare bedroom on the drive when my daughter and family were over from Australia and also after a lovely Christmas Day with my sister and family. We'd also spent a few nights in it on a weekend trip to Filey and a visit to a wine tasting in York (yes, really!).

The joys of being retired meant that we were able to take yet another long break and couldn't wait to pack up the van for our second expedition into Europe. It will come as no surprise, to those of you who were paying attention in the previous section, that preparation for this trip was not without a few dramas! The day before we left we took the van to a vehicle hand wash to smarten it up for our trip; they hadn't done the roof, so Tim put the stepladder up and attempted to clean it as much as possible and to remove some pine needles that had lodged in the recesses of one of the roof lights. Unfortunately when trying to open it the mechanism snapped and we ended up having to tape the whole thing down, aagh! We then decided to fit our recently purchased bike cover. We'd paid for the best one, designed to cover four bikes comfortably and the box labelling confirmed our choice. However, when we unpacked it and tried to put it in place, it became blindingly clear that the contents of the box were not as advertised! It barely covered our two bikes after a considerable effort (involving the stepladder again!) to get it over them; how we were to manage without a stepladder remained to be seen!!

Just to complicate things a bit more, we had also decided (for various reasons) to have a new kitchen fitted whilst we were away, which, of course, meant that we had to completely empty all the cupboards before we left. Consequently, we were living out of boxes for the last few days, as well as packing the van and, the evening before we left, Tim was painting the kitchen ceiling ... I know!!

We had learned a few lessons from last year's trip and invested in a dual gas ring so that we (well, Tim!) could cook outside, and a second folding table that was a bit higher and, therefore, more comfortable to eat at. Having purchased the gas ring though, we struggled to find a supplier of the correct fitting for the external gas point. We were getting a bit worried, as the planned day of our departure was getting nearer, but finally located what we hoped was the right one on-line and paid £10 for speedy delivery. Just typical, they attempted delivery during the brief period we were out, so we had to arrange another delivery the day before our departure; thankfully it arrived safely in time.

France – March

Anyway, we finally set off – yet agin, later than planned – and had a good journey down to visit Tim's family in the south of England, before heading off for the channel tunnel crossing from Folkestone. We arrived in good time, to find that there was an hour's delay, oh no! Some time later we arrived in Calais at a sunny 16°, yes! Sunglasses on, here we go! Sadly, about ten minutes later, fog descended and we were back to 11°. Our satnav friend then guided us expertly to a cheaper fuel station, although, as always, the access to the pumps was exceptionally difficult and we ended up having to reverse in; how do they expect large vehicles to fill up? Answers please!

We gave the coordinates for a nice looking aire just below Orléans to Ms Satnav and off we went. She decided to take us a little closer to Paris than I would have preferred, but we figured she knew what she was doing, so faithfully followed directions and were excited to be treated to a magnificent view of the Sacré Coeur and the Eiffel Tower. A little later, we were, without prior warning, confronted with a two-metre 'soft' barrier (the van is three metres high) and, travelling at around 50mph, with traffic all around us, we were unable to avoid the row of solid foam lumps thudding across the roof of the van, before we managed to swerve on to an alternative carriageway to avoid what was clearly a low bridge ahead. Having just had a new cable fitted providing better access to the TV, we were hoping that this hadn't just removed our aerial altogether!!

We were, of course, now heading in the wrong direction and Ms Satnav kept urging us to turn around or re-trace our steps. We had no desire to hit the two-metre barrier again, so attempted to find our own way. I must say that, after driving in circles for an hour or so, during which we'd seen the Sacré Coeur and the Eiffel Tower another three or four times from different angles, the view had become distinctly less exciting! Finally, we managed to escape and arrived at our chosen aire slightly later than intended.

Thankfully, **Jouy le Potier** was a very pretty, historic, village (much more 'Jouy-ous' than our first 'Mezerey-ble' night on last year's trip!). We found a wonderful Logis and, at a table near the log fire, enjoyed a gorgeous meal of Magret de Canard (duck) with *anais* (parsnip) and sweet potato puree, followed by a selection of cheese (naturally!) with freshly baked bread rolls and, of course, wine. (I feel I should mention that, although we do partake of a little more alcoholic refreshment on our travels than we would at home, we really don't overdo it, honest guv!) The ambience was delightful and the 'lady of the house' (whose husband was the chef) was very welcoming and helpful. (And the aerial on the van was intact, by the way!)

Figure 78 Historic buildings, Jouy le Potier, France

The village boulangerie provided delicious freshly baked croissants for our breakfast and some crusty bread (that we had for our lunch later with some of my home-made houmous (truthfully!)). As we left the village, we were waiting to turn on to the main road when Tim suddenly realised we had been driving on the 'wrong' side of the road, oops! Fortunately, it was Sunday and we hadn't encountered any other traffic.

We then had a 637kms journey, during which we crossed some splendid viaducts, the most magnificent of all being the one at Millau, which is an astonishing piece of engineering, spanning the valley of the river Tarn. It is the third tallest bridge in the world, with one mast's summit at 343 metres above the base of the structure and a total length of 2460 metres.

Figure 79 Millau Viaduct, France

Along the road, we passed a lorry that had the words TRANS GENDRE written on it: we weren't sure whether that referred to the driver, or to the sheep on board! We then made our way to Domaine Saint Hilaire (which was – pay attention at the back – the house belonging to Tim's brother and family), to enjoy their hospitality again, this time in their absence, for a night. We missed the first turning to the Domaine so took the next – narrower and much rougher – road, but, about 100 metres before joining up again with the better road, we realised, too late, that the surface on a small bridge had crumbled over winter. The van grounded, only momentarily but with a very nasty scraping sound, and when we pulled up we found that all the wiring for the lights had been torn apart! It was then that we decided we may need to spend two nights here so that we (the Royal 'we' of course!) could fix the lights!!

Breakfast consisted of delicious fresh croissants and bread again, after which we went to the van to get some of our things out, but as Tim opened the top cupboard, one of our two 'proper' glasses (a gin and tonic just isn't the same in a plastic container!) smashed on to the floor! It must have moved during our brief encounter with the rough road!

Whilst I cleaned up, Tim and a very helpful Domaine employee (Nick Frith) finally managed to connect all the wires up and made the van safe and usable again; fortunately the wires were colour-coded, otherwise we may have had the right hand indicator flashing when we wanted to turn left!

It was a beautiful afternoon, with a temperature around the mid 20s, so t-shirts and shorts were the order of the day as we sat out near the pool to have a drink, then went for a walk through the nearby woods.

The following day we headed off towards nearby Marseillan to fill up with fuel and one or two other basic essentials. We ended up doing a couple of circuits of the town centre as one of the main streets was closed because it was market day and one of the diversion signs had, it appeared, blown the wrong way round! Nothing ever seems to be straightforward does it? Even my trip to the loo in the supermarket turned into an adventure, as, due to building work, I was re-directed via a roller shutter door, but when I tried to exit, I struggled to find the cord that a sign in front of me was directing me to pull. In desperation, I eventually turned round to find an alternative route, only to realise the cord was behind me; oh yes it was!

Before leaving Marseillan, I decided to treat myself to some new sunglasses, as my others were decidedly wobbly. It was such a lovely day, I donned them immediately, but clearly I was tempting fate as within about 10 minutes the sun went in and didn't come out again for the rest of the day!

Spain: Palamós, Benicàssim and Moraira to El Campello – March

We had a 2½-hour drive to our next stop, during which we observed that the French have not held back with renewable energy:

there were hundreds of wind turbines along the sides of the motorways. The last part of the journey was through lovely Spanish countryside villages with names such as Ultramort and Parlava, wonderful! We finally reached our chosen aire for the night, **Empord Area** in Palamós, which was an exceptionally well run aire, accommodating 40 motorhomes (and it was almost full), and with excellent facilities including hot showers and toilets (not usually available on aires). The fee of €12 per night even included electricity and Wi-Fi. By chance we parked up next to the only other British van on the site (an A class (super sized!) Frankia motorhome), belonging to a couple from Plymouth and after our meal we spent a very pleasant evening with them over a bottle of wine.

After breakfast, we unloaded the bikes and cycled down to the lovely sandy beach about a kilometre from the aire. There were very few people around as we cycled along the front, past two large marinas and lots of cafés and bars getting ready for the season to begin.

A very helpful lady at a nearby campsite, due to re-open at the weekend, allowed us to tie our bikes to the campsite railings while we set off on a 40-minute walk along the cliff top to La Fosca, with lovely coves and dramatic coastline.

La Fosca (although also quiet pre-season) is a pretty little town and the sea was a beautiful azure blue as we walked up to the Castell de Sant Esteve de Mar (Steven of the sea? Maybe an ancestor of Sea-sick Steve!). Apparently the earliest record of this castle was in 1063 and it was found to have been erected over a Roman villa.

We walked back to our bikes, then cycled back into Palamós town centre, where we stopped at the Melody Café and partook of their menu of the day: olives, fresh bread, chicken, pasta Bolognese, a glass of beer and a coffee for the price of €9.50 each, excellent value!

On our way back to town, we stopped at the supermarket; I waited outside with the bikes, while Tim popped in to get some bread. We then cycled back to the van and Tim spent the next couple of hours sorting out our music on his laptop, while I wrote my blog.

Having had a big meal earlier, we decided to just have some of our fresh bread with a bit of houmous for an early evening meal. Unfortunately, however, despite searching everywhere, we couldn't locate the bread that Tim had previously bought. In the end we donned our shoes and went back down to the supermarket. Fortunately it was the same assistant and she recognised Tim and handed over the bread that he had paid for but forgotten to take earlier, duh!

Later in the evening we decided to use the excellent shower facilities that required a €1 coin to operate them. I had no change, but Tim said he had two coins so we went up to the shower block and were both all ready to get in the shower before Tim realised that the coins he had were both €2! He went back to the van and fortunately managed to find a €1 coin, which gave us a grand total of five minutes for us both, quite a speedy shower experience!

After breakfast, we stocked up on basic essentials again. I noticed that the toothpaste was advertising, as one of its qualities, *proteccion diaria*, amazing what toothpaste can do now isn't it, I just expected it to clean my teeth! (It actually means 'daily protection'.) We avoided the Bimbo bread and got another lovely baguette, this time remembering to take it with us, before heading off towards Tortosa (pronounced 'tor-tosser'), just less than three hours' drive away. On the way, we stopped at a service area on the motorway and, as it was such a lovely day, sat outside with our lunch. We were joined by a couple from Liverpool, who were also motorhoming to the south of Spain and Portugal and we spent a pleasant half hour or so chatting with them.

We arrived at the aire we'd chosen in Tortosa, but neither the town nor the aire were very inspiring, so, after a bit of discussion we decided to travel for another half an hour to the small town of Peñiscola (a new flavour of cola?!). We headed for a nice looking campsite called 'Stop and Go', and that's exactly what we did, as there were no staff anywhere to be found. Several people were waiting at the bar looking very bewildered and clearly in danger of dying of thirst having gone without a wine refill for more than five minutes. In the end, we got fed up and, having seen another site (**Camping Vizmar**) about half a mile away, decided to head for that. Although the plots were very tight, the site was ok, though rather tired; no Wi-Fi was available, so we watched a couple of old movies on DVD in the evening.

On leaving the site and passing a garden centre called Peñis Verde (Verde=Green! I'll say no more!), I entered coordinates for the **Tauro** campsite in Benicàssim – only about an hour's drive south – and selected the option to avoid toll roads. We were amazed when, a little further along, the road sign for the AP-7 toll road had a huge cross through it! The power of the satnav!! ☺

Eventually, we spotted the Tauro campsite sign on a small road to our left and pulled in, then realised we'd turned a little too early, meaning that Tim had to reverse out on to the main road while I stood in the middle of the road, holding up two lanes of traffic; my knees were shaking when we finally arrived at the campsite, only to find that it was full! Another 5kms drive followed, via some <u>very</u> steep and narrow roads, to **Bonterra Park Campsite**. It was a large, but very friendly and well-run site with a pool, restaurant, shop and other amenities, even including soap and toilet paper provided in the toilets (woo hoo, many sites don't provide them!) and close to a Lidl and a Mercadona supermarket.

In the afternoon we decided to go for a coffee in the bar/restaurant and discovered that there was a stage in there and tables for up to 100 people, so we offered to provide a free concert the following evening. We were advised to check with the manager, who wasn't around until the next day, but a lady (Sue), who was sitting nearby, overheard our conversation and introduced herself. She was a keyboard player in a band who entertained regularly at this campsite and others in the area, throughout the year and she was very enthusiastic about our proposed gig, promising to put the word around to ensure that there was a good audience for us.

After breakfast we set off on our bikes for a ride around Benicàssim. We very soon discovered La Ruta de las Villas: a series of (formerly) grand villas stretching for several hundred yards along the promenade, overlooking the beautiful sandy beach. Apparently, Benicàssim was very popular in the 1920s with the rich and famous and was, for many years, one of the most sought-after places to access the Mediterranean.

After lunch, we called to see the bar manager and met up again with Sue and some of her friends, who'd already confirmed that we could perform in the evening and had been busy passing the word around the campsite! As we were leaving, we noticed a familiar couple sitting outside: it was the couple we'd met on our way down at the motorway services! What are the chances of that? Neither they nor we had had any idea of our destinations over the next few days. Even in Benicàssim there are three sites: we'd tried one that was full and they'd tried one that they didn't like the look of, before settling at this one!

We then, of course, got all ready for the evening and, at 8.30pm, began our performance. We were thrilled to have a really good, supportive crowd of around 70, singing along with us and generally having a great time. After an hour and a half, we wondered whether they'd be shouting for us to get off the stage, but no, we got a standing ovation and, at their request, did a couple of encores. It was the best audience response we've had for our European concerts (see https://www.youtube.com/watch?v=w48TgHLAda4 for a showcase of our performances as 'Shades of Grey')

Figure 80 Bonterra Park, Benicàssim, Spain

After the very late and exhausting (though exhilarating) evening and losing an hour's sleep for European summer time, it was late morning by the time we set off – on our bikes again – along the excellent cycle track that took us all the way (approximately 13kms) to El Castellón. The past few days had been the Festival of Santa Maria Magdalena, today being the final day, but we were not optimistic about seeing anything much of the festivities as, according to our information, they were mostly taking place in the evening. However, by pure chance, we ended up in a large square, full of people in high spirits and fire crackers exploding all around. Having secured the bikes, we got ourselves a drink and realised that people seemed to be gathering along the edge of a security barrier, so we joined them. Several people in traditional costume came by, so we figured there would be a parade.

Figure 81 Ladies in traditional dress, El Castellón, Spain

We were definitely not expecting the pyrotechnic spectacular that followed! The noise was so great that we couldn't hear ourselves speak, the ground shook and the 'booms' reverberated through our bodies as we watched. It went on for over ten minutes and was the most amazing show we've witnessed.

Afterwards, various bands were playing along the street – mostly young people – creating a wonderful, vibrant atmosphere. We weren't sure of the significance of one band's name: All's Sex May Cowen, though we did notice that it comprised of only one girl with about eight young men! Hmmm!

In the evening, we had an excellent, complimentary, three-course meal with copious quantities of wine, at the campsite, as thanks for our previous evening's performance. We'd seen a notice earlier that the England v Lithuania match was to be screened in the bar at 8.30pm, so Tim was looking forward to watching that, but it transpired that somebody had got the time wrong and it had finished a couple of hours earlier, Tim was inconsolable! (Almost!)

We spent the morning cleaning the van and washing clothes (I know, I know, it's such a hard life), then sat outside for lunch, before a quick trip across the road to the *supermercado* (supermarket). After a refreshing swim in the heated indoor pool, our new friend Sue told us that they were having a 'jam' session later, so we went down and joined them for an hour or so, before having our evening meal.

The following morning we cycled along the *Via Verde* (literally 'the green way'), a very pleasant 5kms coastal cycle track (formerly a railway track) to Oropesa del Mar, another nice little seaside town with an excellent beach, and had a couple of drinks whilst doing a bit of people-watching. We continued to try and speak the language as much as possible but, as we noticed last year, there are many local languages in Spain, making it a little more complicated, but also very interesting. For example, I noticed that the Valencian word for 'children' is *xiquets* (*x* is pronounced 'ch'), which is rather sweet! Incidentally, the Castillian Spanish word for children is *niños*, completely different!

We spent the afternoon enjoying the gorgeous sunshine, with temperatures hitting around 30°C, and I had another swim. As it was our final evening at Bonterra Park, we decided to eat in the restaurant again and were joined by the couple we'd met earlier, who were also dining in there.

After packing the van up and saying our farewells, we headed south again, stopping for refreshment at Javea's Arenal beach. Further on, we spotted some more 'ladies of the day' along the roadside (you may remember we saw them last year). I thought I'd take a photo, so Tim tried to slow down sufficiently to give me time to take a photo but without attracting their attention; it was quite difficult as you can't get a good look until you're on top of them.....so to speak!

We had contacted Colin and Sue, whom we'd met for the first time in Seville in May the previous year and later met up with at Dénia (do try and keep up!). They live in Moraira and very generously insisted that we park on their drive for a couple of nights, so, once settled in, we went down to the town centre and had a lovely meal with them, then continued the evening back at their house until rather late!

In the morning, Colin and Sue took us for a ride into the mountains: first stop was the Aleluya Bar in Jalón (*Xaló* in Valencian), owned by an eccentric opera singer, who joined in with Tim singing O Sole Mio, while we had a coffee in the very pretty little courtyard.

Figure 82 Aleluya Bar, Jalón, Spain

I noticed acres of trees in the area with a fruit that looked something like an apricot and was told that they are *nisperos*, similar to plums in texture and very popular locally but difficult to export as their shelf-life is very limited.

We stopped in Parcent, a typical little Spanish village, where the church clock was just striking 12 noon, astonishingly followed by a rendition of Ave Maria! On an information board we noticed that, not far away, at Pla de Petracos, there were some caves that

Colin and Sue hadn't visited before, so headed there to see the cave paintings that apparently date back around 8000 years! The caves were up a steep and fairly rough mountain path but unfortunately the chances of any spiritual feelings of contact with our distant ancestors were pretty remote, as our visit there coincided with a coach full of children aged from three (yes three!) to about 12. I have to say though, that the children were very well behaved. We were particularly impressed when, as we were trying to spot one of the small (very small) cave paintings, a little girl of about seven, who we had just heard conversing fluently with the Spanish children, explained in perfect, native English, exactly where the painting was! (Makes you feel humble.)

By the time we left, the place was deserted; we were probably the only people to have visited for months, typical!

Our next stop was the Coll de Rates restaurant, at the very top of a mountain with fantastic views over the Jalón valley, where we enjoyed a lovely meal.

Figure 83 Jalón Valley, Spain

The steep and narrow, winding mountain roads were full of cyclists practising for coming cycle races; rather them than me I think! Finally, we called at Les Fonts d'Algar, near Callosa: a series of waterfalls that were quite impressive after the heavy rainfall of recent months.

Figure 84 Les Fonts d'Algar, Callosa, Spain

In the morning we visited the local market, before having breakfast at a café overlooking the sea. We then said farewell and headed off on our travels again, stopping off at a Carrefour for a few supplies, where a woman behind us was getting quite irate as we struggled with the self-checkout machine's attempts to thwart our purchases!

After a brief stop in Calpé, to purchase a Portuguese dictionary and partake of a quick coffee, I set the coordinates for our next stop: **El Jardin Campsite** at El Campello, between Benidorm and Alicante. We were only about a mile away when our satnav took us under another low barrier – this time chains at 2.8m – aaaagh!

The road was very busy and I had to steel myself to stop a queue of irate, horn-tooting drivers so that poor Tim could reverse the van far enough to allow us to turn the wrong way up a one-way road to get away! Ms Satnav wasn't satisfied though, she still did her best to get us to turn down impossibly narrow roads or 45° angled corners before we finally found the campsite. We were beginning to think we'd got the days mixed up and today was the 1st April!

A gin and tonic was needed urgently before we could begin the task of cooking a meal. Having regained our composure, we decided to use our new gas hob, and once we finally gave up trying to connect it to the external shower point (!) it worked quite well. Then, after all the trials of the day, Tim felt it was just the last straw when the fish sauce curdled – or 'split' as he refers to it – standards were clearly slipping!

We'd parked next to another English van, whose owners hailed from Staffordshire, so we shared some of our Staffordshire Oatcakes with them. Oatcakes are a type of savoury pancake cooked on a griddle; Tim is familiar with them as his father used to live in Staffordshire and bought Oatcakes from Hanley Market, which is, I gather, one of the best-known places to buy them. Our neighbours, interestingly, hadn't heard of them before, but very much enjoyed them, as we do. Unfortunately, though, they're difficult to get outside of Staffordshire, it seems.

We had a much-needed lie in (I bet your heart is bleeding for us) then cycled down to the wide sandy beach that stretches for miles in both directions. We'd had a brief walk down yesterday evening but everywhere had been very quiet. This morning there was much more activity and we enjoyed a drink at a beach bar at the north end of the town, before cycling around two miles to the south end of the town (Playa de San Juan, almost in Alicante) and then back to the campsite.

There was a lovely atmosphere at the campsite over the weekend. Spanish families clearly enjoy a couple of days at the coast and the site was buzzing with laughter and chatter that grew increasingly louder as the weekend (and, I suspect, the wine intake) progressed! We found it quite amusing, though, that all the holidaymakers from northern Europe were wearing shorts and t-shirts, whilst the locals were dressed in thick coats, trousers and scarves.

Unfortunately, many of the new visitors had also brought their dogs with them and Tim hadn't slept so well, due to one dog's determination to bark all night, setting off all the other dogs. In addition, a brisk wind had blown up that had repeatedly set off numerous car alarms!

The Sunday morning fleamarket was just up the road, so we decided to have a look around, but none of the fleas attracted our attention (although I suspect we attracted theirs!), so we meandered back. We did notice this little piece of equipment on our way though! Tim began to wonder whether he should have a go at making his own satellite dish for the van!

Figure 85 Sky Dish? El Campello, Spain

We chatted to another elderly (we guessed late 80s) English couple, who were parked diagonally across from us, and learned that they had driven, with their caravan, to this site every year for many years from their home in Doncaster; they were very pleased when Tim provided them with some headlight deflectors that we didn't need. We were quite amused, later, to notice a very skimpy ladies' thong hanging on their washing line; good for her!

After getting our own washing done (without problems, phew!), we had a long, lazy, al fresco lunch of chicken, chips, peppers and courgette (known, of course, as *zucchini* in Spain and many other countries) washed down with a perhaps too-generous helping of Rioja (that we'd purchased in Moraira at €1.68 per litre!) and were both overcome by a strange desire to snooze; by the time we woke up, the washing was dry!

A brisk cycle ride into town woke us up. We'd been astonished by the seemingly complex one-way system in El Campello: there were numerous one-way streets and a total lack of directional signs. We could just about cope with that; but when the sign at the end of a road pointed one way, and the road markings were all pointing the opposite way, we struggled!

Our ride took us past a very well-attended spin class being held in one of the squares to the accompaniment of extremely loud music! It seemed that anyone could join in for as long as they wanted (or until they fell off, exhausted); I had to hold Tim back, of course, he was so keen to participate!

Later, cycling along the sea front, we noticed, as yesterday, that even though we were cycling on the section marked as a cycle path, pedestrians seemed determined to walk along it. Having stopped for a drink, and to listen to a band entertaining in one of the sea front bars, I noticed a sign (in Spanish), that appeared to be saying that cycling was not allowed! We were somewhat bewildered, as the cycle path seemed to be fairly clearly marked, so asked the waitress. She confirmed that the council had scrapped cycling along there a couple of years previously and simply hadn't removed the signs! How on earth did they expect us to know!

Tim decided he'd cycle to the local supermarket for some bread and shampoo (as he'd left yet another bottle in a shower somewhere!), while I did another load of washing. A simple task, you might think. Hah! First of all I walked to the washing machine I'd used yesterday (perfectly successfully I should say); it was at the opposite end of the site, but I'd been told it was the better of the two machines available. Unfortunately, as I got there, a woman was just in the process of putting her washing into it, so I trekked back to the other end of the site. The only instructions I could see were figurative and not at all clear to me, so I put my load in, crossed my fingers, closed the door and inserted the required disc. The machine clanked into action; then I realised I hadn't put any washing liquid in, so asked the receptionist next door if it was possible to stop it, only to find that I'd put the clothes in a drier. (Duh!) Well the machines all looked the same, that's the excuse I'm sticking to! To add to my utter embarrassment, whilst I was transferring the clothes from the drier to the washer, a German woman came in and looked at me askance, saying, "You vash again?" (confirming her suspicions about ze crazy English). I rushed back to the van for more money, but the receptionist very kindly gave me a free disc (I think she felt sorry for me) and I put it in and waited....and waited.....eventually I asked a Spanish man how the machine started and he turned the handle (it didn't look like a handle, honest!) to lock the machine door so that it could start! If I only had a brain!

Tim felt he'd better accompany me to retrieve the washing, in case I brought someone else's back or something!

We'd purchased an 'Orange' sim card for Tim's old phone when we were in Benicàssim, with €40 credit on it for phone calls within Spain and for receiving calls from home. However, Tim tried sending a text on it in the morning and received a message that all the credit was used up! Needless to say, we found that rather annoying, as we'd only made a couple of calls and sent about five texts.

After a light lunch we walked down and caught the tram to Alicante, then spent half an hour in the 'Orange' shop trying to sort out what had happened. Apparently, although we'd requested no data, the phone had been using data in the background: to the value of €30 in a week! Thankfully, they agreed to refund that amount.

We decided to visit Alicante's Castillon de Santa Barbara (my Spanish residence, ha ha). The site has been in use since prehistoric times due to its commanding view of the coast, but the first defensive construction was in the 8th century, during the period of Islamic rule.

Figure 86 Castillon de Santa Barbara, Alicante, Spain

We got to the foot of Mount Benacantil, on which it stands, where there was an exceptionally unhelpful plan. In the end, we randomly decided on one of the tracks from there, which turned out to be a <u>very</u> steep track, winding its way around the hill. Eventually, we reached the castle – 169 metres above sea level – and looked around for a bar so that we could quench our thirst. As we sat there, enjoying a drink in the sunshine, we noticed a group of people on a large flat roof above one of the castle buildings directly opposite us, who, it transpired, were doing a photo shoot. I had to shield Tim's eyes when, after photographs of the model wearing one particular outfit had been taken, she walked back to the group and undressed; she was wearing the skimpiest thong imaginable! The bare-faced cheek of it!!

As we were wandering around the castle we saw this notice, which I think the aforementioned model may have taken too literally; fortunately Tim doesn't have a pacemaker!

Figure 87 Note the Warning! Alicante, Spain

We'd noticed that the van belonging to our campsite neighbours to our left had a relatively new tow-bar fitted, that had a supplier's telephone number beginning with a regional code local to our home, so we thought they must live relatively close to us. Tim managed to have a brief word with them, and discovered that they live in the next village to ours, about a mile away from where we lived! Small world eh?!

We'd arranged to pick up our friends Diane and Jimmy (in case you've forgotten, they joined us at the Domaine in France last year), who had booked an apartment in El Campello some time ago and had arrived on Sunday. As we needed some more water and bread, we decided to call at the Carrefour on our way; the road there was exceptionally narrow in places and poor Tim's shirt needed wringing out again by the time we'd manoeuvred past various cars and other obstacles. Parking at these large supermarkets ought to be easy; the car parks are huge, but they simply do not allow space for large vehicles. There are covered areas providing shade for cars, but the covers are only about 1.75m high, so we had to squeeze the van on the end. I do wonder how they expect people with motorhomes to shop!

It was really nice to see Diane and Jimmy again and we headed up to Sella in the mountains. Sella is the lovely, very traditional, Spanish village where Tim and I gave a concert during our trip last year. After enjoying a coffee in the square, we walked down to the old mill, where, again, the waterfalls were very impressive, as Spain had had some heavy rainfalls during the winter. We then walked back up to Bar Maria, where we sat on the balcony with fantastic views of the mountains and enjoyed a wonderful lunch of salad, with calamari and Spanish sausages, delicious paella and, finally, flan de turrón (a bit like a Crème Caramel), with, of course, a bottle of vino collapso! (I should, at this point, reassure you that Tim doesn't drive under the influence of alcohol; believe me, he needs all his wits about him whilst driving the van!)

Figure 88 View from Bar Maria, Sella, Spain

After staggering back up to the van, we sat and put the world to rights over a cup of tea, then drove back to our campsite, where we had another drink and nibbles before walking down to the tram stop with Diane and Jimmy. As we got to the edge of the track, we could see the tram in the distance, so had a sprint of about 200 metres; Tim quickly took the lead and managed to signal to the driver, who very kindly agreed to wait, so that our friends could leap on to the tram with no time for goodbyes! It took us a while to regain our composure and walk back and Diane and Jimmy had four flights of stairs to deal with back at their apartment!

El Campello to Granada – April

Today was national 'Barbara' day apparently, although I didn't know until afterwards! We packed the van up and said farewell to El Jardin campsite, a pleasant site, although the pitches were rather narrow and it lacked a little shop and a decent bar/café.

With Ms Satnav set for Granada we had, unusually for us (!), a relatively uneventful journey to the very pretty campsite **Reina Isabel**, arriving late afternoon. After a mix-up as to which pitches were available, we got ourselves settled and had a nice pre-dinner drink and nibbles. We then discovered that, having paid for three days' worth of Wi-Fi for two devices, we couldn't get either of our laptops to connect and the man on reception was decidedly unhelpful.

The following day, we caught the bus from directly outside the campsite into Granada, 3kms away. Apparently, it's only 29kms to the ski slopes on the Sierra Nevada. If only we'd packed the skis!

By sheer fluke we got off the bus at the right stop and walked along the side of the river for a while, stopping for a coffee on the way, before making our way along a series of very narrow streets winding steeply uphill to the Alhambra. Memories of our visit last year came flooding back: rain, temperatures of 5° and queuing for two hours and still not getting a ticket! Thankfully, although we were there about five weeks earlier in the season than last time, the weather on this occasion was beautiful. We picked up the tickets for tomorrow that we'd reserved on-line (lessons learned) and walked down to the Tourist Information Office, where we could connect to the internet and catch up with messages.

The afternoon was passing quickly and we were deliberating as to whether we should have a meal out or wait until we got back to the van, when we happened upon El Pozo, the little rustic restaurant we'd eaten at last year, run by a husband and wife. This year, we were able to sit in the very pretty little courtyard in the sunshine and enjoyed a four-course meal, with a bottle of wine, for a grand total of €25.50.

Figure 89 El Pozo, Granada, Spain

At the risk of repeating our trip from last year, we then walked through the vibrant Albayzin (Muslim) area and had a cup of herbal tea at the teteria in which Tim had dropped his cup last year; thankfully, he managed to avoid any breakages this time. A little further on we noticed the museum of 'Torture in the Spanish Inquisition' and decided to have a look; I'm so glad that I wasn't around during that period of history! A couple dancing in one of the plazas lightened the mood.

We made it back for around 8.00pm, having done around six miles on foot.

Next day, we set off a little earlier into Granada and followed the same route uphill, this time entering the Alhambra gardens around 11.30am. We had explored most of the site at the Alhambra last year, so we simply enjoyed strolling around and seeing it in the sunshine this year. Eventually, we decided to get into the queue for our scheduled 2.30pm visit to the Palacio de

Nazaríes: the bit we'd sadly missed last year. We stood for about twenty minutes in the queue, behind a German couple.

There was airport-style security to enter the palace, but, at last, almost a year after our abortive attempt, we made it inside. I can tell you that it was definitely worth coming back for; the interior decor was amazingly beautiful; parts of it, I felt, were reminiscent of Gaudí's Sagrada Família in Barcelona (maybe Gaudí was influenced after seeing some of the architecture here at Granada?)

Figure 90 Alhambra, Granada, Spain

Figure 91 Alhambra, Granada, Spain

There were also some lovely, peaceful courtyards amongst the palatial buildings. Of course, we kept encountering the German couple on our way around, along with other groups who'd entered at a similar time to us.

Figure 92 Alhambra, Granada, Spain

By about 4.00pm we were making our way down to the centre of Granada, although visitors were still arriving at the Alhambra; we reckon there must be something like 8-10,000 people per day. We called in briefly at the Tourist Information Office so that our phones could update, then had a much needed drink at a little bar in town, before heading back to the campsite for our evening meal; another 6½ miles on foot!

There had been an influx of French families at the site and a party of Spanish teenagers, who'd arrived during the day, so it was quite a busy scene. After our meal, we watched another old DVD then, just as I paid a final visit for the day to the ladies' powder room, who should be in there (apart from several teenage girls who'd all but taken over the entire area) but the German lady we'd seen at the Alhambra Palace earlier in the day! What a coincidence that they should be staying at the same campsite!

Córdoba, Almería (almost) and Nerja – April

We had originally planned to stay a bit longer in Granada, but made the decision to pack up the van today and head for Córdoba, about two hours west of Granada. Thankfully we had another relatively uneventful journey...apart from a rather rude gesture from a Spanish driver who felt that we were taking up too much road as we were passing cyclists travelling three abreast; perhaps he'd have preferred us to drive into them!

In the Costa Blanca region we'd noticed lots of disused farm land, including olive, almond, orange and lemon trees and vines all left untended, with their fruits sadly going to waste (we'd helped ourselves to a few lemons and oranges that were about to fall and would surely have been wasted otherwise!) However, during the approximately two-hour journey today, we passed acres of farmed land, mostly olive trees and barley fields, with lots of new planting, which was good to see.

We arrived at the **El Brillante** site (which sadly, at the time of writing, appears to have ceased trading) around 1.00pm. It was a municipal campsite and, I have to say, the on-line reviews we'd seen previously hadn't been very complimentary, so we were unsure what to expect; thankfully, we were pleasantly surprised. The person on reception was very helpful, facilities were clean, pitches were private and, although narrow, had a lovely, raised area at the back, where we were able to set up our table and chairs to have lunch in the sunshine. The only drawback was the cost: €32.50 per night, about twice what we've paid elsewhere, but it did include Wi-Fi that worked and it seemed to be the only campsite within a reasonable distance of Córdoba, although we later discovered a very good aire close to the town centre.

We caught the bus from directly outside the site into Córdoba and walked down through the narrow streets, via various large plazas, eventually reaching the *mezquita* (mosque), a UNESCO World Heritage Site. The interior of this building defies description, but I'll try: it is huge, in fact, one of the largest in the world, with a floor area of 23,400 square metres, containing 856 columns of jasper, onyx, marble and granite.

Figure 93 Mezquita, Córdoba, Spain

Figure 94 Mezquita, Córdoba, Spain

It was started around 500 AD, then, after the Islamic conquest of the Visigothic Kingdom, was divided between the Christians and Muslims, who eventually purchased the Christian half of the church and refashioned it as a mosque between 784 and 987. In 1236 the mosque was turned back into a church and alterations

174

continued, the most significant of which was the building of a huge Renaissance cathedral nave right in the middle (which is lost among the columns)!

Figure 95 Christian church within the Mezquita, Córdoba, Spain

The cathedral nave and the other little Christian chapels around the perimeter of the mosque are very beautiful, but we couldn't help feeling, as we did last year in some of the churches we visited, that they seem to be somewhat ostentatious in comparison to the simple beauty of the Muslim architecture.

Seemingly in recent years, Muslims have had repeated requests to the Catholic Church to be allowed to pray in the mosque denied by the Spanish Church authorities and the Vatican.

After leaving the mosque, we strolled through the Triumphal Arch and across the Puente Romano (Roman Bridge) to the Torre de la Calahorra.

The Alcázar de los Reyes Cristianos (Palace of the Christian Monarchs) was, unfortunately, closed, but we were happy to roam the streets in this lovely city, busy preparing for its Palm Sunday parade. After calling for a drink at the Gran Bar (how thoughtful, a bar especially for **Grandma Barbara**?), we made a detour (intentionally of course...not!!!) and came across a small 'Día' supermarket, where we bought some meat, vegetables and, needless to say, cheese, for our evening meal. Once back at the campsite (having clocked up another six miles or so today), Tim made it into a delicious meal, which we ate al fresco.

We used our new mini ironing board (not for ironing minis!) to smarten ourselves up, before walking into Córdoba again next day (we'd realised it was only a couple of kilometres so not worth getting the bus). As we left, a car and caravan were pulling into the site and Tim recognised them as a couple he'd spoken to briefly when they were staying at the same campsite as us at Granada, which they had left a day before us; sometimes it's a very small world!

We headed for the remains of a Roman Temple but were a little disappointed as it mostly consisted of a few columns and a bit of wall. Perhaps we've been spoilt by some of the fantastic Roman remains we've seen elsewhere. The Viana Palace courtyards, however, were well worth a visit: a series of 12 very pretty courtyards surrounding the Palace, with beautiful garden displays and a wonderful aroma of oranges.

Figure 96 Viana Palace Courtyards, Córdoba, Spain

Figure 97 Viana Palace Courtyards, Córdoba, Spain

We then decided to treat ourselves to a meal; we'd hoped to eat at the Gran Bar, but all the tables were reserved (Huh! So not my special bar after all!), presumably as the parade was due to pass by later. The streets everywhere were buzzing with people, many of them holding palm leaves, although we did see one man carrying an entire 4ft branch – talk about one-upmanship – maybe he was from Special Branch! Somehow, we managed to miss the entire procession (!) but then, Córdoba is quite a big place!

We saw a menu outside one of the restaurants, but weren't too encouraged to try the 'ham of fodden', 'ham of acorn', 'blood with onions', 'poor potatoes', 'courgette with imitation elvers' or some of their other mysterious delicacies! We did, however, enjoy a pleasant meal in a patio restaurant, although somehow (is it us!?) managed to confuse the staff as to which menu we had chosen and ended up with a mixture of various ones. Tim had the Revuelta (Spanish for 'scrambled') – asparagus stems and scrambled egg – the same as he'd had in Granada and again, he told me, without any seasoning! Oh my goodness the standards we have to endure! We then set off back, calling in at a church on the way to admire its decor, but became a bit concerned, as, just after we'd entered, they locked the doors behind us, and let us out into an area at the back with iron bars! Thankfully, someone eventually came and unlocked one of the gates; we were beginning to think we were going to be there for the second Spanish Inquisition!

We called for a drink (non-alcoholic!) at one of the little cafés on our way back and returned to the van in the late afternoon, having clocked up another 4½ miles or so (thank goodness for my comfy shoes!). The evening was spent battling with the Spanish internet connections that were painfully slow. Sleep was also a little difficult, as the Spanish custom seems to be to allow young children to play (very noisily!) until after midnight and they're up early in the morning as well; they get the chance for afternoon siestas, which, of course, we don't, when we're out and about. We must make more effort to assimilate this aspect of the Spanish culture! (Yawn!)

I used the furthest shower cubicle in the morning and noticed that there was a nice little area in the corner with a ceramic baby bath built into the worktop; a lovely idea, but what a pity that it was so well-hidden that probably nobody knew about it.

We left El Brillante campsite and called at the Carrefour down the road; yet again, no parking for the van and we must have walked a mile around the block trying to find our way to the entrance and then past the tills to get inside! We got everything we needed except fresh milk; the Spanish seem to only use UHT.

Heading for Almería, on the south coast, Ms Satnav seemed determined to get us to take the longest route, but we rebelled and cut the overall distance by about 50kms! I was a bit perturbed when we stopped at some services to use the toilets and I could hear frantic knocking! It turned out that someone had got locked in the cleaning cupboard; we seem to come across the strangest things!

The countryside around Almería has developed the largest concentration of greenhouses in the world, covering 26,000 hectares, growing more than half of Europe's demand for fresh fruits and vegetables under plastic. Apparently 35 years ago this region was so dry and arid that 'Spaghetti' western films were shot there, but hydroponic systems have allowed it to become an intensive agricultural area, staffed, so we understood, by a hundred thousand immigrants, in dreadful working conditions.

The sea of plastic – as far as you can see in every direction – is so vast that researchers have found that by reflecting sunlight back into the atmosphere, the greenhouses are actually cooling the area. While temperatures in the rest of Spain have, apparently, climbed at rates above the world average, the local temperature has dropped an average of 0.3°C every 10 years since 1983.

We became rather nervous as Ms Satnav took us on a narrow mountain pass, but were amazed when it actually did lead to **La Garrofa** campsite, literally on the beach – a private cove – and it was lovely to be able to hear the waves as we ate our evening meal. The pitches were rather tight and some of the buildings were slightly tired, or, perhaps, rustic. The toilets and showers were exceptionally clean, but with tiny shower cubicles, that meant that drying and dressing had to be done in the communal area. It was quite late by the time we got to bed (cue crashing waves; well, we were near the sea!).

Those of you following our route may well struggle to understand the logic of our next decision! The answer is: don't try! ...well, it was mainly because we'd booked the Alhambra tickets and mis-timed our journey really! Anyway, we packed up and set off along the coast road, arriving at lunch time at **Nerja Camping:** a fairly small site near the coast, about 6kms out of Nerja. We needed bread and discovered from one of the regular campers that the village of Maro was about 2kms away, but, of course, the shops in Spain all close early afternoon and open up again around 4.00 or 5.00pm. Consequently, we got a move on and cycled into Maro – a nice little village – where we got a freshly baked loaf for lunch.

We were thrilled to have the opportunity at last to put down our new outdoor floor covering (little things....) then, having had quite a few busy days, we decided we deserved a rest (I can feel the waves of sympathy) and had a lazy afternoon, sitting out in the lovely warm sunshine and reading. Thankfully, the internet connection there was one of the best we'd had.

The sites do vary considerably and we had begun to question our criteria for a 'good' site; there seems to be some indefinable quality that determines whether we like somewhere or not. Although this site didn't have the advertised pool (well, the pool was there but there was no water!) or cafeteria, it just felt comfortable.

A young couple arrived in the evening and spent well over half an hour examining the pitches before making their decision (we thought they were writing a review of each one). We were, therefore, amazed to find them packing up the next morning! We'd thought they must be staying for at least a few days (maybe they'd mis-timed their trip too!!).

I put a couple of loads of washing in (without incident, although one of the machines cheekily declared that its wash cycle was three minutes; it most certainly wasn't!) and Tim managed to get enough of a washing line up to supplement our handy, collapsible rotary drier. We then cycled to Nerja, about 30 minutes' ride (all downhill, oh-oh!).

Figure 98 Balcon de Europa, Nerja, Spain

Nerja is a very popular and busy resort; the majority of the buildings seem to be relatively new, with some lovely little plazas, most notably the Balcon de Europa, overlooking the beautifully clear sea, where we stopped for a drink.

After we'd had a good look around we made the supreme effort to cycle back to the site (guess what: all uphill!) and enjoyed the campers' sport of watching all the newcomers setting up their various homes for the night/weekend. A Spanish family of four with a small caravan moved in next door to us and were really struggling to get settled, then their gas ring wouldn't work.

181

We felt so sorry for them that we let them use ours, hoping they might remember our kindness if the baby was crying in the middle of the night!

There was a tourist train to the nearby Nerja Caves, that picked people up in Nerja and Maro, but, oh no, that was too easy for us! Buoyed by our success at cycling back from Nerja yesterday, we took on the challenge of cycling the 2 or 3kms from the campsite (all steeply uphill again) in the morning, to visit this amazing series of huge caverns. Stretching for almost 5kms and home to the world's largest stalagmite – a 32 metre high column measuring 13 metres by 7 metres at its base – the caves have formed over a period of around 225 million years, but were not open to the public until 1960.

The cave has one of the richest stores of prehistoric art (sadly not all of it accessible, for reasons of conservation), with 321 recorded items; these and other remains provide evidence of human existence from around 43,000 years ago. Amazingly, an International Festival of Music and Dance concert is held, each July, within the largest cavern. We were astonished by the number of visitors: there were around 100 in the group that we were with and we saw at least another five similar groups during our 45-minute tour around the caves! Our tour guide, though, appeared to be a novice and missed out one section, then repeated another one, typical!

The joy of having cycled there was, of course, that the journey back was much less strenuous and, after a quick cuppa, we got changed and walked into Maro, a very welcoming and well-kept village, with some picturesque little corners and restaurants.

Figure 99 Maro, Spain

We decided to sample the menu del día at La Entrada (literally: 'The Entrance') and enjoyed bread and oil, pasta with garlic prawns, dorada and salad (or Tim's choice of chicken in tarragon sauce, with chips), a dessert and coffee for €8; excellent value, although the service was a bit *mañana*! After our walk back, Tim needed a lie-down (nothing to do with the wine...much!), while I did a bit of sketching.

The large group of people who'd set up camp just behind us the previous day had enjoyed chatting and laughing until around 2.00am; we'd thought about setting our alarm for 6.00am and getting out the microphones and amplifier...but we were too tired!

After much deliberation about what to do today (one of the options was to get the bus to Málaga – about an hour's journey – to see the Good Friday processions there; oh the decisions we have to make!), we finally decided to catch the bus into Nerja and on to Frigiliana, a mountain village 7kms north of Nerja. Unfortunately, our deliberations had taken longer than we realised, leaving us with little time to walk the 3kms or so to the bus stop at the far end of Maro village, so we did a spot of speed walking. Thankfully, we arrived at the stop about two minutes before the bus! The bus timetable that we had was very vague, but it appeared that we had an hour to wait in Nerja for a bus to Frigiliana. Imagine our surprise and delight, therefore, in finding that the bus that was in front of us when we alighted was just about to set off for there (thank goodness Tim thought to check), so we arrived much earlier than we'd expected. I have to hand it to the bus drivers there; getting a large vehicle down some of those tiny streets is not easy!

Figure 100 ...extreme short-stay parking! Frigiliana, Spain

Frigiliana is a very picturesque, though somewhat commercialised, mountain village, voted the 'prettiest village in Andalucía' by the Spanish tourism authority.

Figure 101 Frigiliana, Spain, with El Fuerte in the background

We strolled through some of the lovely streets of the old part of town and stopped for a drink just outside the church of San Antonio. A small crowd had begun to gather, so we thought we'd hang about and see what was happening; we were rewarded with a Good Friday procession from the church led by a small group of children carrying banners and some of the elders of the town chanting. It was a very moving scene in more ways than one: the group of strong men bearing the effigy/float of Jesus were struggling with the weight and almost lost their footing coming down the church steps! It would have been a bit of a disaster if the whole float had come crashing down, but they just managed to stay upright and soon regained their composure!

Figure 102 Spain – Frigiliana's Good Friday procession

Tim suggested that he take my photo standing on some steps adorned with lovely pots of flowers. I put my bag down but was getting a bit concerned as I stood there, as a young man seemed to be edging closer to it. I felt very ashamed of myself for being remotely suspicious when it turned out that it was his house door I was blocking!

We saw a sign pointing up to 'El Castillo' (the castle) and thought it would be nice to have a walk up to see the remains, hah! About an hour later, exhausted and hot, we got to the top of El Fuerte, the mountain (well it felt like a mountain), to find..... nothing, other than a few random stones from a much newer and more recently destroyed look-out tower! Apparently the castle was the scene of the final bloody defeat of the Moors of La Axarquía in their 1569 rebellion and, sadly, some of the Moors reputedly threw themselves from the top, rather than be killed or captured by the Spanish (they probably couldn't face having to do the climb again!) However, we did get some exceptionally good views over Frigiliana and Nerja to the sea beyond. Tim found a 'short-cut' back down, oh oh! We ended up making our way via a disused drainage system, that became increasingly perilous the further along we got, but, by then, turning round wasn't a particularly inviting option either! (Barby's amazing adventures with Tim Tim still survived for another day!!)

After all that exertion we were ready for some lunch and found a nice little restaurant (El Boquetillo, which actually means 'The Mouthful') with a lovely terrace, where we made ourselves comfortable. We were astonished to see that the menu included haggis, then discovered that the Scottish owner and chef was also the private chef for the rock band AC/DC when touring! Needless to say we had a very good and relaxed lunch there...until a couple of families arrived and encouraged their children to sit at a table well away from them (and nearer to us!); another little girl, who was clearly very bored as her family tried to enjoy their meal out, made numerous attention-seeking requests for them to accompany her to the toilet (at least 10 that we witnessed, not that we were counting).

We caught the bus back to Nerja in the late afternoon; the town was busy in anticipation of the Good Friday procession to be held that evening. Unfortunately, the Spanish seem to like to start these things very late in the day – 9.00pm in this case – so we ended up having a few cups of coffee in various places around town until, at last, the ceremonies began, but they were well worth the wait.

As with the earlier, but smaller, procession we'd seen, the most distinctive features were the huge ornate floats (two floats this time: one with Jesus in a coffin and one with Mary on a throne). The floats were carried through the streets by groups of strong men (they need to be strong!), known as *costaleros*, who convey the floats (*pasos)* on their necks and shoulders through the crowded streets. Here, the floats were preceded by a number of bands, that included many young children playing instruments and escorted by groups of penitents wearing long robes with pointed hats/masks and women in black, holding lit candles; it was astonishing that they didn't set fire to each other as their candles were waving around close to their lacy veils. From time to time, the silence was broken by 'spontaneous' singing, with what seemed to be Muslim/Jewish influences, performed from a balcony during the procession. All in all, an amazing and, I must say, moving sight and a fantastic atmosphere.

By the time it had all finished though, it was gone 10.00pm and we had missed the last bus back! Having clocked up seven miles on foot during the day (much of it uphill!), we didn't really fancy walking the five miles or so back. Thankfully, we managed to flag down a taxi: €11 well spent!

After breakfast the next morning, we walked to the other side of Maro (two miles each way) to see the magnificent Eagle Aqueduct (so named because of its weather vane in the shape of a double-headed eagle). It was built at the end of the 19th century as a means of supplying water to the San Joaquin sugar factory on the outskirts of Nerja and was damaged during the Spanish Civil War. Recently restored, it stands 40 metres tall and 90 metres wide and has 37 arches.

Figure 103 Eagle Aqueduct, near Maro, Spain

We stopped for liquid refreshment in Maro, then headed back, noticing, on our way, that there was a footbridge from the centre of Maro to the Nerja caves, that would have saved us quite a distance the other day!

We finally put the awning out on the van (yes, we needed shade!) and enjoyed some fresh bread, with the last of the houmous I had made before we set off and some delicious *queso de cabra* ('goat's cheese').

A few fellow campers were moving on and some new ones arrived in the afternoon; we were intrigued when a group of three young men and one young woman erected a <u>very</u> small tent near us, and wondered quite what their sleeping arrangements would be!

As Tim was cooking our evening meal the gas ran out; well, it had to happen sooner or later (it was the bottle we'd connected up during our trip last year), so the replacement was duly connected.

Afterwards, we decided to have a sing and got out the smaller speaker; Tim was sure he'd put the small set of microphones in (that work wirelessly) but after searching for some time, gave up and we got out the bigger ones with the mixer desk. We had some appreciative comments from our immediate neighbours on each side and a Dutch couple, Claas and 'Yoga' – well that's what it sounded like! – came over to listen, so we invited them to bring their chairs and share our Spanish brandy and we chatted with them between songs. They recorded some songs and asked if we had a CD, so Tim promised to send them some of our performances, but was somewhat perturbed to note that their email address contained the word 'Joke' and wondered whether they were not being serious. (I later learned from my Dutch/English speaking niece, Carol, that 'Joke' is a common Dutch name that is pronounced 'Yoga'; who'd have believed it?! ....well, most Dutch people presumably!)

After about an hour, we sang our last song for the evening, just as one concerned father came to ask us to keep the noise down (oops!) and, as we were packing away, Tim found the other microphones, exactly where they were supposed to be, duh!

A couple more loads of washing were done and hung out the following morning before we set off for another cycle ride to Nerja, which is not the most cycle-friendly town I have to say; the roads are narrow, with no cycle lanes and some of the grates are positively lethal. We arrived as the clock was striking 12 noon, just in time for the Easter Sunday parade; a rather less sombre procession than those we'd seen on Friday of course, and this time with three floats! Again, it was a lovely atmosphere and we marvelled at the young children playing their instruments in the bands and the amazing costumes of the penitents, particularly the conical hats!

Figure 104 Easter Sunday float, Nerja, Spain

Our cycle ride back to the campsite was just as gruelling as last time, so we were glad to have a nice cool drink and a change of clothes before walking down into Maro for a meal at one of the restaurants there. Yet again we'd just got nicely settled and relaxed, when a family with four children came and sat next to us; we do seem to attract them! Two of the boys were very mischievous and put on an impromptu floor show for us, much to the embarrassment of their parents!

We ambled back in the late afternoon to find the place almost deserted, so we had the rest of a nice, peaceful afternoon.

A good breakfast in the morning sunshine set us up for our task of cleaning and packing up the van ready to move on from this pleasant, though somewhat expensive, campsite. We were gradually gathering more accessories (collapsible dustbin, external gas hob, groundsheet...), but that, of course, meant that it took longer to pack them all away. Our problems seemed fairly insignificant, though, compared to a car and caravan who were attempting to leave, when the caravan unhooked itself and careered backwards down the hill, very fortunately avoiding other people and vehicles, and coming to a safe stop embedded in a large bush!

Once packed, we said goodbye to a couple on the site with whom we'd chatted and who had been very helpful with their advice. We also said farewell to Claas and Yoke and were very touched and honoured to learn that they had spent all the previous evening listening to our recordings and had sent us a lovely email thanking us for our entertainment.

Yet again, there was no access for a vehicle like ours at the Mercadona in Nerja: very frustrating! We managed to park at the side of the road and went to another, smaller, supermarket. However, when we went into the back of the van there was a strong smell of gas that was a little worrying! We finally traced it to the used cylinder that had been outside the van whilst at the campsite. During our investigations, though, we realised that the shelf under the bed had collapsed, so we ended up having to do some repair work before we could set off again! There always seems to be something!

Málaga – April

We had only a short distance to travel, as we'd planned to stay a couple of nights near Málaga. I set the coordinates as usual for an aire near there; Ms Satnav's attempts to say some of the Spanish place names and road names continued to make us laugh; she pronounced all the 'ã' sounds as 'aah', resulting in such things as: 'Maahlaahgaah' for 'Málaga', and some of the street names sounded very strange. The route led us down a very narrow, winding road, with no signs, so, rather than end up having to reverse out, I walked up to try and find the aire, but found nothing! We eventually found a different one: a caravan/motorhome storage area close to the airport, with places for tourers, that was, in any case, slightly nearer to Málaga (apologies, I didn't make a note of the name of it).

Once settled in, we tried to find the bus stop (allegedly only 100 metres from the site) and, after a couple of trips along the side of the busy road, with no path, we found it, beside a slip road, underneath the fly-over, with nowhere to stand except directly in the path of traffic turning to join the motorway above. We were very thankful when the bus eventually came at 5.20pm, as usual its timing bearing no resemblance to the timetable given. (The timetable said that the first bus was at 7.00am, then every 30 minutes throughout the day, with the last bus at 10.40pm! Work that one out!).

The journey into Málaga took about 40 minutes (€1.30 each) and after the obligatory visit to Tourist Information, we stopped for a drink in the Plaza del Obispo, close to the Episcopal (Bishop's) Palace (1762) and the huge cathedral, then explored some of the streets in the old town.

Our next stop was the remains of a 1st century Roman amphitheatre and then to the 11th century Alcazaba, the Muslim palace fortress built on the remains of an older Phoenician fortress. The Alcazaba was very well-preserved and contained some beautiful patio areas (some of the decoration being reminiscent of the Alhambra palace), as well as some interesting artefacts.

Figure 105 Alcazaba, Málaga, Spain

We were pleasantly surprised by the amount of green spaces in the centre of Málaga as we walked down towards the port, that, today had a couple of cruise ships in, as well as what appeared to be a sailing ship. We were even more surprised when we got to the bus stop to find that the bus we needed was there and ready to leave. Unfortunately, we were also surprised to find that the return stop was about half a mile further on than where we'd caught the bus, so it was an even longer perilous walk back along the busy roadside.

After our evening meal, we settled down to sleep, lulled until the early hours of the morning by the sound of traffic on the motorway nearby, aeroplanes taking off, lorries coming and going at the distribution depot next door and work being carried out in the nearby workshop; not the best site we've stayed at, but it was secure and cheap and we did actually eventually manage a reasonably good sleep!

I'm ashamed to report that, having had the van for over a year at that point, at least five months of which had been spent living in it, this was the first time we'd actually used the shower. For some reason, we'd been reluctant to try it, thinking it would be messy and ineffective, but it was actually a really good shower, very easy and clean to use. We decided we'd use it again soon!

After yesterday's unpleasant experience waiting for the bus, we decided to try the next stop today; the walk along the road was no better, but at least there was somewhere off the road to stand and wait. We were intrigued to pass, on our bus journey, a Hindu/Italian restaurant, something you don't find every day!

Incidentally, we'd overheard various Spanish conversations and had begun to notice that there are certain Arabic inflections in the language in that area of Spain. We also noticed that a pack of butter we bought there had its name written in Spanish on one side and Portuguese on the other; so we learned our first two Portuguese words: *barrar*, 'to spread' and *manteiga*, 'butter'.

Once in Málaga, Tim went to get his hair cut (interestingly, at a place called 'Tupe'; he was a bit nervous, wondering whether that's what they would resort to if the cut didn't go well!), whilst I visited the house of Pablo Picasso's birth, in Plaza de la Merced. Picasso's father, José Ruiz Blasco, was an art teacher, so Picasso was mixing with other artists throughout his childhood and it was interesting to see some of his father's work also on display, along with various artefacts from Picasso's childhood and later life. At the other side of the Plaza is the Church where Picasso was christened.

Luckily for Tim, a toupé wasn't required, so we enjoyed a light al fresco lunch of paella, interrupted by numerous musicians, each asking for a donation after 30-seconds of 'entertainment' (not that I'm cynical or anything). Once replete, we visited Naisha's Day Spa for our appointment, booked yesterday by phone. It seemed a very dodgy-looking shop, where an equally dodgy-looking man sat behind the counter and we were both more than a little worried as to what we'd signed up for! However, once upstairs and through another door, everything was very well organized and we both felt that our massages had loosened up our aching backs and shoulders that had bothered us for a while.

Next, we visited the cathedral and its museum. Work on the cathedral started in the 16th century, on the site of an Arabian mosque, but the south tower is still unfinished (talk about mañana!) and consequently the cathedral is known as La Manquita (the one-armed lady).

A quick coffee gave us a bit more energy, so we tackled the 25-minute walk up a steep mountain pathway to the Castillo de Gibralfaro, constructed in the 14th century. We were a bit sceptical after our disappointment at the lack of a castle in Frigiliana, but we were able to walk on the ramparts of this huge fortress, with fantastic views over Málaga and explore some of the areas within it. The only thing we felt was lacking, as yesterday at the Alcazaba, was some kind of explanation as to what we were actually looking at!

By the time we'd made our way back to the van we'd covered another five miles or so again today (according to my phone's step counter). We enjoyed some delicious local fish for our meal, followed by – oh no – Tim was distraught as we finished the last of our Stilton cheese and we were on the last packet (having brought five!) of cheese biscuits (must be crackers ☺); we were going to have to ration ourselves (the Spanish just don't seem to do 'proper' crackers).

We were so thrilled with our shower yesterday that we decided to have another. We probably needn't have bothered, as, having discovered that the site had a proper vehicle-washing point with a gantry and long-range nozzle, we decided to wash the van, resulting in us both ended up soaking wet through anyway, but the van did look cleaner.

Cádiz and Jerez – April

Our quest for groceries ended up as frustrating as ever, with a distinct lack of parking for large vehicles, but we survived. The countryside, as we headed towards Cádiz, was much greener (more rain?!) and we passed various signs advertising ferries to Algiers, just across the sea.

It's always interesting, as we're travelling along, when the signs tell us which river we're crossing but it became a bit much after crossing the same one at least 20 times as it meandered beneath the road, with a sign at each bridge! Eventually we managed to find a little spot away from the motorway to stop for lunch and had some *pan de abuela* – literally 'grandma's bread' – with cheese. We'd noticed that the wind had become much stronger as we were travelling and the bike cover was flapping loose, but hadn't realised quite the strength of the gale until the van door was very nearly ripped from its hinges, along with Tim's arm, when he opened it!

Las Dunas campsite near Cádiz was rather unwelcoming, but very clean and efficiently run. We decided to have a walk along the sea-front, as we both needed sand-blasting again (!) then settled down for a quiet read before our evening meal.

We were troubled with the wind throughout the night (must have been the garlic) and the van was violently rocking, but thankfully not rolling! However, we saw the man opposite (whose 'set-up' we'd remarked on yesterday as it seemed very well established) battling with a caravan awning in the wind and noticed later that he'd lost the battle: the awning and poles in a heap told their own sad story.

After breakfast, we walked the mile to the ferry port in Puerto de Santa Maria, but disappointingly, due to the high winds, our much anticipated catamaran crossing to Cádiz was being replaced by a bus. However, we were rewarded with a trip across the fantastic Constitution 1812 Bridge – named after the site of the signing of Spain's constitution two centuries ago – linking Cádiz to Puerto Real. The bridge, nicknamed La Pepa, opened in September 2015, at a cost of over half a billion Euros, having taken more than eight years to complete, and is apparently longer and higher than San Francisco's famous Golden Gate. It is over 5kms long and stretches across a body of water 3.09kms in length and, at a height of 185m, it is one of the tallest in the world, allowing ships as high as 69 meters to pass beneath it. Its width of 36.8m allows a dual carriageway for traffic and double tramlines.

Figure 106 Constitution 1812 Bridge, Cádiz, Spain

Cádiz stands on a peninsula jutting out into a bay and is almost entirely surrounded by water. Named Gadir by the Phoenicians, who founded their trading post in 1100 BC, it later became a thriving Roman port, attaining great splendour in the early 16th century as a launching point for the journey to the newly discovered lands of America. It was raided by Sir Francis Drake and, later, managed to withstand a siege by Napoleon's army.

Once in Cádiz, we made our way (thanks to Tourist Information, who we amazingly managed to find whilst it was still open!) through the medieval part of the city, then found a little tapas restaurant in a narrow street away from the wind.

Next stop was the huge cathedral, built between 1722 and 1838, but never finished: one more case of the Spanish *mañana* ethos? This was another astonishing example of the baroque style (although incorporating other styles due to the length of time over which it was built), with beautiful choir and chapels within it – one of them containing an amazingly enormous silver casket – and the crypt had such fabulous acoustics we fancied doing an impromptu concert there. Unfortunately, though, the roof and some of the walls were in need of some TLC compared to previous cathedrals we'd visited (and we'd visited a few!). We also went to the top of the Levante tower (over 300 steps), from where we had panoramic views of the city, provided we could stand upright for long enough in the howling gale that greeted us up there!

The Roman amphitheatre in Cádiz, dating from the 1st century BC, is one of the oldest and biggest theatres of the Iberian Peninsula; in its heyday, it held 10,000 spectators. We were able to walk through the gallery beneath the seating area, known as the 'vomitorium': Roman lager louts, we mused? Well, no! Apparently, popular culture states a vomitorium is a room where ancient Romans went to throw up lavish meals so they could return to the table and feast some more. In fact, vomitoria were the entrances/exits in stadiums (or, if we're being consistently true to the Latin, stadia) or theatres, so named by a fifth-century writer because of the way they 'spewed' crowds out into the streets, so I understand!

Figure 107 Amphitheatre, Cádiz, Spain

Figure 108 Vomitorium at the amphitheatre, Cádiz, Spain

We enjoyed roaming through some of the streets and historic areas, with a coffee here and there when we could find somewhere on the pleasant plazas that was out of the wind! It almost took us off our feet at times, reaching up to 100kmh throughout the day.

Finally, we made our way back to the van – having walked over 6½ miles again today – feeling thoroughly windblown, and settled down for the evening.

Our sleep was disturbed by the wind yet again (must take something for it). Tim went out during the night to remove the bike cover as we feared it may blow away; consequently, we were a little late up in the morning. By the time we'd had breakfast and showered, we had only 35 minutes to catch the train to Jerez, otherwise we had another hour to wait for the following one. We decided to give it a shot, but the station was almost two miles away. We made it in 30 minutes, with the wind against us and got on to the platform less than a minute before the train arrived, phew!

The trains and buses there were exceptionally comfortable and clean and not at all expensive: this was €4 each, return. How do they manage it? The station at Jerez, which opened in 1854, was also extremely attractive.

Jerez is the 25th largest city in Spain and largest in the Province of Cádiz; famous for flamenco, sherry, horses and motorcycles, it had been the European Capital of Wine in 2013. There are some beautiful buildings, but unfortunately many of them were in a poor state of repair. We stopped for some tapas: peppers stuffed with fish, cheese with anchovies and kidneys in sherry (really good, not at all 'offal') washed down, of course, with amontillado sherry: well you have to when you're in the home of sherry don't you? (*Jerez*, of course, is the Spanish word for 'sherry'.) Whilst we were there, a group of university students came and entertained us; they were very good so we didn't mind being asked for a donation. I did notice a man at one of the tables with a t-shirt bearing the slogan 'leave me alone' but it didn't work!

Whilst walking around the town, we were intrigued by the fact that lots of the buildings seemed to be called 'Manzana' (which means 'apple' in Spanish: maybe Apple Macintosh were quietly taking over?). We were curious as to why that was, but after a little research I found that *Manzana* is also the name for a block, enclosed by streets; we learn new things every day!

The Alcázar was a beautiful, well preserved, building, dating from the 11th century and including the only mosque remaining in Jerez, from 18 former mosques. Unfortunately, a food fair had taken it over for the day, so we couldn't see much of the interior. That might have been okay, except that they were having their siesta at that time, so we couldn't even sample the food! You may wonder what the difference is between an Alcázar and an Alcazaba, well we did anyway. Apparently an Alcázar is a castle, palace or fortress for a king, whereas an Alcazaba is a Moorish fortification principally for the troops; of course, it's obvious, the troops would need a 'bar' wouldn't they!?

The cathedral is a mix of Gothic, Baroque and Neoclassical styles and was built in the 17th century; the decorative stonework around the main entrance was astonishing. Formerly a church, it was elevated to the rank of cathedral in 1980; we didn't go inside though, as we were beginning to get a bit 'cathedralled out'!

We'd hoped to be able to have a small sherry tasting at the Tio Pepe bodega, but they were charging €15 each for a full tour round on a little train, along with the tastings. We just didn't have the time left for that, so decided we'd catch the next train back, which meant another speed walk! Once again we got to the station with just a minute to spare, before the train arrived heading back to Puerto de Santa Maria.

During our mad dash to the station in the morning, we'd noticed some historic buildings in this town, so we decided to have a look on our way back and discovered that Cristobal Colon (Christopher Columbus) actually lived here, along with Juan de la Cosa, who created the first map of America in 1500. The Iglesia Mayor Prioral was the main church of the town from the end of the 15th century, but is now sadly in disrepair and the Castillo de San Marcos, originally a Muslim mosque, built in the 13th century, was eventually converted into a Christian church. The clouds were gathering though and we'd felt the odd spot of rain, so didn't hang around too long.

Back at the campsite we were going to try out the supermarket but were told by the proprietor, who was just coming out of the door, that it was closed, despite contrary information on the advertised opening times on the door! Clearly they weren't too bothered about having customers! We got back to the van, having covered almost nine miles on foot; we certainly weren't idling around there you know! Astonishingly, we'd just got the kettle on for a cuppa, when the heavens opened, now that was lucky!

We couldn't believe that the wind had been gusty again during the night, having settled a bit during the previous evening, but the day was much more pleasant and warm, with temperatures back into the 20s, as we packed up the van and moved on again.

Another stressful Carrefour fuel-station visit followed – the exits are always narrow and at peculiar angles – and, as always, there was nowhere to park for motorhomes at the supermarket. I did feel like contacting Carrefour to ask them why they torture motorhomers in this way, I would have thought they would be glad of the trade and it surely wouldn't take much to provide some accessible parking areas! In our attempt to find a space, the one-way system forced us on a circuit of the town, but, as a result, we happened upon an Aldi with an accessible car park, so replenished our groceries in there and decided to buy some nisperos, the plum/apricot-like fruit that we had seen growing in quantity in Spain last year.

Portugal: Manta Rota, Silves, Monchique and Alvor – April

We crossed the border into Portugal (and put our clocks back by an hour) and I persuaded Tim that we should spend a night in **Manta Rota**, where we stayed last year. Dedicated readers may recall that we encountered a male naturist on the beach there and Tim was convinced that was why I was so keen to return! This time, there was room for us on the aire there, although facilities only comprised of a very basic service point (chemical toilet disposal, tap and drain; no toilets, showers or electricity). However, Manta Rota was just as peaceful and beautiful as we had remembered it and we wandered along the boardwalks to the gorgeous sandy beach in the evening sunshine, feeling instantly relaxed. We spotted a woman whose t-shirt bore the slogan 'get a grip' across her chest; fortunately I don't think anyone took it literally!

The next day was again beautiful, so we sat outside for breakfast of croissants and coffee, with our last jar of Tim's mum's homemade marmalade. We then walked to one of the little bars along the boardwalk for another coffee (and to take advantage of their toilets; there is a lovely public toilet in Manta Rota with pretty flowers outside the door but every time we tried to use it, it was firmly padlocked, I guess that cuts down on the cleaning!), before settling down on the beach for a relaxing few hours in the sun, after which we had a walk along the water's edge; the beautiful beach stretches for miles in both directions.

Figure 109 My collage/painting of the beach in Manta Rota, Portugal

We'd been trying to learn a little bit of Portuguese but finding it much less easy than Spanish (where all letters and vowels are reasonably consistently sounded); it seems that you need to have a cold and be somewhat inebriated to get the correct pronunciation: lots of nasal and 'sh' sounds (eg Portugueshe).

We were quite impressed to find a 'state of the art' touch screen in the square with information on everything for miles around, which was fortunate as the Tourist Information did not open over the weekend; maybe they also had the key for the public toilet! They didn't even open on the Monday, but when we asked why, at the bar nearby, they told us that the Tuesday was a public holiday (celebrating the anniversary of overcoming an authoritarian, non-democratic government with flowers instead of guns), so they probably wouldn't bother to open on the Monday either! There really isn't any sense of urgency or customer satisfaction there! Nonetheless, Manta Rota seemed to somehow cast a spell on us so that we loved it anyway, despite its shortcomings!

After a cooked breakfast we went on our way. Whilst checking the tyres at a service station we saw a wagon with washing hung on a line beneath the open bonnet of the cab; now that's what you call resourceful, as long as the driver doesn't forget and put the bonnet down on it! Soon we arrived at the lovely **Algarve Motorhome Park**, where we quickly settled in and did a load of washing before walking into Silves, about 10 minutes away. In the 14th and 15th centuries Silves was the Episcopal capital of the Algarve and is a very pleasant city, with an impressive castle at the top of the hill, random sections of city wall remaining around the streets and a cathedral, sadly looking a little dejected now. Apparently, Silves suffered a decline from its former glory until it became a major cork producer at the end of the 19th century.

The area is also famous for piri-piri sauce, so we bought some and added a tablespoon to our meal........after we'd doused the resulting fires in our mouths it took a large pot of yogurt to make it just about palatable!

We were amazed at the number of storks there were: nesting on the top of every available post and lots of other strange places and their nests were huge, as, of course, were they. We did see one flying towards us carrying a large package so we shut the doors and windows and hid, hoping it wouldn't then leave us a message on the windscreen!

Figure 110 Storks nesting near Silves, Portugal

As we walked back to the aire, we noticed a sign saying *pequeniños*, apparently a playgroup; it reminded us of the British lullaby 'go to sleep my baby.......time for little picaninnies (pequeniños?) to go to sleep'. It's fascinating how languages overlap and influence each other.

After our evening meal, we finally tried the nisperos and were decidedly underwhelmed; no wonder they don't export them! I don't know whether we'd just been unfortunate in getting a bad batch, but I have to say they were pretty flavourless and lacking in juiciness.

The next day didn't get off to a good start: we tried to log on to the internet that was provided free at this aire but it turned out they were having problems with the new router they'd got yesterday; next, I decided to try one of the showers – 50c for five minutes – as I needed to wash my hair. It seemed to take ages to warm up and there was no indication as to how the time was going, but I'd been reassured by neighbouring campers as to how long the shower seemed to last. Just my luck: the shower stopped abruptly while my hair and body were still covered in lather! I had to scamper across to the van in my towel and finish the job under our shower, aagh! I thought it was the last straw when the hair drier then kept cutting out as the electricity supply was only six amps! My hair had to dry 'au naturel', not my best look!

But our eventful morning wasn't yet done. Having already been three times to check whether there was a washing machine free, I was thrilled to find, on my fourth attempt, that one was available and was in the process of loading it, when a woman came in shouting 'non, non'....etc (in French), pointing at my washing! I didn't know what the problem was, but then she seemed to indicate that she'd made a mistake and left, laughing nervously, so I assumed it was ok and continued loading. Next thing I knew, she re-appeared with the receptionist who explained that her washing, propped up in a carrier bag against the wall (I hadn't even noticed) was in a 'queue' for the next machine and I'd 'pushed in'! I apologised and offered to remove mine but in the end she said she'd wait! Blimey, you think this is easy, but oh my goodness, the traumas we have attempting to get accustomed to different protocols!

Once the washing was hung out, we walked up to the castle – the biggest in the Algarve and (so they say) the finest military monument in Portugal, from the Islamic period – on the site of Roman fortifications from the $4^{th}/5^{th}$ centuries and built in the characteristic local red sandstone. The walls were very intact and gave us some great views of the city and there was a huge underground cistern that had originally been used for water storage to supply the castle and city. Sadly we were barred from entering an area that had been excavated, though it had clearly been intended for visitors, with walkways and information boards (this has happened at other sites we've visited).

Figure 111 Castle at Silves, Portugal

After leaving there we watched part of the celebration in commemoration of the uprising in 1974 and then visited the archaeological museum, which included lots of artefacts from the area; its centrepiece was a well that was actually in its original position, having been filled-in and built on in the 16th century and recently re-discovered.

We sampled some of the tapas at a little restaurant before walking back through the town to have the rest of a quiet afternoon and evening.

After a morning trip to the Continente supermarket, very close to the aire – which, we were very impressed to note, actually had signs indicating parking places for motorhomes; typical when it was in walking distance – we packed up and said goodbye to some of the other travellers who we'd chatted to during our stay.

We then headed along mountain roads with seemingly never-ending potholes to an aire (**Camping Vale da Carrasquiera,**

I think!) we'd chosen near Monchique, up a very winding, unmade, road and, just as we arrived, it started to rain. However, the facilities were good, including decent Wi-Fi and the views were beautiful.

On the way, we'd noticed one particular bus stop at the side of a very narrow road, on a blind corner, with nowhere to stand off the road; you'd be taking your life in your hands waiting there we thought!

Luckily, it was just a brief shower, so we sat outside and had lunch, then decided to cycle to Monchique, the nearest village. The winding track from the campsite to the road was all downhill, but from then on we were cycling uphill, in the lowest gear possible almost all the time. After about half an hour, suffering from severe exhaustion, we stopped for refreshment at a roadside bar, only to be told that we still had about 6kms to go! We considered giving up, but stoically decided we should keep going. It ended up being a very tough cycle ride – we reckoned around eight miles all uphill – and the only thing that kept us going was that it would be downhill all the way back!

On our way we passed Caldas de Monchique, where there are four springs that are known to have existed for more than 1000 years. We also passed a sign for Aljezur – where we were planning to visit in a week or so – and started to get really worried when we got to a road sign for Lisbon; how far were we cycling?! After all that effort, we finally reached the village of Monchique and can report.....well, it really didn't feel as if it had been worth it (we had wondered why the bar man who'd told us it was another 6kms had looked at us as if we were crazy; we were!) Monchique has approximately 600 inhabitants (and we passed eight vehicle repair workshops in the village; maybe the vehicles wear out with going up and down mountain roads all the time!) and very few shops. Thankfully, we did find a reasonably pleasant little square and collapsed in the café there with a drink!

As anticipated, our ride back was exhilarating though somewhat scary: one slip could have had very nasty consequences that I didn't dare think about as we whizzed back round the bends at speeds around 30mph Tim reckoned; it felt a lot more to me! Thankfully, we made it back to the campsite safely, having walked some of the way back up the final rough track.

We definitely felt that we deserved our lovely evening meal of steak, chips and mushrooms, but decided to eat inside, as the clouds were gathering and, later in the evening, the rain finally came.

After yesterday's exertion and the weather still being a bit unsettled, we decided to have a quieter day and, later in the afternoon, walked down the rough track and had a drink in the bar/restaurant by the roadside. We'd noticed they had 'black pork' (a local speciality) on the evening menu and were deliberating whether to walk back for a meal later, but the rain descended again not long after we returned to the van and made our minds up for us. It was no hardship though (not for me anyway!); as the rain poured, we sat down to a meal of roast chicken with new potatoes, courgettes and cabbage, accompanied by giblet gravy, that Tim amazingly produced using only our very small oven and three-ring hob, yum!

In the morning, we said farewell to new acquaintances, who very kindly gave us some addresses for sites farther North and headed the short distance to Alvor, where we'd booked ourselves another massage at the Swan Day Spa and very relaxing it was too! From there it was a short distance to **Camping Alvor**, where we settled on a pitch before heading down to the Pingo Doce (literally 'sweet drop') supermarket, just five minutes' walk away. They had amazing offers on for the Bank Holiday weekend, but we were more than a little amused to notice that all the offer signs around the store included the word *poupou* and we bought lots of products that had been *poupou'd*, including a five-litre box of 13.5% abv red wine for €3.64! We discovered that the verb *poupar* means 'to put down'. As I've already mentioned, we're both fascinated by language and wondered whether that's where the English term 'to *pooh-pooh* (ie 'put-down' or denigrate) something' has come from? Whilst looking up that word I also noticed that *pinça* (pronounced 'pincer') means 'tweezers' and we'd seen, at the castle in Málaga, that the Spanish word for a short sword is *daga*; see what I mean? The English language is, of course, very flexible and comfortably accommodates additions from all over the world.

After a bit of lunch, we got the bikes down and cycled down some narrow streets to the sea front in Alvor; the beach there is lovely and we sat and had a drink overlooking the pretty little harbour before cycling back. We were feeling that we needed to settle somewhere for a few days (what we needed was a holiday!), having been on the move quite a lot recently but somehow, although the facilities were very good and the cost fairly low at €13/night, this campsite just didn't 'do it' for us.

As always, it seems, during the night there was a distant dog, barking continuously; maybe it's the same one that's following us!?

We couldn't resist another trip for more *poupou* products (I know, we're so childish!). The supermarket was even more packed today, but it never seems to concern the till operators, they still chatter happily to all the locals and each other and are in no hurry to get the queues moving; on this day all the tills (about half a dozen) were open, each with 12 or more customers waiting, but on other busy days we've seen the same situation with only one or two tills open. In the same vein, we've noticed cars blatantly parked on double-yellow or zig-zag lines or 'no parking' areas but no one seems to bother!

Lagos – April

Our next destination, **Turiscampo Yelloh Village** near Lagos, was only about half an hour away. This site seemed a bit more like our hoped-for longer-term place to stay and we soon got ourselves settled in on a nice pitch. The sun was much warmer than it had been the last couple of days, so we went for a look around; the toilet and shower blocks were described as 'luxurious' in the blurb and I'm afraid we were a tad cynical about that description, until we saw them! There was also a lovely outdoor pool, where we sat with a drink for a little while before lunch.

The campsite was a bit more expensive at €17/night, but with a good mix of transient holidaying people from various countries in contrast to some sites we've visited and, although it's nice to have English people to talk to, we also enjoy meeting people from elsewhere. On our travels, we have also noticed that a lot of people return to the same site every year and many sites have permanent residents with their pitches marked out by picket fences or hedging, complete with anything from pot plants, garden gnomes and fairy lights to cane garden furniture and, on a recent site, a statue of Venus with its own spotlight.

The activities board indicated that tonight was a Jazz night, so after a nice relaxing afternoon, we got changed and went for a meal in the bar, overlooking the stage, only to find that the Jazz night had been a month ago! Another example of their lack of attention to detail! Anyway, we enjoyed a delicious fish stew for two, whilst three young children (aged about seven, five and three) were happily doing some dancing routines on the empty stage, keeping us entertained for a little while, bless them! Desserts were €3.50 per person, which included the option to return to the dessert selection as many times as you like; obviously, we just had one portion each (not likely!!!).

We had a late, cooked, breakfast in the sunshine, before cycling into Praia da Luz. Memories came back of a week I spent in Lagos with my elder daughter Helen 12 years ago, when we walked along the cliff top to Praia da Luz and narrowly avoided serious injury slithering down the very steep cliff side, grasping plants and trees to steady us on our descent, as we couldn't find a path down to the beach!

Despite my protestations (oh how I objected!), Tim was keen for us to share a litre jug of Sangria and some spicy chicken wings in a lovely café by the beach; resistance was futile, so I gave in! We then had to cycle – and it was almost all uphill – the 2.5kms back to the campsite and needed to sit down and relax for a while with a cup of tea, feeling strangely lethargic.

It had been a Bank Holiday weekend so lots of the motorhomes and caravans on site were leaving today; was it something we said? We decided to wash the bedding, so, while I roamed the campsite with my two carrier bags looking for an empty washing machine (it seemed that everyone who remained on site had decided that today was wash day), Tim put up a washing line diagonally across the adjacent pitch; we figured that as there were so many vacant pitches it wouldn't matter.

We got the first load hung out and were just sitting down to lunch when an American couple walked past, looking for a pitch. Out of courtesy, Tim ventured that we could move the washing line if they preferred that pitch, but the woman said that there was no need. Five minutes later, a **huge** Mercedes van (3.5 litre engine, so Tim informed me) – about a metre higher and two metres longer than ours, plus extending panels at the side and end – began reversing into the pitch and although the American woman was still reassuring us that our washing was not in the way, we quickly removed it before it ended up flapping around the end of their van!

While I went to retrieve the second load of washing, Tim managed to get the line running along the awning to the fence, and that, along with our little rotary drier, managed to accommodate the lot! We later saw the Americans going out on their bikes and admired the rear view mirrors and microphones on their cycle helmets, so that they could see and speak to each other when cycling: definitely something to consider!

After such a busy day, we felt like we needed a treat (!) so we had a nice little drink and some tapas on the sun terrace by the pool before our evening meal.

The following day we caught the bus from outside the campsite into Lagos. I have to say we were impressed with the public transport there: the buses were luxurious, prompt and inexpensive! We found our way through the old part of the town to the city walls; there were some beautiful areas, but also some rather run down parts. We visited the old fort – where there was an exhibition of installation art related to the fishing industry, that we felt was a bit disappointing – and the museum, which housed various artefacts and exhibits of local culture, plus the most unbelievably gaudy chapel, dripping with gold. Tim was examining one of the exhibits and tried opening the drawer; it shot out unexpectedly quickly and clattered to the floor, oops! Thank goodness it remained intact and no-one seemed to have noticed! We moved on very swiftly.

We did like Lagos and felt very relaxed meandering around the streets and the market stalls. The cliffs of the Ponta de Piedade headland are said to be the finest natural features of the Algarve, with a dramatic coastline of tall rocks, caves and rock arches that has been formed due to erosion of the limestone cliffs over millions of years.

Figure 112 Ponta de Piedade headland, near Lagos, Portugal

Next day, we packed our rucksacks and set off into Praia da Luz with the intention of finding the cliff top path that had eluded my daughter and me on our previous trip. The Portuguese don't give any secrets away though and we roamed around in ever-decreasing circles in our quest. After an hour's walking we ended up by the beach, and refreshed ourselves in one of the bars. We finally discovered a path (well, one of many, it eventually turned out!) that started nearby; it was a bit of a relief to know that the paths really did seem so hard to find though, as Helen and I had questioned our sanity in being unable to detect one!

We noticed, incidentally, that all the pavements and formal pathways we'd come across so far in Portugal were made of flat stone cobbles. They must have been exceptionally labour-intensive of course, but will definitely last much longer than tarmac.

We set off on what was something of an uphill slog in the heat and not the easiest ascent, but we did have a beautiful view over Praia da Luz from the top, before setting off on our lovely cliff top walk.

After another hour or so we ended up in yet another lovely beach resort: Praia do Porto da Mos, where an ice cream helped us on our way. The path, though, disappeared and it took a bit more detective work to find it again. We came across some steps down to Praia do Canavial, one of the many gorgeous little coves around there and Tim spent a couple of hours relaxing while I did another pastel sketch.

Figure 113 Pastel sketch at Praia do Canavial, near Lagos, Portugal

We continued along the path, that became less easy to follow – I think some of the cliffs must have fallen away recently – and we finally walked into Lagos, where we were pleased to get some liquid refreshment before catching the bus back. This time, we avoided getting off too early, only to find that the next stop was almost as far beyond the campsite! Our mileage today came to just over nine and much of it, of course, had been up and down, so, as neither of us felt much like cooking, we availed ourselves of the 'luxurious shower facilities' then had a bar snack on the sun terrace.

Our American neighbours were there, so we chatted to them and learned that they had had their motorhome shipped to Southampton from America two years previously, before beginning their current European tour!

Having decided to move on the next day, we needed to get another load of washing done so I ended up getting some funny looks again, as I did another couple of circuits as 'the bag lady' before finding a vacant machine.

In the afternoon, we enjoyed a short walk in the sunshine to the adjoining village of Espiche, a very pretty little spot, where a drink of the local beer – Sagres (the eponymous town being close by) – definitely had our name on it (no, our name isn't Sagres!!), at a nice little bar/restaurant called the Grape Vine.

Having decided to leave, we had a busy afternoon ahead of us: well, I had to finish the book I'd borrowed from the internet room/library and get the blog done! So much to do and so little time.

The forecast rain materialised during the night, so we felt quite smug that we'd put all the outside furniture away the previous evening. We managed to get the remaining jobs done in breaks between showers, then said farewell to our American neighbours.

We had been very impressed with the standard and breadth of facilities at this site: everything was kept spotlessly clean and there were lots of playgrounds and other activities for children, as well as adults!

We headed for Lagos, where we'd previously spotted an Intermarché supermarket with fuel and a parking area that we could get into easily. However, we hadn't realised how expensive the supermarket would be; maybe that's the price we motorhomers have to pay for being able to park!

Lisbon – May

Once fully stocked, we set the coordinates for Lisbon, our next port of call. We'd considered calling at Vila Nova de Milfontes on the coast, as one or two people had recommended, but the weeks were flying by and we felt we'd better get a bit further along.

Ms Satnav, however, seemed determined to take us miles out of our way; we eventually persuaded her to take us on a scenic route through the mountains, where a lot of the landscape was very much like the British countryside. The final stretch was on the motorway, where we noticed we were still being 'storked': there were lots of them nesting in the pylons by the side of the road.

As we joined the motorway Ms Satnav was saying 'keep left' and, before we knew it we found ourselves going through one of the unrestricted toll entry points without having taken a ticket. On entering Portugal, we'd pulled into the large lay-by there, and had registered our credit card in the machine; we weren't sure, at the time, whether that was just an entry charge or whether it meant that we'd actually registered for the motorway tolls. So we were panicking a bit when, on leaving this motorway, we were told that, without a ticket, we'd have to pay €72!!! Having no desire to fork out that much money, we hastily reversed out of that lane and drove through the unrestricted exit lane, which would be ok if we had registered for the tolls but, if not, we'd have a huge pile of fines waiting on the doormat at home! Time alone would tell. (Luckily, it turned out that we had registered for the tolls and only had some very small charges on our credit card bill.)

Getting across the massive Vasco de Gama bridge that crosses the Rio Tejo into Lisbon (the second longest bridge in Europe at over 10 miles long) amongst the Friday evening traffic was the next stressful part of the journey and coming across three accidents in the space of about 10 minutes didn't help; we're convinced that part of the problem is the fact that they have exit and entry slip roads leaving/joining not just the slow lane, but also the fast lane, which seems like a recipe for disaster. Tim's shirt needed wringing out again by the time we reached **Lisboa campsite** just on the edge of the city, especially when a power steering warning light came up on the dashboard; we'd already lost part of a windscreen wiper on the way too, aagh!

Thankfully, the campsite seemed a very secure, well-equipped and well-organised place, with pitches amongst mature woodland. Next door to us was an old English van (1982 vintage) that had clearly been there for a long time and wasn't going anywhere in a hurry. The sole male occupant (plus dog) had quite a 'pad' there: settee, inflatable hot tub, two motorbikes and a small 'workshop' behind his awning. I've mentioned that we've seen permanent holidaymakers at lots of the sites; many, as in this case, are single men whose mobile homes have long since ceased to be roadworthy and who seem to be living quite happily on their chosen campsite.

Sleep hadn't been too easy, due partly to the campsite's proximity to the motorway and airport. It might also have been due to the fact that, despite having done our best to level the van, it was still on quite a slope; we had to leave the table out to hold on to in case one of us broke into a trot down the van! I must say, though, that otherwise the pitches were very good: hard standing and each with its own drinking-water tap, drainage, electricity, picnic table and bin. Unfortunately, though, I couldn't say the same for the showers/toilets, which, compared to the luxurious ones at Yelloh village, were 'bathetic'!

After a 200-yard sprint to the bus stop, we just made it in time for the 45-minute journey into Lisbon (we weren't far out of town, but the bus route was circuitous). Contrary to the forecast, it was turning out to be a very hot day, so we called at Café Nicole in one of the big squares, which, according to their advertising, was the best café in Portugal in 2000. I don't know what had happened since, but they were still charging on that basis: €8.40 for an orange juice and a small beer!

The Castelo de São Jorge, overlooking the city, was our first visit; we've noticed before that the Portuguese don't like to make things easy and although (after walking up countless steps and steeply sloping streets) we knew we weren't far away, there was no sign for the castle until it was in full view. The Moorish castle dates from the medieval period, although the first fortifications known to have been built there were in the 2nd century BC and excavations show that humans have been present there since 6th century BC. As with most of Lisbon, the castle has been largely rebuilt following a devastating earthquake in 1755, but some elements from earlier times were on display and we were able to walk around the walls that were mostly original and provided a fantastic view of Lisbon. It's interesting to notice that, whereas in UK cities there are usually some upmarket areas distinct from poorer areas, in Portugal there seem to be very dishevelled buildings shoulder-to-shoulder with some of the classiest shops.

After leaving the castle, we called in to a little wine bar, where we had a platter of meats and cheeses, along with a couple of nice glasses of specially selected wine; I must say that the proprietor was (justifiably I think) very enthusiastic about his products! Our next visit was across town to the former Roman Catholic convent founded in 1389, now known as the Carmo convent; apparently by 1551 it contained 70 clergy and 10 servants, but sadly was largely destroyed in the 1755 earthquake, leaving only a skeleton of the huge Gothic church. Some repairs were carried out in 1800 after which it was occupied by the Police Royal Guard, but the church was never fully rebuilt and was rented out as a sawmilling shop in 1835, before the religious orders were expelled from the country. In 1864 it was donated to an Archaeology Association and became a museum.

After admiring its amazing artefacts, we made our way to another of the many large squares down by the water's edge. There was a great atmosphere generally in Lisbon and we loved the many colourful tuk-tuks and the lovely old trams on the 31kms network serving the city.

Figure 114 A Lisbon Tram, Portugal

We should have planned our afternoon in Lisbon a little better (no surprise there!). As you may have realised, it's quite a hilly city and we recklessly decided to head back up to the square near the Carmo convent, having spotted a lovely bar there. However, the climb was worth it as we listened to an excellent group of young people playing jazz, whilst we sat in the sunshine enjoying a long drink. When the time came to make our way back down from the dizzy heights of the Carmo area, we went to investigate the Santa Justa lift (so that's how Santa gets up the chimneys!), a strange looking neo-gothic construction over the road that was built at the turn of the 20th century, to connect the *baixa* (Portuguese for 'low') streets with the higher Largo do Carmo area. Originally powered by steam it was converted to electrical operation in 1907 and in 1973 was integrated into the city's historical tram network. In 2002 it was classified as a National Monument and reopened in February 2006 as a tourist attraction. We didn't use the Santa Justa lift, but descended in the more modern lift provided and were amazed when the doors opened up and we were at the

220

back of a shop, that we then had to walk through to get back on the street; it felt a bit like going back through the wardrobe from Narnia!

By then we were feeling quite weary so we caught the bus back to the campsite, having clocked up another 7½ miles on foot!

At the campsite the area around the café was packed: it seemed that there was a party going on and we were kept awake by some of the revellers still making their way back in the early hours!

We'd decided to move on the next day, but, before leaving, had a walk round the large outdoor shop nearby. As we were leaving Tim was stopped by the security guard as the machine beeped! This has happened before and we've never really known what it was, but this guy was more thorough and pinpointed a label on Tim's hoodie that clearly hadn't been removed after we bought it in England before leaving; we hadn't even noticed it! Honest guv, it wasn't stolen! Luckily, they gave him the benefit of the doubt and didn't call the police!

As we left the site, there was a large group of about 100 girls and boys, all late teens at a guess. About a third of them were standing at one side of the entrance, wearing black ceremonial gowns with white shirts and black ties; the remainder of the group were standing in lines facing them, with their heads bowed – possibly in prayer – for at least half an hour. It was quite a sight and we were intrigued as to whether the gowned ones were leading the prayer, or whether the ungowned ones were taking some kind of oath before being allowed to wear a gown? Perhaps they were the guilty late-night revellers who were on trial! We shall never know!

Our journey out of Lisbon was thankfully much quieter than our entrance had been – and, touch wood, the power steering warning light didn't come back on – in fact, the roads were almost deserted and when we stopped at a service area for lunch there wasn't another vehicle there. The staff in the restaurant looked extremely bored!

Aveiro and Porto (almost!) – May

Having spotted some cheap fuel – and it did seem to vary considerably – we pulled in to fill up, only to find that the computers had broken down so we were unable to use the pumps! Hah! They probably put the price up when the computers were working!!

We arrived at **Costa Nova do Prado** on the coast mid-afternoon: the campsite was one of the ones recommended to us by the couple we'd met at Monchique and it was a lovely site, on a narrow spit of land, just yards from a beautiful sandy beach that goes on for miles at one side, and alongside a river just across the road at the other side.

We had a gorgeous meal of salmon with pasta, sundried tomatoes, garlic, onions & pine nuts – à la Tim – then sat outside with a drink, listening to the waves crashing on the sand nearby. As the evening wore on, I began to feel very restless and by mid-evening, I was itching to get my clothes off; I just couldn't wait any longer, so Tim quickly followed me into the van and I hastily disrobed..........I'd been viciously attacked by some hungry insect/s, with a grand total of 28 insect bites on my bottom and the back of my legs (so Tim reliably informs me, as I couldn't actually see them)!! We had sprayed repellent, but I hadn't quite sprayed it that far so I don't know whether the little **** had crawled up inside my shorts or had been on the chair when I sat down. Suffice to say I was not very happy about it and consequently spent a rather disturbed night, with a tube of antihistamine cream as my bedfellow!

We were a bit late setting off to catch the bus to Aveiro the next day and ended up doing another speed walk for the good half mile to get to the bus stop (we seem to make a habit of this!), breaking into a jog as we saw the bus coming. Fortunately, the kind driver saw us running and stopped for us, even though we hadn't yet made it to the stop.

Aveiro was a nice little town, with – as you might guess from its tourist information title of Little Venice – canals running through the centre, complete with gondolas. After a wander along the waterways, we spotted an array of restaurants in some of the squares close by. Tim had been fancying trying the black pork (a local delicacy, from the black Iberian pig, only found in Portugal) since we'd first noticed it on menus a few weeks ago, so when we saw that it was on offer here we decided to give it a try and it was delicious!

Having washed it down with some rather nice wine, we were feeling quite indolent by the time we'd finished and decided to get the next bus back, which was due to leave at 4.35pm according to our timetable. We ambled back through the town, reaching the corner of the bus stop at 4.25pm, just in time to see what turned out to be our bus disappearing; apparently our timetable was wrong! As the next bus wasn't due for another 1½ hours (although, with the unreliable timetables, another might have come along at any time!) we went crazy and got a taxi back to the site, where I made sure I was well covered up before the evening midges were out, and we chatted to an Australian couple who keep their van in England and return regularly to spend time touring Europe.

Sadly the sky was distinctly overcast and very windy and our planned relaxing beach/cycling day wasn't going to happen, so we decided to leave and head for Porto. We still needed fuel, so tried to find a garage that Tim had spotted yesterday; after some frustrating wrong turns we eventually did, but then it wouldn't accept the card and, as it was unmanned, we still couldn't fill up! Nothing seems easy! Thankfully, we found another one not much further on.

It was a short journey to **Campsite Orbitur Angeiras**, north of Porto, where we arrived in the early afternoon, but I have to say we were a bit disappointed. It was expensive and, apart from having nice clean showers/toilets, there was not much else to make the cost feel worthwhile: the pool and supermarket weren't open yet (out of season) and the Wi-Fi was only available at reception.

We had a walk down to the sea front, which boasted a nice sandy beach, but it was a very quiet little town, so we headed back to the van, luckily just in time before the rain arrived.

Violent thunderstorms and rain during the night had disturbed our sleep a bit, but not, I imagine, half as much as for a German couple who were in a tent nearby; we noticed they'd dug trenches from the tent overnight to drain the water away!

Although we'd planned to visit Porto, the prospect of a 1½ hour bus-ride each way, as well as having to contend with the pouring rain, held little charm, so we decided that it was a good day to travel. First of all we found a Pingo Doce supermarket; you may recall our previous experience of their *poupous*. Unfortunately the poupous here were smaller than those we'd encountered previously, but nonetheless impressive.

We finally set off on our journey, but Ms Satnav seemed to think it would be great fun to divert us about four miles from the motorway to visit a sewerage works, then tell us to retrace our steps to the same motorway! Sometimes I think she's just attention-seeking.... but we were completely at a loss as to why that had happened, I think I must have inadvertently touched that location on the screen!

Spain Again: León, Potes and Bermeo – May

The rain continued for the whole day as we travelled north, eventually crossing the border into Spain. Tim had to carry out some further Heath Robinson (the term, I gather, comes from a cartoonist called William Heath Robinson, known for his drawings of whimsically elaborate machines to achieve simple objectives) repairs to the ailing windscreen wiper, using blu-tack and a rubber band. We'd randomly selected an aire in León to head for – it looked quite pleasant, it was free and was situated by the riverside – right in the centre of town, and 400kms seemed like an achievable goal for the day. We'd forgotten that the clocks were an hour ahead of Portugal in Spain, so ended up arriving at the new time of 6.30pm and took the last available space.

The rain had continued throughout the night but it seemed to be brightening, so we thought we'd explore León. We'd passed a very interesting-looking old building as we drove in yesterday and decided to investigate it. As we were walking I spotted the back of an old-looking building and suggested that that might be the place. Tim, however, was insistent it was just a church, saying, "If that's the building, I'll do the washing up for a week"; tee hee, guess who was on washing-up duties for the next week?!

The building turned out to be the former Convent of San Marcos and home of the Order of the Knights of Santiago, dating from the 12th century and said to be one of the most important monuments of the Renaissance in Spain. Part of the building was being used as a hotel and other parts constituted a huge church and museum, but apparently it only just escaped demolition in 1875. The darkest period in the monastery's five centuries of history was during the course of the Spanish Civil War, when every available space was used to imprison and torture up to 7,000 men and 300 women.

We walked into the town of León, former capital of the Kingdom of León (later the Kingdom of Castilla and León), not expecting to see a great deal more, and were completely amazed by what we found.

The Gothic cathedral, Santa Maria de León, erected around the 13th century, was built on the site of previous Roman baths of the 2nd century. It features no less than 1800m² of beautiful medieval stained glass windows, with the great majority of them dating from 13th to 15th centuries: apparently, a rarity among medieval gothic churches. Consequently, it is known as The House of Light.

We also visited the Royal Collegiate Church of San Isidoro: a magnificent complex of buildings in the Romanesque style.

The basilica, located on the site of an ancient Roman temple, was dedicated to Saint Isidore in 1063; the Royal Pantheon – the funeral chapel of the Kings of León (no, not the band!) – contains vaulted ceilings decorated with frescoes from the 11ᵗʰ century that were amazingly clear – despite never having been restored – as it seems the techniques they used have stood the test of time.

Figure 115 Frescoes in Royal Pantheon, León, Spain

The museum section of this building also housed the magnificent, jewel-encrusted, onyx Chalice of Doña Urraca, with provenance dating it from around the 1ˢᵗ century AD, and known to have been stolen from Jerusalem by the sultan of an Egyptian caliphate; as you may imagine, it is another claimant to the title of Holy Grail. Apparently there are 200 chalices with that claim, of which we'd now seen three, but the provenance of this one did seem to be more plausible: a document is said to exist that suggests the cup was given to Ferdinand I in the 2ⁿᵈ century, and was later mounted and decorated, before being presented to the church in León. Also in the museum was a selection of ancient and beautiful caskets made from various materials, a bible dating from 960, a huge bell from the 11ᵗʰ century and a massive Iranian cockerel from the 7ᵗʰ century; grains that were found inside it when it was taken down for restoration proved its date and origin: Iran (Persia).

León continued to amaze us: large sections of Roman wall; many lovely plazas; the 17th century classicist-baroque style town hall in the Plaza Mayor; the Casa Botines, a late 19th century building designed by Gaudí, with elegant facades on all four sides and a turret at each corner; and numerous interesting churches, such as Nuestra Señora del Mercado (literally 'our lady of the market') that dates from the early 12th century and stands on the Pilgrims' Santiago de Compostela route.

By then we'd walked about 6½ miles so made our way back to the van for a chicken dinner, mmm (Tim, of course, had some humble pie ☺).

Preparing to depart the next day, we decided to defer emptying the chemical toilet – as the disposal point was a hole on the pavement where people were walking – and set off on our travels again. Our route took us through a beautiful valley, alongside and across the huge Embalse de Riaño (reservoir) and then up into the Picos de Europa, part of the Cantabrian mountain range, along unprotected narrow, twisting roads with sheer drops at one side and imposing rock faces leaning into the road on the other. To say that it was a 'hairy' journey would be an understatement, but what a fabulous route it was, with the most fantastic views; they would have been even better if the sun had been shining, but hey!

We arrived at the town of Potes in the early afternoon and found a nice pitch at **Camping La Viorna**, at the foot of the Viorna Mountain.

After lunch we walked down into the town (about 2kms) and had a look around. It was clearly a very popular place, but for very good reason: the scenery, of course, but also some very picturesque medieval houses and a pleasant town centre. We visited the Gothic Torre del Infantado (14th century), which included an excellent exhibition of illustrated manuscripts dating from the 9th to the 13th centuries, then meandered through some of the lovely back streets of town before returning to the van.

The sun was shining the following morning and we decided to try one of the many walks around there. We found the correct path and headed uphill passing a hermitage, then continued higher up into the mountain along some tricky, but very pretty, paths. We were rejoicing that the signs were very easy to follow, but then came to a fork, where the direction to take was very unclear, typical! I wasn't too keen on getting lost up there as bears and wolves roam the mountains in that part of Spain! We tried both directions, neither of which seemed to be going what we thought was the right way, and ended up scaling a cliff side of about 100m high and a gradient of about 1 in 1! Well that may be an exaggeration (so uncharacteristic of me!) but I was literally using my hands to hold on to rocks and grass and had visions of slithering all the way back down again: not quite my idea of a 'cliffhanger'! Once at the top, though, we had some fantastic views over Potes and the mountain range surrounding us.

Figure 116 View over Potes, Spain and the mountains

228

Thankfully, after a lot of to-ing and fro-ing, we found a path of sorts and made our way back down the mountain passing a huge number of cork trees, many of which had had some of the cork bark removed. We also noticed quite a few enormous spider nests hanging from the pine trees; I wasn't too keen to meet their inhabitants!

It was something of a relief to reach Potes again and, after all that exertion; the final uphill 2kms back to the van seemed much harder than it had yesterday! We'd walked for about five hours and reckon we'd covered at least 10 miles, possibly more, it certainly felt like it!

We'd seen a few Fiat 500/600s (and Seat copies) in Potes when we were there, but were amazed when, the following morning, a rally of about 100 of them passed the campsite, sounding horns of all kinds as they went!

It was another beautiful day and we managed to get a couple of wash loads done and hung out without incident! We didn't fancy walking too far today but later in the afternoon walked up the hill to the Monastery of Santo Toribio de Liebana about 1.5kms away. We knew very little about the monastery; simply that we'd seen lots of people heading towards it and had also seen numerous signs in the area proclaiming that this was Jubilee Year.

The church itself was not architecturally remarkable; it was built in 1256, on the site of a former monastery, in a very simple style that is apparently characteristic of the monastic order responsible for its building. What we hadn't grasped until our visit was that its fame is related to its contents: firstly the remains of Saint (Bishop) Toribio, that are believed to have been in the monastery since 1316 or before; secondly, and most importantly, it contains what is said to be the largest known piece of the True Cross (part of the left branch, with the hole where Christ's hand was purportedly nailed), believed to have been brought from Jerusalem, along with the remains of Santo Toribio, in around the 8th century, and now incorporated into a more ornate cross. After a Papal decree in 16th century (that was extended by Pope Pablo

XI in 1967), the Jubilee Door is only opened on years in which St Toribio's day (16th April) falls on a Sunday (as it did this year, hence the Jubilee Year), when visitors to the monastery are able to touch the Lignum Crucis: the 'true cross'.

Tim and I listened to a solemn lecture in Spanish – not understanding much of it sadly – then queued, along with the other people there, to touch the cross (we elected not to kiss it, as many before us had done). I know that for some this would be very spiritual, whilst others would regard the touching of a supposed fragment of the cross with a degree of cynicism. I have to say that we both came away with very mixed feelings but cannot deny that it was a very special experience that we were glad to have been a part of.

In the morning we drove through some very pretty little villages to Fuente Dé, about 23kms away, where we took the cable car (Teleférico) to the top of the Picos Massif mountain, above the snow line at around 2000m (the highest peaks are over 2600m); the views were amazing.

We'd discovered that it was possible to walk down from the top, via routes of varying difficulty and we'd understood from our neighbours at the campsite that they'd done it the day before. They didn't seem like they were regular walkers, so we figured it couldn't be too hard – and all downhill (obviously!) – and we set off along the very well-made path, reaching the Hotel Aliva about 3.6kms later, where we stopped for a coffee. About a couple of hours from leaving the cable car we came to a boundary, after which things went decidedly 'downhill'! The path became very narrow and uneven and included lots of unexpected uphill sections (!), with some very steep drops, where one misplaced foot could have resulted in a premature end to this story (or, as Tim suggested, a potential change of author!). The scenery was beautiful, of course, but we definitely needed to watch our step. We had a few brief stops for rehydration and arrived back at the van after a total of just over four hours, having covered around nine miles, over half of which had been in very difficult terrain. We were very pleased to have a cup of tea in the van before going back to the campsite, where we discovered that our neighbours had only walked round at the top of the mountain and then come back down in the cable car!

As neither of us fancied doing any cooking, we had a nice meal at the little restaurant on the campsite.

In the morning, we left the La Viorna campsite – a very reasonably priced site, with good clean facilities, a nice little shop and restaurant and friendly atmosphere – and headed north east.

After a brief break in a layby, we reached Bermeo on the north coast of Spain (just east of Bilbao) for an overnight stop at an aire. We walked down into Bermeo, which is a busy little fishing port, then had a quiet meal in the van. Well, I say quiet, but in actual fact there were lots of vans on the aire/car park and a huge number of Spanish 'promenaders', providing quite a pleasant atmosphere.

Back to France: Moliet Plage (via Bayonne), Mimizan Plage, Lacanau Ocean and Île de Ré – May

We managed to get a reasonably early start (for us!) for our journey towards Bayonne. As we needed some fuel we specified 'no toll roads' with Ms Satnav, but changed our minds and ignored her frequent suggestions for changes of route; we could tell she was getting tetchy and laughingly wondered how she was going to get her own back this time (another random diversion to a sewerage works?).

As we skirted the edge of San Sebastian we managed to fill up with fuel before crossing into France (where fuel is at least 20c more per litre than in Spain), arriving in Bayonne in the early afternoon, and I (rather unceremoniously) shoved Ms Satnav into the glove box. Tim managed to negotiate some very tight turns and squeezed us into a car park, close to where the rivers Adour and Nive converge and we headed into town – walking some of the way along the walls, parts of which date back to Roman times – and into the huge Gothic Saint-Marie cathedral that stands on the Pilgrimage Way of Santiago de Compostela. The original Romanesque cathedral was destroyed by fires in 1258 and 1310, apart from some sections of the cloister that date back to 1240. Construction of the current cathedral started in the 13th century and was completed in the 17th century, except for the two spires that were not finished until the 19th century; no rush then?!

I was quite fascinated by the buildings in the old part of the town where the tall town houses with shutters and exposed timbers illustrate Bayonne's Basque history. Unfortunately, Tim had had intermittent tummy problems over the previous few days, so we didn't linger in any of the nice looking little bars, as we might otherwise have done.

We had to pay for parking at the booth before leaving the car park, so I hurriedly tried to put in the coordinates for our destination but Ms Satnav was obviously upset and ready with her moment of revenge, refusing to respond to my frantic taps on the screen! In the end, fearing that we'd go over our period of grace before leaving the park, Tim just had to follow his instincts (that are generally very good I must say) to get us out of Bayonne, and I resorted to good old-fashioned map reading to navigate to Moliet Plage. We arrived at **Saint Martin Campsite** around five-ish and were very impressed that, on request, we were given free Wi-Fi access to all four of our devices.

Once settled in, we had a look around, returning to the van just in time before the heavens opened.

The torrential rain continued throughout the night and for the next couple of days, so we spent some time each day in the indoor pool (one of the reasons we'd chosen this site, as we'd seen the forecast!!), which we had pretty much to ourselves, probably because there was a fault: the water was colder than it should have been and the Jacuzzi was extremely cold! The sauna, however, was nice and warm. During brighter intervals we explored the lovely sandy beach one day – the longest in Europe at almost 200kms – and the nearby woods another.

At last a bright and sunny day dawned, so we cycled into Moliet et Maa, a pretty little village, then got a couple of miles along the busy road to Léon – no, not 600kms back into Spain, this was another small village, with some more half-timbered houses – before we realised there was supposed to be a cycle path, which we did eventually manage to pick up.

We'd been craving some of the local delicacies (eg Foie Gras, Confit of Duck, Armagnac) and thought today should be the day to try some. Tim had enjoyed a meal in Léon some years ago and was keen to find the same restaurant but, despite our efforts, we failed to find it. As we started to cycle back we noticed a sign for Maison Tenoy, advertising itself as a *ferme auberge* (literally a 'farmhouse inn'), so thought we'd give it a try. After cycling for a good 10 minutes along a country road, we were about to give up, then noticed another sign in the distance. We were so pleased we hadn't turned back! The restaurant was nestled in the woods and had a lovely ambience with around 14 other diners (all French). We chose the Assiette Tenoy menu for €24, which comprised: Salade de gésiers (which we later learned means 'gizzard salad', it was delicious!); then Tournedos de canard au foie gras, that was beautifully presented with asparagus, carrot fondant, aubergine and slivers of courgette wrapped around an unidentified but very tasty treat! The dessert was Tourtière: an apple tart heavily laced with alcohol, accompanied by a glass of wine.

Figure 117 Maison Tenoy, Moliet et Maa, France

The restaurant was run by a French couple, who are, apparently, among the 5% of French artisans who continue to raise, feed and cook duck in the traditional way; what a treat! We were so pleased to have found it, but it was definitely a slightly more wobbly 45-minute bike ride home, whilst loudly singing through all the French songs we could think of!

Feeling strangely lethargic again (it just comes over us every now and then!), we sat out in the sunshine and 'relaxed' when we got back!

The people near us packed up their tent that, rather weirdly, was erected on the car roof; there are many different ways of camping!

It was a beautiful day so we spent most of it on the lovely beach, then, after freshening-up, ambled along the bars near the campsite. A few of them were offering cocktails at around €8.50 each; I settled for a crêpe instead, and Tim had a beer, before heading back to the van.

The following day we cycled about four miles to Messenges along the excellent Voie Verte (French version of Via Verde), then headed a couple of miles further to the beach. However, it was rather blustery and the café was very busy, so we had a hot chocolate back in the village of Messenges before cycling back for another session in the pool.

We packed up and left Le Saint Martin campsite, a very pleasant site and very reasonable (€17 per night with the ACSI card), considering the facilities that were available, but we were dreading what was going to happen when we tried Ms Satnav again. Tim had checked her over the previous evening but couldn't see what was wrong, apart from a mark at one side of the screen. It turned out that we could, in fact, go anywhere, as long as it only included letters on the left hand side of the keyboard (QWERTY; ASDFG; ZXCVB), so maybe our next visit would have to be some obscure village in Croatia or southern Russia? Tim accused me of having 'stabbed' the screen too vigorously, but I think I must have trapped it in the glove box door the other day in Bayonne (oops!).

Having had such a lovely meal at the Maison Tenoy the other day we thought it would be a great place to try the Confit of Duck, another regional speciality. Unfortunately when we got there, although the doors were open, it was empty and we couldn't get anyone's attention. A little further on our journey, though, Tim spotted L'Estanquet restaurant at the side of the road so we pulled in to the car park. I'd got out to check for Tim while he reversed; all fine, then the van started rolling backwards into the car behind, aagh! The van's overhang was over the car's bonnet and heading rapidly towards its windscreen as I hammered frantically on the side of the van! Thankfully, and with about a millimetre to spare, Tim heard my frenzied banging and realised he hadn't put the handbrake on...and I realised that stupidly I was pushing at the back of the van, like I could have stopped 3½ tonnes!

After all that, the meal was very nice: a gorgeous duck and vegetable soup to start, and the confit of duck was lovely, but its accompanying vegetables were a bit of a let-down and it certainly wasn't in the same league as Maison Tenoy; nonetheless a very pleasant meal.

We drove through Bias (but it was all one-sided) to our next destination: **Club Marina** at Mimizan Plage, again very close to the beach. We chose pitch number 13 (tempting fate?) and, once settled, had a look round to get our bearings. There was only one toilet/ shower block open on the site; the campsite had opened for the season last week and all of the other blocks were in various states of renovation, but otherwise it seemed a very pleasant location.

After our evening meal, we had a walk down to check that the beach was just as beautiful and it was; no problem finding a place to put the beach towel!

Figure 118 Mimizan Plage, France

In the evening, Tim decided he'd have another 'look' at Ms Satnav, eventually, after removing various bits, declaring her a hopeless case; she was last heard uttering the immortal words "Turn around when possible" (and as we threw her in the bin I'm sure I heard her say, "Only joking").

Incidentally, on the subject of technology, my phone had mysteriously turned itself off a few days previously and refused to turn on (aagh!). I was desperate to repair it (how reliant we have become on these little gadgets) and, after quite a lot of searching, found some good information on the web. Unfortunately, we didn't have the tiny screwdrivers needed to remove the back and I was cautious about Tim tackling it after seeing Ms Satnav's demise! I have to say I felt bereft without it – incommunicado and no word games, I was having withdrawal symptoms – whatever was I to do? In the end we just had to talk to each other!! ☺

During the night we were reminded of some of the drawbacks of camping amongst pine trees with various cones and other bits of tree detritus raining down on us! Tim decided to take matters into his own hands and removed a couple of unruly branches with his trusty camping knife saw!

In the morning, Tim went to empty the toilet cassette; he was unsure where the emptying point was, so decided to follow another man doing the same thing and followed him back to his own van, oops!

The bottle of champagne we'd brought with us was calling and, as we'd recently bought some smoked salmon and it was another gorgeous day, we took our minds off pine cones, technology and toilet cassettes, by tucking into a breakfast of smoked salmon & scrambled eggs with bucks fizz. The base of one of the plastic champagne flutes had broken on the journey but, hey, who needs to put their glass down!

Obviously, we needed a little break before setting off tomorrow, so we had a nice relaxing afternoon on the beach, then back to the lovely pool for a cooling swim. Oh it's a hard life!

As we were packing the van up, Tim ricked his back, oh no! Consequently, it took us a bit longer than usual before we were able to set off. Of course, with no satnav, I now had to map read, so I can't really blame anybody else as we took a rather long 'scenic' diversion around the (very beautiful) lake at Sanguinet (bloody place, ha ha!).

When we arrived at **Les Grands Pins** at Lacanau Ocean (another Yelloh Village, like the site we stayed on in Lagos), I thought Tim was getting his own back when the remains of yesterday's (very solid by now) baguette fell off the shelf above us on to my head!

It was a holiday weekend in France, so it was exceptionally busy and took us about an hour to get checked in, but finally we got a nice pitch under the pine trees (oh oh!) and had a look around the site after a late lunch.

The next day was another beautiful, hot day (actually reached 40° in the sun, but officially about 30° in the shade) and we considered putting our awning out. We then realised that, as well as having had a visit from 'special branch' (more twigs and detritus on the roof and around the van) during the night, everything was covered in a sticky resin, so we decided it might not be the best idea.

In the afternoon, we headed down to the beach and walked past crowds of people who'd settled close to the access area, before getting to a much quieter section. The waves were exceptionally powerful, as we found to our cost when we ventured a paddle up to ankle depth only to both be completely knocked off our feet by a huge wave that seemed to come from nowhere! Some of the surfers here are very adept I must say; I'd love to be able to join them, but I'm not too keen on the process of learning! The crashing waves made a very pleasant background noise when we were in bed.....lulling us to sleep of course!

The sun was still very hot as we walked back in the early evening and sat outside again for a lovely Tim-cooked meal of duck breast with potatoes and courgettes. I think we may be exhausting the duck supply around here soon.

We were curious about the priorities given to certain basic requirements at the different sites we'd visited. For example, the previous site – Club Marina – handed out rubbish bags to everyone, and collected them every morning from each pitch, but there was only one shower/toilet block available. At this site, there were lots of shower/toilet blocks, but we couldn't find any proper bins, just two kitchen-sized swing bins at each shower block and recycling bins at reception. There seemed to be only one area with washing machines here too, but it was a large one with ten machines, each of which worked as washers or driers depending on the setting and payment, plus free ironing facilities, woo!

We decided to have a short walk into the busy little resort of Lacanau Ocean, where we treated ourselves to some moules frites. The campsite required us to wear identity bracelets and we felt a bit like prisoners out on licence for the weekend! (Hmm, maybe that's why special branch had dropped in?)

Strolling along the beach the next day we were anticipating a nice siesta in the shelter of the dunes, when along came a thunderstorm! We had to put our picnic blankets over our heads so as not to end up completely soaked; that wasn't the idea at all. Of course, after hurrying back, out came the sun again and we ended up with another scorching afternoon and evening – hah – well, at least we were able to listen to the excellent band playing in the evening.

It was, apparently, the end of the French Bank Holiday and it seemed there was a mass exodus. Thankfully, that, of course, meant it was much quieter on the site, so we spent the morning at the Zen pool, well away from the fantastic slides and watersplash area and only open to adults of 18 years and over, to ensure that we could 'relax in tranquillity'. Just our luck, then, that a French couple had seen fit to bring their 10-ish year-old son with them, who enjoyed dive-bombing in the pool and practising his swimming, much to his parents' delight. I did point out the sign to them, but they seemed to think it just meant that unaccompanied children were not permitted and I'm afraid the language barrier prevented any further discussion! Ah well, I did manage a good few lengths anyway and we had a session in the Jacuzzi section too.

After lunch and with temperatures well into the 30s again, we enjoyed a few hours on the beach.

We packed up the van next morning and left Les Grands Pins campsite: an excellent site for families, with good entertainment and facilities and of course, close to the lovely beach.

As we left it started to rain, again testing our repairs to the windscreen wiper! The rain soon cleared though and we travelled along miles of wonderfully straight and quiet roads, through acres of pine forests, with a quick supermarket trip en route.

In the afternoon we reached Pointe de Grave, where we had our lunch whilst waiting in the queue for a ferry across La Gironde estuary. The crossing to Royan only took around 25 minutes, and then we were heading north again. Amazingly, despite the fact that there were no direction signs until we got well out of Royan, we had managed to take the right road!

We had thought about going to the Île d'Oléron, but fancied visiting La Rochelle, so headed for a campsite on the Île de Ré, the smaller of the two islands – just 26kms long and 70m wide at its narrowest point – which is accessed by a huge road bridge, arriving at **La Tour des Prises** just in time before the site office closed. We found a nice little pitch and proceeded to set up, only to find that we had left our step at the previous site! Noooooo! We made a frantic call to see if it was possible for our former neighbours to take it back to the UK with them, but were not sure whether that would happen. (It didn't ☹) We ate our evening meal feeling very cross and upset with ourselves.

We were cheered up a bit when another beautiful day dawned and we had fresh bread delivered to the door; what a lovely service!

Later we cycled the 10kms along fantastic cycle paths by the coast into Saint-Martin de Ré, the largest town on the island.

The town is famous for its fortress, apparently the finest example of its kind, having been designed by Vauban, Louis XIV's military architect, and listed as a UNESCO World Heritage Site in 2008.

Figure 119 Fortress, Saint-Martin de Ré, Île de Ré, France

The port at Saint-Martin de Ré is very pretty and the town itself has some lovely streets, as well as the ancient church of Saint Martin, originally built in the 11th/12th centuries, but destroyed in various wars over the years and eventually rebuilt in the 18th/19th centuries. We were able to go to the top of the bell tower (117 steps), with some fantastic views over the town and harbour, and got up close and personal with the bells (thankfully it was after noon).

We'd taken a picnic with us, so we found a seat overlooking the harbour. After a while we were joined by an older couple, who were waiting for their daughter and her French husband. We ended up having quite a conversation with them all: the man was born in Scarborough and his father had been the headmaster at the school that Tim had attended many years later! We parted with an exchange of email addresses and an invitation to visit!

We then cycled back past the fortress – part of which is now a prison – before heading for La Couarde-sur-Mer, apparently popular with show business figures during the inter-war years largely because of its long sandy beaches and pretty little streets.

We got back to the campsite around 5.00pm, with time for a relaxing swim and lounge by the pool, before our evening meal.

We packed up a picnic again and cycled into La Couarde-sur-Mer, where Tim had his hair cut, while I did a very quick sketch of the square. We then realised that to get to Ars-en-Ré, we had to cycle back past the campsite, so we ate our picnic at the van! We then cycled along the excellent cycle paths (more like cycle motorways, they are so popular), past all the salt marshes, to Ars-en-Ré, which is listed as one of France's most beautiful villages (the criteria for which are that there are fewer than 2000 inhabitants and at least two protected sites and monuments). There were, indeed, some pretty little streets in Ars-en-Ré, but we felt that Saint Martin and La Couarde were prettier. I couldn't contain my mirth, though, at their translation in the booklet we were given at the Tourist Information Office, so will quote directly from it: "Ars benefits from an opening on the sea (Fier d'Ars)...", you couldn't make it up!

As we walked around, Tim received a message on his phone (my phone still being out of order) from 02 that, from 15th June, using the mobile network in Europe would be free; oh whoopee, that's the day we were due to travel home!

The Saint Étienne church in Ars-en-Ré combines the Romanesque style of 11th century and Gothic style of the 15th century but, as we have noticed with other churches in France, was in a poor state of repair, although still very beautiful. It is noted for its tower which is painted black and white to serve as a landmark for sailors. Apparently a famous French film, Cycling with Molière, was filmed in Ars-en-Ré and we had a drink in the Hotel Le Clocher ('Belltower Hotel') just across the square from the church that apparently figured prominently in the film and, perhaps still on the strength of that, charged us a grand total of €7 for half a litre of beer! The other main monument is the Seneschal's House, dating from the 16th century, whose original owner was a lawyer, judge and, surprise, surprise, a seneschal (an officer having full charge of domestic arrangements, ceremonies, the administration of justice, etc, in the household of a medieval prince or nobleman).

We cycled back for another swim in the lovely covered pool before our evening meal, then decided we'd have a bit of singing practice in the games room for an hour.

France to Home: La Rochelle, Vannes, Le Mans, Rouen and Home – May to June

We decided to pack up and head a little closer to La Rochelle next day (the campsite was about 30kms, which felt a bit too far to cycle!) and said goodbye to new acquaintances and to the very friendly campsite, heading back over the bridge and, amazingly, finding the campsite at La Rochelle quite easily; it must have been a fluke. We were quite amused when we pulled up at **Camping Beaulieu**, to find that an English couple had been following us thinking we knew where we were going; if only they knew!

We got settled (and considered that we'd actually got 'perfect pitch', ha ha!) and, after lunch, got the bus from outside the campsite into La Rochelle, though we were a bit concerned when on the display it said 'next stop: 11 November' and a little later we pulled up at Allemagne (Germany)! Once in La Rochelle, we figured the best thing would be to find the Tourist Information Office and were very impressed that it was well signed, so off we went. About half an hour later we were still walking and eventually got there, only to find we could have walked it in about 10 minutes if we hadn't followed the traffic signs!

Armed with a map at last, we had a look around the old port. The fortunes of La Rochelle appear to have varied somewhat over the centuries, as French and English forces battled for supremacy into the mid-15th century. However, the slave trade and later the fishing industry restored its prosperity and, in particular, it now boasts the largest marina in Europe. Sadly, the beautiful Mairie, or Town Hall, was destroyed by fire in 2013 (maybe because it was on Grille Street?) and is currently being rebuilt; only the tower remains of the original.

We managed to get the right bus back to the campsite and had noticed earlier that there was to be entertainment at the campsite restaurant this evening, so we put on our glad rags, planning to eat at the restaurant and enjoy the entertainment.

We had a little while to spare, so Tim went around to the supermarket close by for some essential supplies, and I got my laptop out to update the blog, having paid €9 for an internet connection.

Sadly, by 8.15pm I had to face facts: the internet connection was one of the worst we've experienced on the whole trip (including the free ones); and the restaurant wasn't going to open! Consequently, Tim had to start preparing a meal for us (that was very nice of course) and the evening ended up being quite different from that planned!

Another wash-day dawned and Tim got creative when putting a washing line between the trees, using his shoe as a weight to lasso the branch! He spotted the proprietor of the restaurant (here, as with many campsites, the restaurant is run independently of the site) and told her of our disappointment last night; she explained that the entertainment is on every Thursday in July and August, but was quite apologetic that this wasn't made clear on the advertisement, which she promptly removed. She also told us there would be karaoke that evening, so we booked a meal.

We eventually got the bus again in to La Rochelle, which, my daughter Helen reminded me, was the setting for the French language textbook Tricolore that she had used at school.

We went straight to visit the towers that had been part of the port's defences since the 14th century and were spared when other fortifications were destroyed in 17th century. Our first call was to the St Nicholas tower, used originally for defence as well as residential quarters – including bedchamber, harbourmaster's hall and private chapel – and from 16th to 18th centuries as a prison. The tower has a double spiral staircase so that soldiers and residents could go about their lives without ever meeting.

From there we walked along the old city walls and past the small beach, then strolled through one of La Rochelle's many green areas that we were surprised to find contained an animal park.

After that pleasant diversion, we returned to the second tower: The Lanterne Tower, the former residence of the ship disarmer (he removed the arms from ships entering the port). This tower was also used as a prison in 17th and 18th centuries and was made into a military prison in 1820. The tower is built from sandstone and amazingly there were around 600 very interesting graffiti inscriptions on the walls, made by prisoners, around a hundred of which included extremely detailed drawings of sailing ships.

The final tower – the Chaine Tower – was also used as a residence until 1472 by the harbourmaster, (he controlled the chain that enabled the port to be closed on the orders of the mayor, hence the name, of course!). The tower was destroyed and remained open to the heavens for 300 years, but had recently been restored, and housed an interesting exhibition regarding the departure of emigrants to Canada in the 17th century.

After a drink in one of the bars overlooking the port, we wandered back through the old town with its half-timbered medieval houses and Renaissance architecture, including passageways covered by 17th-century arches that apparently were erected to protect shoppers from the sun. Finally, we called in at the Saint Louis Cathedral; built in the 18th century, it was somewhat unremarkable from the outside, but with an interesting interior and has been a national monument since 1906.

After all that walking we needed a refreshing swim in the lovely pool, before strolling around to the restaurant, where a large party of young people (well, under 40 years old, that's young to us!) was gathering, seemingly to celebrate some occasion but we never found out what! Based on some written reviews in reception we were expecting a really nice meal, but sadly were disappointed: Tim's steak was so tough he nearly broke the knife, my chicken was lacking in size and, although our chosen menu included coffee, we were never offered it. We wondered whether the reviewers had been offered the incentive of a discount to leave positive comments! But we weren't downhearted: the karaoke was setting up, unbelievably using records and an overhead projector! We keenly scanned the pages to see what we could sing. Alas, there were only a couple of brief pages of songs that we recognised at all! We eventually chose Top of the World and then, later, Summer Nights and I'm pleased to report that they were both very well received, which was quite a relief as we were clearly the only English people there!

It was a bit cloudier the next day, so we had a look around the huge shopping mall nearby, then had a lazy afternoon. A group of about nine French lads (early 20s I reckoned) arrived in the two chalets opposite our van, gradually getting louder and more raucous as the afternoon progressed into evening and continuing until well into the small hours.

Having been kept awake most of the night, there was no chance of a lie-in as some other French lads (presumably the ones who'd gone to bed a bit earlier?) were singing loudly outside their friends' windows. Tim was busy planning his revenge while I sneaked off to sit outside the restaurant so I could use the free Wi-Fi, expecting it to be deserted, only to find myself, a little later (still in my pyjamas, on a What's App call to my daughter in Australia), amongst about 30 men who, it transpired, had come to take part in a poker tournament!

Once the remaining bleary-eyed French boys had emerged, Tim got out our busking speaker and microphones and we put on a special performance for them; we were actually quite amazed that they enjoyed it and even asked for more (that wasn't the idea at all!).

After another wash-load was hung on the line, we spent the beautiful afternoon at the swimming pool.

It was time to move on from Camping Beaulieu: a pleasant site with a lovely pitch and pool and good access to La Rochelle, but a disappointing restaurant, only one toilet/shower block and the only dustbins right at the far side of the site. I must say though, to their credit, when I complained about the standard of the Wi-Fi, the €9 fee was waived.

With only about ten days to go before going home, we decided to have our last big supermarket shop and bought enough (we hoped) to keep us going, filling the fridge up completely. Imagine, then, our desperation when we realised (with a journey ahead of us, just on that day, of around 250kms) that the fridge would not run from the engine battery when we were on the move! After much fretting and gnashing of teeth etc, we established that it would, at least, run on gas, so decided we would just have to leave the gas on, although it's not recommended when travelling; also we were already concerned whether our last gas bottle would last the holiday. However, we felt much less sorry for ourselves when we passed some fellow-motorhomers, whose van had burst a tyre and appeared to have grounded on the motorway; there were bits of plastic, metal and rubber all over the place. How awful!

We finally pulled up at **Flower Camping** at the very end of a finger of land near Vannes and Tim very kindly reversed a little to let another motorist through, only to find that we'd reversed into a concrete flower-tub, cunningly concealed but just at the right height to make another hole in the back of the van, nooo! Thank goodness we hadn't replaced the panel after last year's similar incident!

I went to the office to check in and, as usual, was asked for some details. Having answered a few questions, the receptionist asked, "Do you have ze basicals?" I asked her to repeat the question a couple of times and my mind was racing, thinking, "...well, we've got gas and water, I've already asked for electricity...", but I just didn't know what she was getting at, until she said, "Ze basicals to ride on ze basical track"...ah *bicycles*!

Just to finish things off, the heavens opened whilst we were setting up. However, it was a lovely site, with a wonderful view over the lake, a good pool, free Wi-Fi and plenty of shower blocks and bins!

Tim phoned the van suppliers for help to fix the fridge but sadly, despite their guidance through the checking of various wires and connections, we had no success.

We took the van out (gas on!) and drove to Carnac (following directions previously downloaded on to the computer as we were, of course, without our little friend Ms Satnav). Some fresh bread was needed for our lunch, so we walked into the town centre; Carnac is a lovely little town, with the most beautiful church of Saint Cornély (the patron saint of horned animals!) that dates from the 17th and 13th centuries and contains some exquisite fresco paintings covering the wooden vaults.

After a quick lunch in the car park, we went to look at the largest collection of megalithic standing stones in the world, comprising of more than 3000 prehistoric stones cut from local rock and erected by the pre-Celtic people of Brittany between around 3300 BC and 4500 BC.

Figure 120 Standing stones at Carnac, France

Figure 121 Standing stones at Carnac, France

There are three major groups of stone rows (with stones varying from around 2ft to 12ft high), which possibly once formed a single group, stretching for around four miles, but which have been split up as stones were removed for other purposes. At other points there are menhirs (single stones), tumuli (grassy mounds) and dolmen (generally considered to have been tombs, constructed with several large stones supporting a 'capstone'). Bizarrely, and despite much research, the purpose of all these stones is still not known; maybe the druids were just having a bit of a laugh and setting us a poser for eternity?

After leaving the amazing stones, we drove down the peninsula leading to the town of Quiberon, a pleasant little port, but we didn't linger as it was getting rather late, and drove back along the Côte Sauvage ('wild coast'), that was very much living up to its name when we stopped to have a closer look. We could see both coasts quite clearly at the narrowest point along this finger of land and the difference between the two was amazing, with the 'savage' Atlantic coast lashing against the coastline and the millpond-like, gentle tide of Baie de Quiberon, only about a hundred yards away.

Next morning we caught the bus from directly outside the campsite into Vannes. Again, we found the Tourist Information Office straight away and headed off, via the town gate, St Vincent Ferrier, to follow the walking-route around town. A very extensive market was being held in the Place des Lices (we were getting very itchy!) and we bought some award-winning strawberry jam! Some of the houses there were half-timbered and I started taking some photos of them, then realised that the town of Vannes is an absolutely amazing medieval town, with street after street of beautiful half-timbered houses!

The town hall is just outside the vast medieval quarter, but was well worth seeing. It was built between 1881 and 1886 and is a copy of the Parisian town hall.

Back among the medieval houses, we came to the cathedral: a huge building, combining Romanesque (belfry, 13th century), Gothic (façade, 14th century) and Renaissance (chapel, 16th century) sections, but we didn't really feel that the interior was remarkable for anything other than its vastness.

We popped into a lovely little café, the Dan Ewen, and had Galettes Blé Noir (meaning 'made with buckwheat flour', that has a distinctive, mild, nutty taste). The decor was very much in the Breton style. In fact, the area is very evocative of Welsh/Cornish tradition, the Breton language having been brought from Great Britain by migrating Britons during the Early Middle Ages; hence it is very closely related to Celtic languages, particularly Cornish. It has apparently declined from having more than a million speakers in 1950 to about 200,000 now and is classified as 'severely endangered', although more children are now learning it at school. Certainly the Breton language is very prominent in that area, with all the road signs written in French and Breton. We discovered that *priveziou* means 'toilets', *bountit* means 'push', *Gwened* is 'Vannes', *kreiz* is 'centre' and *ker* is 'town'; there were so many places called *ker*-something, we were thinking maybe Ker-Plunk was invented there!

Thanks to the help of a man working on the erection of tents in the beautiful gardens there (clearly for an upcoming event), we found our way on to the ramparts, with a view along the city walls, parts of which date back to the 3rd century. Unfortunately, the aforementioned event meant that we were unable to walk through the gardens, which contained the very extensive washhouses that are one of Vannes' best known monuments, dating from around 1817.

As is often the case, we spent quite a while familiarising ourselves with the whereabouts of public toilets; as previously mentioned, I think we could write a Guide to Toilets in France and Spain!

We made our way back to the lovely marina and had a glass of vin in Vannes, before returning to the van.

In the evening I went to use the French computer in the reception office to load my photos on to the blog; sadly, my efforts were in vain and severely compounded by the fact that the keyboard was decidedly not QWERTY!

We'd called in at the Leclerc and Carrefour supermarkets as we'd passed them yesterday, but had failed to find gas bottles in the size that would fit our van, and finding some was becoming more of a priority, so we asked the receptionist to check whether Intermarché had some in stock and they had, whoopee! Following directions on the laptop we arrived, located the gas near the fuel kiosk and somehow managed to make the non-English-speaking attendant (well so she said) understand what we needed. Unfortunately, we hadn't brought our empty French gas bottle from last year (well, you wouldn't bring an empty one with you!), so needed to complete a form. Keen readers may recall that our gas purchase last year was also fraught with problems, resulting in us buying gas without completing a form; sadly we weren't going to get away with it this time, but the woman said she couldn't find the right form and suggested we come back in the afternoon when her colleague was on duty! Tim complained to a non-English-speaking manager who really didn't want to help, so we had to leave empty-handed and somehow managed to navigate to the Super-U supermarket. They had bottles of the right size but the woman (again no English) was insistent that she was about to leave for lunch, so, under considerable pressure and with a little concern that this was a different type, we bought a bottle, along with fittings.

Having now purchased some gas, we relaxed a little and drove to the town of Auray, where the lovely little harbour of Saint Goustan had some more medieval houses (although some of them had been altered very unsympathetically) and a very old bridge (The New Bridge!), dating from the early 13th century. In the main town centre there was also the 17th century church of Saint Gildas and a few more, better-preserved, medieval houses.

Back at the campsite, Tim went to fit the new gas bottle, only to find that he couldn't, huh! Consequently, panicking about the gas running out, we daren't put the kettle on for a cup of tea, so we just had to drink wine! Life's a gas!

So, back to Super-U, where the woman (still no English spoken; we were certainly brushing up on our French-speaking skills!) did at least refund our money without too much of a problem. Again, we managed to navigate back to Intermarché and were greeted with delight (NOT!) by the same woman who'd been on duty yesterday morning. All she could say (in French of course) was, "Why didn't you come back in the afternoon?" and rudely closed the door on us. We again went in to see the manager, who simply repeated that message and even suggested that we try Leclerc or Super-U; I pointed out in my best French that she had the gas we wanted, but to no avail. So we returned very dejectedly to the van and had some lunch. To pass the time whilst waiting, we had a walk down to the little harbour of Conleau, on the tip of land close to the campsite, and were pleasantly surprised that it was a very pretty little place with more medieval houses and some lovely restaurants.

Back to Intermarché again, and beginning to feel like we knew the route backwards, Ms Satnav would be proud of us! This time, thankfully, it was a different person on duty, who greeted us with a cheerful smile, got out the appropriate gas bottle and – guess what – the same form that the other woman had said was the wrong one, which we then filled in. Job done in five minutes! Tim fitted the gas bottle whilst we were there, just to be sure!

Feeling very relieved, we decided to make the most of another enforced trip out in the van. We passed some stones via Crach (!) – but it wasn't all it was 'crached' up to be – and, avoiding Troc and Puces(!), visited the lovely Trinité sur Mer, one of the places that had been recommended to us. It was a beautiful afternoon and we walked past the huge marina and down the headland (most of the places in the Golfe du Morbihan are on little peninsulas) and back along the beach. I then realised that, as we were parked opposite the Tourist Information in town, I might just be able to upload some photos to the blog, so I spent the next 45 minutes doing just that.

We drove back via Carnac, for another look at the amazing alignments of megaliths there and stopped at the site of

Le Quadrilatère, a rectangle (approximately 20 x 5 metres) of smaller standing stones and Le Géant du Manio: a single, enormous, megalith, around 2.5 metres high. Yet again, you just have to marvel at these stones and imagine what their original purpose was!

Figure 122 Le Quadrilatère at Carnac, France

Another lovely day dawned and we tried the fabulous 25m pool on the campsite and did about 30 lengths; we then got on the bikes and cycled along a very pleasant cycle path into Vannes. We did consider running back and calling it a triathlon, but thought better of it.

We had another vin in Vannes, then went round to the gardens that were now thronged with people, so we thought we'd investigate. It turned out to be a book fair, where numerous authors were present; our French has improved, but not to that extent! However, as entry was free, we went in and were able to see more closely the washhouses that we'd seen from afar the other day.

I'd taken my sketch book with me, so, later, Tim left me at a suitably-positioned café in the medieval quarter, while he went in search of oranges to make a sauce for our evening meal.

Figure 123 Pastel sketch in Vannes, France

When Tim returned he was still reeling, having paid €2.40 for two oranges; he hadn't realised until too late that he'd found a 'bio' fruit and vegetable shop and, of course, anything that's 'artisan' or 'bio' generally means adding at least €2 to the normal price. However, the resulting duck with orange sauce was delicious and it was a fabulous evening, so afterwards we had another stroll down the peninsula to Conleau harbour.

It was a beautiful day the next day, so we visited the protected wildlife area around the estuary close to the site. Later, we had a lovely meal at one of the restaurants in Conleau (I had foie gras profiteroles and Tim had salmon and prawns; we both had magret de canard – I know, yes, again – then cheese and biscuits), with a

255

beautiful view over the harbour, before finally making our way happily back to the van.

We made an early start and left the very friendly, clean and good value Camping Le Conleau and headed for Rochefort en Terre, another place recommended to us, and classified as a Petite Cité de Caractère; another of the 'most beautiful villages in France' and also recognised by Villes Fleuris for its environmental efforts and tourist facilities. I'd had a look online to see if I could find out any information in advance and the blurb said, "..the best way to see Rochefort en Terre is to wander the streets on foot...", so I had to hastily cancel our plans to paraglide and, as we approached in the van, we were very impressed that there were actually clear directions to a motorhome parking area. It most certainly was a very pretty village, with some beautiful medieval houses. Clearly there was about to be an outside broadcast about the village's award-winning status, as there was lots of equipment in the square and everyone was hanging baskets outside and filling up their flower-tubs ready to be filmed!

Figure 124 Rochefort en Terre, France

We had a look in the Notre Dame de la Tronchante Church, which is unusually located on a slope in the lower part of the village, apparently because a priest had hidden a holy statue in the location in the 9th century, which was discovered 200 years later and seen as a 'sign'. The old town, where the poorer people (tanners, potters, etc) would have lived, is located below the grander houses, but contained some beautiful old houses.

We left via Pleucadeuc (and as you've probably gathered a few ducks have been plucked around here recently!) and raced to the **Pont Romain** campsite at Le Mans. Having found a lovely pitch, we settled down for a quiet evening, sitting outside in the sunshine, with the birds singing and a little red squirrel hopped across the grass in front of us, before scurrying off into the wood. After about an hour a single man on a vintage motor-bike came and pitched up close by, then another two men, then another single man in a camper, then some more motor-bikers and, near the toilet block, five, what I can, sadly, only describe as archetypal English yobs; we don't consider ourselves to be anything special, but they were incredibly obese, topless, loud and coarse men, who used the f* word almost every other word, despite being very close to the main thoroughfare through the campsite; they made us ashamed to be English, particularly as they were from Yorkshire! (Tim referred to them as the 'blubber boys'; well, they did seem to be having a whale of a time!)

Curious to know what was causing this influx of male travellers, Tim went across to the Wi-Fi area and asked Google, who told him that the main Le Mans 24-hour race was on that weekend and we hadn't even realised!

After our evening meal we noticed that one of the sauce bottles had tipped upside-down in the overhead cupboard in transit (no, I know, it's a Fiat ☺) and its contents had leaked through the cupboard on to the seating and curtains below, cue cleaning up session!

The village of Yvré l'Eveque was close to the campsite, across the eponymous Pont Romain, which, we discovered, was built in the 16th century on the foundations of a Roman bridge. Our plan to catch a bus to Le Mans, however, was less straightforward than we'd imagined it would be; isn't everything!! It required an extensive search, not only for the bus-stop, but for which side of the road to catch it! As we were searching, assisted by a very helpful French lady, our dilemma was resolved: the bus went by... on the opposite side of the road! Consequently, we had another half-hour to wait for the next one.

Once in Le Mans, we had more searching to do, this time for the Tourist Information Office, and another very helpful French lady (who spoke no English) came to our assistance and kindly walked us straight to the door! We felt very proud of our French conversation as we chatted to her on the way.

We hadn't been too sure what to expect in Le Mans – especially having discovered that the main event was imminent – but we were in for a treat. St Julian's Cathedral, whose construction dated from the 6th through the 14th century (on the foundations of an earlier church) partly with money provided by William the Conqueror (who was, of course, the Duke of Normandy), was immense and extremely beautiful. It is noted for its exceptional stained glass windows, 20 of which, in the nave, date from the mid 12th century. At its highest point, the new choir stands at 34 metres, (the old choir, 24 metres high, is now the nave) and the total length of the building is 129 metres; the flying buttresses on the outside are something to behold!

Figure 125 St Julian's Cathedral, Le Mans, France

We decided to have a Croque Monsieur and chose a lovely café just outside the cathedral and opposite a large square where a collection of old cars was on display. We were just enjoying the tranquillity of the moment, when two council men came and began cutting the grass directly adjacent to the café, only a few feet away from where we were sitting – they were wearing ear-protectors, but we could hardly hear each other speak – just our luck!

Continuing our trip around Le Mans, we came across the city wall, built with ornate red patterned stones in the 3rd century, to reflect the resurgent power of Rome. It has been declared a UNESCO world heritage site and is said to be the best preserved of all the ancient Roman Empire.

Figure 126 Roman Walls at Le Mans, France

The many medieval streets in the Plantagenet area of Le Mans are more amazing examples of their kind; some have sadly been allowed to perish, or been altered somewhat, but the majority are breathtakingly beautiful and exceptionally interesting in their variety and design, dating from between the 14th and 18th centuries.

As we meandered back to the bus stop, there were lots of preparations going on in readiness for the weekend's big event, including crowd barriers, marquees and a big army and police presence. Finally, we made our way back to the campsite and enjoyed a nice relaxing evening.

We had originally planned to stay near Le Mans for three nights, but with the racing event looming, and having realised we still had about 400kms to go to Calais we decided to move to **Campsite Les Terrasses,** near Rouen, although there was not much information available about it. We passed lots of English vehicles heading for Le Mans, but without Ms Satnav we were unsure whether we'd find the site, so I was thrilled to be able to get us there without too much trouble. Unfortunately, though, it looked very shabby and run down and there was no one on reception, so we turned around and Tim suggested heading for Rouen centre and trying to park there, with the intention of heading for an aire later in the day, hah! Every car park we came across was so full it was impossible to fit a motor-bike in there, certainly not a 7.5 metre-long motorhome. We were on the point of giving up on Rouen and just heading on to another site or aire, when I spotted a camper site sign, so we followed it.

After what seemed like ages, we felt sure that we must have missed the next sign and were feeling despondent, but then, just in time, spotted another sign and another and eventually arrived at about 2pm, at **Camping de l'Aubette**, a beautiful, rustic campsite (not far from Boos!), reasonably priced, with electricity, showers/ toilets etc and a bus close by into Rouen. A quick lunch followed, before we found the bus-stop and headed into Rouen.

Our first stop was what we thought at first was the cathedral, but turned out to be the Abbey of St Ouen, the building of which began in 1318 but, interrupted by the Hundred Years' War, was not completed until the 15th century. The Gothic Abbey is a huge structure, 137m in length with 33m high vaults and its beautiful stained glass dates to the 15th and 16th centuries, giving the church a brighter interior than is typical of Gothic churches. Sadly, the Abbey had fallen into disrepair and needed a great deal of work.

After a frantic search for public toilets again and finally having to queue behind a school party that had just arrived (!), we went to visit the Notre Dame Cathedral, with sections dating back to various points in history, the oldest surviving section being 11th century. The cathedral was seriously damaged during the Second World War and had undergone considerable restoration before re-opening in 1956. It was an enormous structure, dominated by three towers: the Tour Saint-Roman (c.1145); the Tour de Beurre (Butter Tower: named because it was built from donations from parishioners for the privilege of eating butter during lent!), built in 15ᵗʰ century and standing at 250 feet; and the Tour Lanterne (1876) that contains 56 bells and rises to almost 150m (500 ft) – the largest spire in France – but which was, at the time of our visit, in the process of restoration. However, although the exterior was beautiful (the façade – also the largest in France – having been immortalized by Claude Monet in his paintings, of course), the interior of it somehow lacked the charm of the Abbey, we felt.

Rouen – capital of Normandy – is yet another city with an amazing medieval section, containing around 2,000 half-timbered houses, about half of which have been restored. 227 houses are listed as historical monuments, some dating back to the 14ᵗʰ and 15ᵗʰ centuries, making Rouen one of the first six cities in France in terms of historic architecture, despite serious destruction during the Second World War. Beautiful though they are, we have to admit to being a bit 'medievalled-out' by then!

We had a drink in the square, close to the place where Joan of Arc was burnt to death in 1431, and visited the Gros Horloge, a huge clock (which is, of course, what *gros horloge* means), with one of the oldest mechanisms in France, the movement having been made in 1389, cast in wrought iron. At 2.5 metres in diameter, it is thought to be the largest such mechanism still extant. The beautiful façade was added in 1529 when the clock was moved to its current position. We went up to the top of the bell tower, with some superb views over the city and on the way down the bell struck five and nearly made me jump out of my skin!

Figure 127 Gros Horloge in Rouen, France

After a pleasant walk down to the River Seine, we made our way back to the site, then sat outside for our last evening meal of the holiday. It was an absolutely gorgeous evening and we felt so lucky to have found this site in such a random way, for our last evening away.

We packed the van up, planning to set off for around 10.30am and with around 200kms to go, hoped we'd be in Calais for about 1.00pm. Tim joked that we might still be finding our way out of Rouen by then, as we weren't sure of the way back to the motorway; how we laughed! Only a few minutes after leaving the site, we saw the sign for the motorway, yippee! Our joy was short-lived, however, as when we reached the exit, it was closed! There were no diversion signs whatsoever and we did an unintentional (and, to be fair, unwanted) additional circuit of Rouen, still not seeing any mention of the direction we needed. We ended up going a very long way out of our way and probably didn't fully appreciate some of the very pleasant (and often curiously named, eg Pissy Pôville) French towns we went through! Just to add insult to injury, we had to pay a toll for our journey on a section of road that we didn't even want to be on, and an hour and a half after leaving the campsite we were still 200kms away from Calais!

Thankfully, we eventually found the right road and made good time to Calais. Back in the UK, we spent a lovely evening with Tim's family who'd kindly formed a welcoming party.

The next day, on our final leg of the journey home, we set off to have the reversing sensors and the fridge fixed at the place we'd bought the van. The fridge duly fixed, they announced that the van was ready and, on enquiring about the reversing sensors, we learned there had been no problem, they just hadn't been switched on! So, it transpired that we'd driven 10,000 over our two holidays (and backed into two low-level concrete planters), when the thing was perfectly ok, but the van now required a complete new end panel fitting! I should point out, lest you should think we're a bit thick (how could you?!), that the switch was near the front of the van, in a little cubby hole behind the passenger seat and underneath one of the table seats, so it was certainly not obvious! Ah well!

Unfortunately, due to an accident, the M1 was completely closed, so it was about 1½ hours later than we'd anticipated before we pulled in to Selby market place and got some fish, chips and mushy peas, that we hungrily devoured in the van, parked outside the fish and chip shop.

Finally arriving home about 7.30pm, we were thrilled to see the brand new kitchen that had been fitted in our absence; but it was some time before we finished going through the heap of mail – phew, no fines – and putting away all the pots, pans, groceries, cutlery, crockery etc that had been stacked in the dining room! We also had to work out how to use the new microwave and cooker and particularly the heating/hot water system, as the boiler seemed to be working continuously despite the searing heat outside and the fact that it quite clearly stated, "heating: off" and "water heating: off". Happy Days!

We did, of course, arrive home with no satnav, only one (working) mobile phone (sadly, I have to report that my phone was irreparable), no step and, oddly, three teaspoons fewer than when we set off; we can only assume they'd been thrown out with the washing up water!

The Third Trip:
France, Germany, Switzerland, Italy, Sicily and Spain – September to December

Through France, Germany and Switzerland – September

I guess Tim and I had caught the travel bug and certainly wanted to make the most of our lovely motorhome, so we journeyed south to call on Tim's family for the weekend, only realising, on our way, that we'd forgotten to get the bread, potatoes and onions out of the cupboard. A phone call to our wonderful neighbours was needed or we'd have been arriving home to some rather unpleasant smells in the kitchen! We also realised we'd forgotten to pack the microphones that work with our busking speaker. Thankfully, we do have others, but ended up deciding to leave the speaker with Tim's brother, as it didn't work well with the other microphones.

Finally the day came to head for the Channel Tunnel for our crossing and we put our new satnav to use; you may recall that our previous one had met a tragic end! The new one was a special motorhome edition, into which we could put the van's dimensions, ensuring that we wouldn't encounter any more low bridges or exceed weight restrictions (fingers crossed!). In addition, we were able to search for campsites already programmed into it: all our problems were solved!

After about an hour or so, the screen went blank, oh no! Not another satnav failure? After a frantic moment or two, we discovered that one of the 12-volt sockets on the dashboard had stopped working, which was, at least, better than the new satnav being broken, but, as we had that in one socket and a dash cam in the other we had to make a decision, so unplugged Ms Satnav whilst in the UK and hoped it was just a fuse that could be easily fixed. The tunnel crossing was, as always, efficient and brief and we arrived in France in bright sunshine. Our joy was short-lived though; about five minutes later the rain was battering on the windscreen and the wind buffeting the van, and as we headed south the temperature plummeted to about 11°C!

The coordinates were set for an aire in Reims but after a trip around the city, we ended up at a private car park! As we sat there, totally bewildered, a very nice French man (who spoke impeccable English), on noticing that we appeared to be lost, stopped his car and approached the van. We were quite amused that it was only after he'd interrogated us as to our opinion on Brexit and we had sworn that we hadn't voted to leave (well, we weren't actually in the UK at the time anyway), that he very kindly escorted us by car to the right place (about 100 metres behind us, but as we were on a one-way street we had to do a circuit to get there). I noticed that we were only a few hundred metres from Reims Cathedral, so we were looking forward to walking across after a much-needed cuppa.

Unfortunately, as we sat with our drink, we became aware of a group of 8-10 somewhat unkempt-looking young men, who made us feel rather intimidated; they were leaning up against our van, making it rock and we heard one of the socket covers on the outside click as if someone had opened it and let it go. They left on foot after about 20 minutes or so and we went to look at their, much smaller, van, parked next to us; it seemed as if they were all sleeping in it! Feeling a bit nervous about having them as neighbours overnight, we decided to head for an alternative site – sadly missing the cathedral visit – about an hour away at **Camping de Chalons en Champagne**.

Our new satnav let us down again though, abandoning us as we battled through Reims ('drive to road', thanks!) and brightly piping up again once we'd reached the right road! Then, as we approached the site, she took us around to its back gate, which was locked; again we had to find our own way round a housing estate to the main entrance. By the time we got there, it was 7.00pm and reception had closed, so we found a pitch and plugged in, glad to use one of our new additions for this trip, an electric kettle: much quicker when we are on a site!

The site itself was rather 'tired', the showers and toilets were grubby and the television room had just a hole in the wall where the television should have been! The book had said there might be some 'disturbance' from grape-pickers in September (we were in the

Champagne region of course); we hadn't realised that meant there'd be rather a lot of young men sleeping eight or more in transit-type vans! Presumably that's what the men we'd encountered in Reims were, so we might as well have stayed there. Oh well, we live and learn and felt guilty at having judged them as we did.

Anyway, we were too tired by now and there seemed to be lots of other tourists' vans on the site, so we had a walk to stretch our legs then headed back to the small bar/restaurant on the site and sampled their speciality of lamb shank with chips and a glass of wine, that the very helpful young man kindly put in foil dishes so we could eat in the van.

We made an early start next morning and Tim called for some fuel, while I popped to the Carrefour to replenish our root vegetables; a simple task, you may think. Hah, think again! Firstly I attempted my purchase at the wrong self check-out (I was told I needed a loyalty card of some description!), then the one I was sent to would only accept credit card payment and Tim had my card for the fuel! Feeling embarrassed, I joined another queue, shoved the eventual receipt in my bag and made for the exit, only to have to then hastily unearth it from my bag as I needed to scan it to open the barrier; it is me isn't it!

We passed Troyes by – but I couldn't see the wooden horse – and Nancy didn't tickle our fancy at all, but finally, as we approached the German border, we had to put the air-con on as the temperature reached the dizzy heights of 21°C! We drove along the side of the beautiful Rhine through Germany, then into Switzerland, but what with the Ausfahrts, Belchen and a sign for lateral wind, we were beginning to feel a bit nauseous!

Around 5.30pm, we thought it was time to look for a site and headed for **Campingplatz Gerbe**, a farm site near Luzern that sounded nice in the description. This time, Ms Satnav got us to the right place, but we were not impressed with what we saw. There seemed to be a lot of litter around, the 'pool' was a plastic, rigid-sided construction (containing positively disgusting-looking water covered in green algae), alongside which was a warped table-tennis table, and – guess what – the wooden horse of Troy! Seriously, it was a huge wooden horse – around 15 to 18ft high – presumably designed for children to play on, but looking rather mouldy and unwelcoming.

Needless to say, we didn't fancy staying there (maybe we're getting a bit picky), so we reluctantly set the coordinates yet again for the nearest campsite en route (according to our book), two hours away! On the way, we saw a campsite sign and left the route to check it out; the access wasn't suitable, but we then couldn't get back on the motorway and yet again were abandoned by Ms Satnav; we're beginning to wonder whose side she's on!

Our rather dejected mood was lightened somewhat as we passed through some of the most amazing scenery: huge lakes surrounded by imposing mountains. Eventually, we went through an exceptionally long tunnel, about 20kms, coming out into Italian-speaking Switzerland (there are three main languages: German, spoken by about two-thirds of the population; French, spoken in the west of the country by about a quarter of Swiss people; and Italian, spoken in the southernmost parts of Switzerland by around 8% of the people) and we reached the picturesque **Acquarossa Campsite** by around 8.00pm.

We awoke to some lovely sunshine and a stunning view from our van. The toilets and showers were immaculately clean, but we discovered that we needed a token to operate the shower and, as reception was a good half-mile walk from our pitch, we decided to eschew a shower until our next stop. As it was advertised at €19 per night, we got a bit of a surprise when we were charged €26 and were told the extra was taxes! Language barriers prevented much discussion, so we paid up and set off for the next site, arriving at around 3.00pm.

Italy: Lake Garda – September

Our pitch at **Bella Italia Campsite** was about 30 metres from a shingle beach at the edge of the beautiful Lake Garda and, joy of joys, the temperature was about 25°C, so, after a walk round, we sat outside in shorts and t-shirts, enjoying the warmth.

The following morning, having checked the bus times, we went for the 11.45am to Verona, which arrived at the bus stop at noon, completely packed, with no chance of us getting on. An English couple, who were also waiting, told us there was a train at 1.00pm so we walked to the station in the nearby town of Peschiera, arriving in Verona after a 15-minute journey. Thanks to Google maps on our phones, we found our way into the centre and visited the amazing Roman arena, completed in the 1st century AD, which seats 30,000 people. Sadly the operas are held there only in June, July and August every year so we were just two weeks too late.

Figure 128 Roman arena in Verona, Italy

We then called at the Casa di Giulietta (Juliet's gaff) and saw the balcony where she allegedly called for her beloved Romeo. They were, of course, entirely fictional characters and the house was chosen in the 1930s as 'hers'. The wall leading to it was completely 'plastered': couples proclaiming their love by writing their names on sticking plasters, which was a new one on us! The lovers must have really been stuck on each other! Walking on, we passed through some wonderful piazzas; lots of the buildings are, or have been, covered in frescoes, it must have been even more stunning when they were all intact. In a brief visit to the Chiesa di Santa Anastasia, Verona's largest church, we saw the elegantly decorated and vaulted ceiling, dating from 13th-15th centuries.

Our next visit was across the Ponte Pietra: a Roman bridge over the Fiume Adige, to the Teatro Romano, built just after the arena was completed and also still in use. From the upper courtyard we had some good views over the city. By now we were quite footsore and weary, having walked almost 10 miles, so we didn't go inside the Duomo, Verona's 12th century Romanesque cathedral. A desperately-needed drink in the Piazza del Signori gave us an opportunity for a bit of people-watching, before we made our way back to the train. The forecast today had warned of possible showers, so we'd packed our kagoules, thank goodness, as, about two minutes after getting off the train in Peschiera the heavens opened. Our walk back took us about 25 minutes, by which time our feet were squelching in our shoes!

The sky was overcast in the morning, but rain wasn't forecast till the evening, so we decided we'd risk a load of washing and hung it out before setting off for a lakeside walk to Peschiera, a very quaint little town that actually has quite a history. At the time of Pliny, during the Roman Empire, it was called Arilica and already had considerable importance. In the centre there is a huge pentagon-shaped fortress that, apparently, played a prominent part in most military campaigns conducted in northern Italy after 1400. The town is encircled by massive Venetian defensive systems that had recently been declared a UNESCO World Heritage Site. There were lots of lovely restaurants and, along the lakeside, plenty of facilities for water-sports. After a wander around we stopped for a glass of 'spritz' – the Italian drink – consisting of prosecco with aperol and soda, then a cup of coffee at a nice little café overlooking the lake. The clouds were gathering so we headed back and got our washing in then went to the internet café, where, for €1 per hour, I tried unsuccessfully to upload some photos to the blog. Meanwhile, Tim checked out the internet at reception and it seemed ok, so we went to try it there, only to find that we needed to show our booking form to get access, meaning we had to walk to the van and back (at least half a mile each way) before I could post the blog photos! Thankfully it was much better internet, but cost €1.50 for an hour.

The rain came with a vengeance in the evening, so we had to set up washing lines in the van; it was getting very steamy in there!

We were a bit worried that we might be floating out by morning, but we managed to get out quite well, thankful we'd put everything away before the rain had started. We'd enjoyed our stay at Bella Italia, an enormous site with lots of chalets as well as pitches, a fantastic pool area, lots of activities, bars and restaurants and plenty of clean facilities too; we'd saved €33 altogether with our ACSI card, on the marked price, what good value!

Venice – September

It was an uneventful journey to **Serenissima Campsite**, near Venice, where we arrived around lunch time. Tim got out to plug us into the electricity and came back in with his leg covered in bites; they work quickly around there clearly! This site was much smaller than the previous one, but again with plenty of clean facilities, a nice pool, small supermarket and restaurant and, literally just across the road, we were able to catch the bus into Venice: €3 return for a 25-minute bus ride.

Alighting from the bus at the Piazza le Roma, we had a good half-hour walk through some less exciting, but nonetheless interesting, parts of the city (a wedding was being held in one of the churches we passed), before crossing the Rialto Bridge and into the main tourist area. We enjoyed the ambience whilst drinking a rather expensive glass of spritz at one of the bars opposite the Doges Palace, where there was a four-piece band playing, then had a look around the city. It seems that most things in Venice are rather expensive; even the public toilets were €1.50 and they were far from immaculate!

We decided to try a pizza in what appeared to be a little corner restaurant away from the centre; it turned out to be a huge restaurant, but the pizza was very nice. We then made our way back to the bus station, passing through the midst of a large crowd of protestors on the way (don't know what they were protesting about!) and got the bus back, realising during our journey that, in the dark and being unable to see out of the windows very well, we hadn't a clue where we were. Luckily, a helpful Italian saw our plight and told us where to get off (!!). According to my pedometer, we'd done around five miles today.

The next morning was beautiful, so we hung out another load of washing (oh, it's a hard life!) and decided to live dangerously, getting the bus into Venice without taking a waterproof with us! This time, we found a different, more interesting route into the centre, passing, on our way, at least 40 different shops selling masks exclusively; it really is a big thing there! Interestingly, the Spanish for 'mask' is *mascara*, Italian is *maschera* and, in French, *masquer*, which gave us the word 'masquerade'. Masks, made from papier maché and ornately decorated, have, apparently, been made for centuries in Venice, where they were initially intended to ensure that everyone could be treated equally, since their identity could not be detected. However, their use gradually was taken advantage of and they began to be used to protect the wearer's identity during promiscuous or decadent activities. Eventually, they were banned, except for a short period each year that became the annual Carnival (which, itself, means: 'remove meat' and was the word for pre-lent celebrations), originally a pageant and street fair celebrating hedonism, but nowadays a cultural celebration.

Figure 129 Masks on display in Venice, Italy

On our visit to the city yesterday we had learned that rucksacks cannot be taken into St Mark's Basilica, so we put Tim's in the luggage locker before going inside the extraordinarily beautiful church, the interior of which is covered in gold leaf and mosaics. It was built in the 10th century but had to be rebuilt a couple of hundred years later having been destroyed by fire (and the place is surrounded by canals!). After exploring all the very interesting areas downstairs, we went upstairs to the museum, where, amongst other fascinating treasures, were the original golden horses (that had been over the main door until the 1980s when they were moved for their protection; they've been replaced by copies); apparently they have been carbon-dated to the 4th century BC, astonishing!

Figure 130 St Mark's Cathedral, Venice, Italy, with the Doges Palace in the background

Some liquid refreshment was needed by now (you know how it goes) so we decided to try a different bar in St Mark's Square, again with a four-piece band playing and we had our glasses of spritz, along with some, admittedly very generous, helpings of olives, crisps and nibbles, whilst sitting in the sunshine, with St Mark's Basilica and the Campanile as a backdrop; it was beautiful and we soaked up the atmosphere. Once we saw the bill, we decided that that would have to be lunch: €36, ouch!

Adequately refreshed, we walked along the Grand Canal past the bridge of Sighs (so called because the prisoners were taken along there to the death sentence). Tim's grandson had persuaded him, last weekend, to download Pokémon on to his phone, and we were amazed that they were everywhere, even around St Mark's Square! What was more astonishing, though, was that the mapping on the Pokémon game seemed to be better than on our new satnav!

277

We then went to the top of the Campanile (bell tower) where we got some amazing views of the city.

Figure 131 St Mark's Square, Venice, Italy

We really enjoyed Venice, particularly the area around St Mark's Square and the Doges (Duke's) Palace, and the many beautiful buildings and piazzas, but they certainly knew how to get money out of the tourists, many of whom arrived on the massive cruise ships we saw there. Venice has, I gather, had its share of troubles over the years, but currently its biggest threat is said to be from rising tides.

Finally, we stopped at another nice little out-of-the-way restaurant and had a pasta dish, before deciding (at around 7.15pm) to try to make the 7.25pm bus. We hadn't far to go so did a bit of jogging, but somehow got completely off track and by the time we finally got to the bus station, ended up having to wait half an hour for the next bus, by which time it was dark and, again, very difficult to tell where we were on our journey.

Very luckily, someone else had requested our stop and it was only when the bus had actually stopped that I noticed we were at our campsite, otherwise who knows where we'd have ended up!

Fano, Campobasso and a visit to Isernia – September

We left the Serenissima site at Malcontenta (feeling very contented), having had an enjoyable stay, and headed south, passing a sign for Samaritari Eros: the Samaritans of love? We decided we didn't need their services today so continued towards Ravenna. According to the 'Lonely Planet' book, Ravenna has eight UNESCO Heritage sites containing amazing collections of 4th to 6th century mosaic artwork that we thought would be worth a look. We put in the coordinates for a campsite nearby, but it was much too far out of town, so headed for a town centre aire, which, having faced the rigours of town-centre traffic, we were frustrated to find was completely full. The sky was very dark, so we decided to abandon our plans and head further south, down the coast. We passed some 'ladies of the late afternoon' and Tim spotted one changing into her 'work' clothes on a garage forecourt; there was another woman with her, so we wondered whether it was shift changeover time!

Whilst driving along the equivalent of our A-roads, the surface was so rough in some places that I was beginning to think my teeth might fall out, and they're not false! We encountered rush-hour when going through Rimini and passed painlessly through Anas before squeezing ourselves into a very busy aire at **Fano** that some people clearly called home! There were only the most basic of amenities (water, drainage and dustbins) but once we'd shut the blinds and settled down to watch an old DVD, whilst eating our Bolognese (we were not far from Bologna, so it seemed appropriate), it didn't really matter!

Both of us had been itching all day: I think our half-hour wait in Venice bus station must have been tea-time for the mosquitoes!

We were glad of the tarmac surface on the aire, as it rained all night, so, once we'd filled up with fuel at one of the cheaper service stations near the town, we decided to get on to the motorway to make faster progress. Unfortunately, two hours later we had only covered about 40kms as we'd been queuing for about 1½ hours due to a horrific accident; we were thankful we weren't involved in it. Just as we'd emerged from the queue, an Italian car shot past us at around 70-80mph and from our elevated position in the motorhome, we could see that he was texting: crazy Italian drivers!

We passed a sign for Vibrata – must be the rough roads – and at last the sun came out and the temperature reached 23°C as we passed lots of small seaside towns, some nice-looking beaches and the gorgeous turquoise sea.

At Termoli, we turned inland, crossing an amazing viaduct over the beautiful Lago del Liscione, before reaching the **Dominick Ferrante Aire** in the town of Campobasso. Having travelled for several hours today, we were disappointed to find that it appeared to be locked and deserted; there weren't even any other vans there. However, in desperation I went to investigate and found that the gate wasn't locked, so I pushed it back and we went in. It was very neglected, but had electric points, waste water disposal and fresh water, as well as a – clearly disused – large club-house/bar and kitchen area. We were having a look around, when a man came from the house opposite. He didn't speak any English and we told him – in our feeble attempt at Italian – that we didn't speak Italian so, through gestures and a very limited understanding on our part, he explained that it was €10 per night, which we paid to him, although he might have been some random chap who was just making a nice little earner out of an abandoned piece of land for all we knew!

Anyway, it was worth it, as we were able to charge up our various appliances, heat the water and use the electric kettle and the new George Foreman grill (as well as the gas hob of course) to make a lovely meal of pork chops with stir-fry vegetables and potatoes.

The next morning, after a shower in the van, we headed (past the Centro Marmitte: didn't realise Marmite was so popular out here!) for the nearby site of Altilia Saepinum, which, according to the Lonely Planet book, is one of the best-preserved and least-visited Roman remains in Italy; we can tell them why it's the least-visited, there was not a single shred of information or signage for it until we actually got to the site, where there was a small sign! It was clear that they get very few visitors, particularly in motorhomes, around there; we got some very inquisitive looks!

Figure 132 Altilia Saepinium, Italy

Anyway, it was indeed a very interesting site that was, apparently, a well-established town by the 2nd century BC, continuing to be inhabited until at least the 4th to 5th centuries AD, when it suffered an economic crisis following an earthquake and the Gothic War, and was eventually abandoned in around the 7th century AD. Three of the four city walls were relatively complete and it had a wonderful amphitheatre and forum, where we were able to roam around without fear of interruption from other visitors, as were completely alone!

We then decided to head for Isernia – about 20 miles north of Campobasso – which was actually in the wrong general direction, but, again according to the Lonely Planet book, there was a paleolithic site there, and we felt that it would be a shame to miss it when we were so close. We were heading for the centre of the large town of Isernia with not the faintest clue where we needed to be and, again, no mention whatsoever of La Pineta paleolithic site. Thankfully, Tim spotted a Lidl, so we were able to park in there and get some fresh bread for lunch, which we ate in the car park; oh we do eat in some romantic places!

After much frustration asking Google maps and other phone-mapping devices, we eventually got directions for a walk of around 30 minutes to the site; again there was no mention of it until we actually arrived. The site was exceptionally well-presented though; it consisted of an exhibition around the remains of a 700,000 year-old village – one of Europe's oldest – discovered in 1979 when a new road was being built, and excavations have been ongoing since then. In 2014 the tooth of a young child was carbon dated to around 586,000 years ago (it makes the Roman ruins seem positively modern!) and there were remains of bone, not only from early humans, but from many animals, including elephant, rhinoceros and hippopotamus.

We'd really enjoyed our visit, and were just about to leave when Tim realised that he didn't have his sunglasses with him and was sure he'd had them on when he'd arrived. Consequently, we spent another 30-45 minutes searching all the places on the site; we'd been the only visitors (due to lack of signage?!) so felt sure they must be somewhere, but they were nowhere to be seen and eventually we had to leave without them.

We put in the coordinates for the only aire we could find in our information – **Sannio Camper** at Benevento, about 50 miles away – which looked like it would be very suitable for the night. On our way we passed a pub and cocktail bar in the middle of nowhere it seemed, then, just a few yards further, Pista Go Kart, well, you would be if you'd just been to the pub and cocktail bar I suppose!

By the time we got to the aire – which looked very clean – we were ready for a nice quiet night, but the gates were locked. There were lots of motorhomes inside but no sign of life. We tooted our horn and rang all three of the telephone numbers given on the notice, all of which went straight to answerphone. There didn't seem to be any other sites of any kind close by and Ms Satnav confirmed that the nearest site was about 50 miles away. I suppose we could have wild-camped, but we didn't know the area and the van was a bit big to sneak in anywhere. Pompeii and Naples were only around 50 miles away, so we decided we might as well just head there for the night, and off we went with Ms Satnav in charge. It was motorway most of the way and we were making good time...until the road ahead unexpectedly ended, diverting us off to the right. We followed Ms Satnav's directions, then, about 10 minutes later, realised we were back in exactly the same place! I'm sure she'd have been quite happy for us to still be doing the circuit, but we asked her for an alternative route and boy, did we get one! She took us along a narrow, bustling road, through a busy town (we later realised we must have been on the outskirts of Naples) and, we think, through a dodgy red light district. There were people and cars all over the place – coming out of side streets and literally turning straight across in front of us – it was utter mayhem and wasn't helped by the fact that Ms Satnav told us to make turns down roads that didn't exist, or at traffic lights that weren't there!

Pompeii – September

After what seemed like eternity, we got back on to a 'normal' road, but our detour meant that we didn't arrive at **Campsite Zeus** in Pompeii until around 8.45pm. The man in reception was decidedly unwelcoming, the restaurant was closed (we'd thought we could maybe get a take-away as it was so late) and the pitches were extremely tight, making it quite difficult to get sorted out in the dark. We were completely exhausted by the time we'd cooked and eaten our evening meal!

The showers at our new site were definitely past their best, but worked fine once we'd realised that hot and cold were the opposite way around to the indications on the taps, then, after breakfast, we had a look around and found there was a much bigger pitch just round the corner from where we'd parked overnight, so we thought we'd quickly move the van there. As I was winding up the electric cable, Tim pulled out, but caught the back of the van on one of the very annoying trees (with sturdy branches jutting out just at the height of the top of the van) that they seem to plant at most European campsites, and pulled one of the back panels out of place, aaaaagh!

We parked the van at the new pitch and Tim spent quite some time trying to fix the panel, mostly successfully, but clearly something that should hold it in place had snapped, so it was still in danger of falling off again. We also realised that the rear light cover had disappeared and spent ages searching for it, helped by some very kind French and Dutch people, sadly unsuccessfully.

Feeling quite despondent, we walked down to the Carrefour, a few hundred metres away, for some fresh bread, then, after lunch outside in the beautiful sunshine, decided to visit Pompeii.

The campsite was only about 100 metres from the main entrance to Pompeii, so we didn't have far to go and we spent the rest of the afternoon roaming amongst the amazing buildings and monuments of Pompeii: a huge city of, in its heyday, around 20,000 people, founded in 7th century BC, and, of course, buried under a pile of volcanic ash from the Vesuvius volcano eruption in AD 79. It really is breathtaking and the work that has been done – and is still ongoing of course – is excellent. Some parts have been reconstructed to show what they were like, which does help enormously. Seeing the arena, the baths, the wonderful frescoes and some of the everyday things like the counter tops in shops (see photo) and advertisements etc on walls was really astounding.

Figure 133 Pompeii, Italy

Figure 134 Pompeii, Italy

Four hours and a total of 8½ miles later (we did six miles yesterday), we were definitely ready to relax with a gin and tonic (and a slice from a fresh lime we picked from the nearby tree) and some nibbles before our evening meal.

Next morning, we made an early start and had a quick al fresco breakfast – it was another beautiful day – before getting the express train (the station is literally just outside the gate of the campsite) to Naples. We chatted to an English couple on the station, who were staying at a nearby site, then, on arriving in Naples, walked along Via Carbonara (honest!). Drivers in Naples seemed completely crazy and crossing the road at various points was like playing Russian (or Italian) roulette! We finally reached the safety of the Archaeological museum and Tim had to leave his rucksack in the cloakroom or *garderobe* (from the French *garder*, 'to keep', and *robe*, 'clothing'; the origin of our 'wardrobe' but it was also the word for a store room or a toilet in medieval times). There were lots of exhibits from Pompeii: many frescoes, paintings and mosaics, as well as numerous fascinating artefacts that really helped us to imagine what it would have been like. It was early afternoon when we emerged, so we stopped to have a slice of delicious pizza and a coffee at a nice little street-side café, €8 for the lot!

We then headed towards Subterranean Naples, which, again, we'd read about in the Lonely Planet book, and stood in the queue for a while, before we realised that the tour we were queuing for was in Italian! The next English tour was another 1½ hours' wait, so we called at the Pio Monte della Misericordia – a church museum – for which the famous artist Caravaggio had been commissioned to paint the famous altar piece (La Sette Opere di Misericordia: The Seven Acts of Mercy), which inspired some of the other paintings on display in the former church, made into an art exhibition in 1601.

A cool beer and a bit of people-watching passed half an hour for us, before re-joining the queue to explore what turned out to be an amazing underground area comprising of two million square metres of space, apparently originally excavated by the Greeks 5000 years ago, who used the stone for building. The area was then taken over by the Romans who used it as water storage and it continued as such until the late 19ᵗʰ century, when a cholera epidemic, blamed on the water supply, broke out. For 50 years after that the Neapolitan citizens just threw their rubbish down the various wells, then, during WWll, when Naples was under heavy bombing raids, it was decided that the caverns would make good air-raid shelters. There was, by then, rubbish about six metres deep that was impossible to remove, so they simply made a flat surface of it and covered it with other materials. For around three years during the war, many Neapolitans lived down there, sheltering from the bombs; there were some household items and children's toys still down there that really made the experience quite poignant. Part of the area was under the San Paolo Maggiore Church and the nuns lived in the underground caverns until the early 1950s, making their own wine; apparently there was a secret passage where they were able to meet up with the monks from an adjoining church, for prayers of course!

Amazingly, the tour then took us to a private house built over a Roman amphitheatre! The house had been occupied for several hundred years, using the cellar for wine and other goods, its occupants not realising that the 'cellar' was part of one of the biggest and most important amphitheatres of its time! The modern city of Naples had been built on top of it and there are so many houses built over that area, it is impossible to open it up completely, although excavations are continuing. We were able to go into the house's 'cellar', which was, in fact, part of the lower corridor around the amphitheatre. Further up the street, a former carpenter's shop is sited in what was the upper ring of tiers from the theatre, where Nero performed in the 1ˢᵗ century BC, astonishing.

The tour was extremely interesting and the guide very good, but it had taken much longer than we'd expected, finishing at 5.35pm and we'd been told our express return train was at 6pm (there were other, slower ones, available later, but we'd bought a return ticket for that train), so we ran for 15 minutes across the centre of town, dodging traffic coming from every direction amongst a constant cacophony of car horns and sirens, and bringing our total mileage on foot to 5½ miles today. We made it back to the station just after 5.50pm and then found out the train didn't go until 6.08pm, so had a moment to regain our composure.

When we got back to the van, a large party of French people had arrived as part of a guided motorhome tour; there were about 30 people chattering and drinking at trestle tables set up at the van next to us, so we certainly weren't alone as we ate our evening meal outside; it was a lovely – and lively – atmosphere!

Later, we joined another English couple, who'd been at the site for a few days longer than intended as their car had broken down (they were in a caravan), and enjoyed a drink or two with them.

We made another early start and got the train again, this time alighting at Herculaneum. Having missed breakfast, we found a nice café and sat in the sunshine enjoying coffee and delicious croissants, before heading for the ruins of Herculaneum.

The first thing we noticed when entering the site was that this was a much smaller site than Pompeii and there were many buildings that retained a second storey. The town of Herculaneum had, of course, been destroyed in the same eruption in AD79 but here the buildings were covered in mud around 15-20 metres thick (much thicker than the ash covering Pompeii), which then solidified and became what is called 'tuff', with an almost concrete-like consistency. The 'tuff' had, in fact, protected many of the materials – even papyrus and food items survived – and there were some excellent examples of carbonised wood beams etc, still in place.

Figure 135 Herculaneum, Italy

The task of excavation must be immense and it was clear that this town, in a similar way to the Roman amphitheatre in Naples, had simply been built upon (it is much lower than the new town, as the photo shows), making it even more difficult to excavate; there is clearly a great deal more to uncover. The colour has been retained in many of the remaining columns and frescoes, which, along with the presence of upper storeys, made it a very different experience from Pompeii, but an equally thrilling and enjoyable one.

After leaving Herculaneum, we called for a nice refreshing beer, before making our way back to the station. We had considered getting a bus to Vesuvius and walking to the top, but it was getting rather late in the day, so we decided to head home.

A cup of tea was calling and we then made a quick trip to Carrefour, before another lovely al fresco meal and quiet evening in, blogging and reading!

A couple of loads of washing were hung out before brunch the next morning, then we set off again for the ruins of Pompeii, as we really hadn't seen all of it on Thursday. This time we went in the opposite direction once inside and our first call was at the Villa of the Mysteries, a huge complex of 60 rooms, which is one of the best-preserved sections. The frescoes are breathtaking and really give a feel for the opulence of these great houses.

Figure 136 Villa of the Mysteries, Pompeii, Italy

We then continued, admiring the many amazing features of various houses along the way, as well as the fantastic streets, rutted by cart wheels 2000 years ago, as the photo shows. Astonishingly, we once more bumped into the couple we'd met at Pompeii station and again at Herculaneum, who suggested we call at the very interesting exhibition on our way out, which we did.

Figure 137 Pompeii, Italy

After a short rest – well, we'd done another five miles today – we decided that, as we were planning to leave tomorrow and rain was forecast overnight, we (I'm using the Royal 'we' here of course) had better fix the panel on the van. We needed to reach the top corner (three metres high) to try and secure the panel somehow, so I suggested that if we turned the van around, we could back it up to the wall and Tim could climb on there to reach the top. We started manoeuvring between the low-branched trees and suddenly had an audience of about a dozen of the French people who, I presume, thought that they were helping us leave the pitch altogether, all offering advice and helping to guide the various angles of the van and shouting out if there was anything too close; they were very helpful, but I think we really confirmed their suspicions of the 'stupide' English, when we then reversed back into the pitch, up to the wall. Unfortunately, none of them spoke very good English, and I lacked the French vocabulary to explain, so I don't think they understood what exactly we were doing!!

Somehow or other Tim managed to lever himself up on to the roof and glued the top part of the panel, then proceeded to cut off a piece of 'gaffer' tape to ensure it was secure, only to find that there was only about 2cm left on the roll! I asked our French friends, who were still standing around, no doubt marvelling at the crazy English couple, but they didn't have any. Finally, an English chap, travelling alone, came up with the goods and we got the job done, hoping it would last until we could get a proper repair!

We left the Zeus campsite – with its grumpy receptionist, tight pitches (!) antiquated showers and toilets but perfect location – and (no thanks to Ms Satnav) found our way to the motorway, going beyond Angri (!) and keeping the windows firmly shut as we passed through Eboli! Ms Satnav continued to make things difficult, firstly telling us to turn left as we were driving along a motorway, then, as we were going through a very long tunnel, she said there were animals crossing ahead! A little further along, the display showed us in the middle of nowhere, with the marked road some way to our right!

We rejoiced as the temperature reached 27°C as we headed south, but 20 minutes later it was back to 15°C and raining as we headed across the mountain tops! Thankfully, it warmed up again as we descended. We'd covered around 250 miles by around 3pm, so we had a look to see where the nearest campsite was and ended up along a very dodgy road to **Villaggio Camping Mimosa**, near Rosarno. The road was so rough that all the pillows bounced off the bed, the clothes jumped off the rail and the front panel of the radio/CD fell off the dashboard on to the floor!

The campsite was pleasantly rustic, right on to a lovely beach and we had our own personal toilet/shower cubicle (well, a tin shed really but it did the job!). We had a lovely meal in the deservedly popular restaurant; there were about 30 people dining and it was only a small, half empty, site. We chatted to a couple from Lancashire, who were a good 10-15 years older than us, touring in a slightly smaller campervan, but who made us feel like a couple of wimps! They'd been to all sorts of awkward places, including wild camping at the top of Mount Etna!

Sicily – September to October

After leaving the site, we headed south again and at last Ms Satnav redeemed herself in getting us to a ferry route from Villa San Giovanni to Messina on Sicily. We fought our way through the traffic in Messina and were in a queue (we thought) to turn right, effectively blocking the road to following traffic (because of our size), prompting more horn-blowing from the natives (with whom we've had a few altercations, occasionally exchanging words as well as gestures!). We then realised that we were behind rows of vehicles – including a coach – that were double-parked!

A few miles further on, the road was diverted due to a landslide which, having come through miles of roads tunnelled into the mountainside, made us a little nervous. Eventually we reached Taormina, which was roughly where we were headed, but Ms Satnav took us on a 15-mile detour through the town and then back again; we just didn't understand what had gone wrong there!

Luckily, we happened upon Camping **Lido Paradiso.** It wasn't in our book; we were actually on the way to another site, but this one was much nearer to Taormina and we were so glad we found it, as it was beautiful, next to the beach, with every facility we could wish for (except perhaps site-wide Wi-Fi) and scrupulously clean showers and toilets.

Having got set up (with our new groundsheet and mats), we were about to relax with a drink in the sunshine, when we switched on the internal power and the kitchen tap began to gush (and I do mean gush) with water, from the joint not from the spout. We hurriedly turned off the power again and set about dismantling everything around the sink in the hope of finding a way into the tap, without success. In the end we phoned the very helpful man at Elite Motorhomes (where we'd bought the van), who explained how to undo the tap 'handle' so that we could tighten the collar around the joint and eventually it worked! We can only assume that the collar had been loosened with all the rough roads we've travelled along.

We really enjoyed our relaxing drink, but it wasn't long before the skies darkened and it began thundering and pouring with rain. Consequently, we ate our evening meal of turkey teriyaki (one of Tim's culinary creations) indoors.

Our first experience of the showers the following morning was that, although clean, the water was very cold; we wondered whether, as the heating was solar-powered, it was just bad luck! We then had to dry off the groundsheet, mats and chairs before we could sit outside for breakfast, before enjoying a lazy hour or so, sitting outside in the sunshine reading and blogging.

As it was such a lovely afternoon, we decided we'd walk along the roadside into Letojanni, the nearest town, about two miles away. We'd just reached the town when the heavens opened and we were treated to yet another thunderstorm; fortunately, I'd taken the precaution of popping a couple of plastic capes in my bag that saved us from getting completely drenched (I was a Girl Guide and try to 'be prepared'). We took cover in a little café until the worst of the rain had passed, then set about our task of finding a supermarket. Letojanni is a really pleasant little seaside town and we roamed around its maze of streets on our quest; phone mapping didn't help very much on this occasion, sending us round in circles. Eventually we found a small store, but it was, of course, shut! We hadn't realised that the Sicilians have an exceptionally long lunch, about 12 noon till 5.00pm it seems!

Later on we found an open grocer's shop with fresh milk, vegetables and some local cheeses and we bought some Pecorino (spicy pepper) cheese. Then, just around the corner, we spotted a butcher's shop and stocked up with some meat; it had now got to 5.00pm and there seemed to be supermarkets and grocery stores everywhere! Having bought all the supplies we needed, we waited about 20 minutes for a bus but, as none came, we decided to walk back. Needless to say, the bus passed us when we were about half-way back, followed swiftly by another downpour, just before we reached the site, typical! We tried the campsite showers again in the evening and I wish I could say that they were hot! Warm would be an exaggeration I'm afraid!

The following morning we had an early start, catching the 8.35am bus into Taormina, where we met up with my niece Carol and her partner Erik, who are staying in Taormina for 10 days or so. Attentive readers may recall that we stayed with Carol and Erik at their home in Holland for a few days at the end of our first trip away last year.

Our priority was breakfast at a café near the bus station, then we had a look around Taormina, very popular with tourists for good reason: it's a beautiful medieval town (the capital of Byzantine Sicily in the 9th century), with picturesque streets and numerous historic buildings as well as lovely beaches. First stop was the Greek theatre, built in the 3rd century BC and still in use for arts and film festivals; it is dramatically situated on a hill top, with Mount Etna in the background and stunning views over the town and Ionian coast.

Figure 138 Taormina's Greek Theatre, Sicily

After a pleasant stroll along Taormina's Corso Umberto (main thoroughfare), we stopped at a lovely little restaurant where we whiled away a couple of hours and missed another cloudburst! We then found ourselves drawn to Castelmola, a hilltop village with a ruined castle, that turned out to be much more of a climb than we'd anticipated, but we did have some amazing views once we'd reached the top and recovered our composure! We were exhausted by the time we finally got back to the campsite, having covered over seven miles (a lot of it steeply uphill!) on foot.

We caught the early bus again the next morning, meeting Carol and Erik at the bus station, this time boarding a second bus to take us to the very beautifully-decorated railway station at the other end of town, from where we took a train, arriving just before 12 noon in Syracuse, founded around 734 BC and home to Archimedes; it was considered to be the most beautiful city of the ancient world.

The town is split into two sections: the mainland 'modern' town, and the ancient adjoining island of Ortygia that has a real charm to it, with historic streets and alleyways, and beautiful buildings – many dating from 13th century – as well as the baroque Duomo, built on a 5th century BC Doric temple. We spotted a restaurant alongside the bustling market stalls and settled there for an excellent lunch, whilst doing a bit of people-watching and lots of chatting of course!

After a bit more wandering along by the sea and then back through the streets of Ortygia, we crossed over the bridge again and made our way to the Greek amphitheatre, built in the 5th century BC. It is the most intact Greek theatre in existence and is still used for classical theatre productions, seating 16000 people; a truly awe-inspiring place. It was made from limestone quarried from the adjoining area, which was apparently used as a prison for many years.

Figure 139 Greek amphitheatre in Syracuse, Sicily

One of the nearby caves is 23 metres high and extends 65 metres into the cliffside; it is known as The Ear of Dionysius, as the acoustics are so good that Dionysius was said to be able to hear everything the prisoners were saying! (A Greek nosey-parker!)

On leaving the Greek theatre, we passed the ruins of the Ara di Gerone (a huge sacrificial altar, where apparently up to 450 oxen could be killed at one time, lovely!) on our way to the Roman amphitheatre. Built in the 2nd century AD, it was originally used for gladiatorial combats and races, etc. Sadly much of the stone from here was taken in the 16th century to build the city walls; however, it is still an impressive site.

We were all pretty tired by now, so stopped for a refreshing drink then had to run for the train back to Taormina, arriving about 8.15pm. As Tim and I would have had well over an hour's journey (including waiting time) to get back to our van by bus, we decided to splash out on a taxi, so we were back about 15 minutes later. Just as we walked back through the gate, it started to rain again; we were beginning to think there was a cloud hovering over the campsite, as we later learned from Carol and Erik, who were staying about five or six miles down the coast from us, that they'd had hardly any rain whilst they'd been in Taormina, whereas we seemed to keep getting caught in heavy showers in between the sunshine. Perhaps the huge mountain behind us was creating its own micro-climate?!

After a happy (!) couple of hours cleaning all the mud and detritus that the overnight rain had deposited on our lovely new groundsheet again (incurring the wrath of the campsite 'madonna' when we tried to hang it over the fence to dry!), we definitely felt we deserved our nice lunch in the sunshine, which we did manage to fit in between a few light showers. We had been quite amused to note the various ways (besides walking and driving) that people were finding to move around the site: one chap used a skateboard, and another – whom we had nicknamed 'the oldest swinger in town' – went up and down on a 'segway'; the man and wife owners had, respectively, a motorbike and a bike, and it was only about 500 metres from one end to the other! We enjoyed another pleasant walk into Letojanni in the afternoon, managing to avoid the showers!

The next day we had another early start, but sadly, at breakfast, Tim broke one of my 'B' cups: one of a matching pair (pun intended!). We were picked up at the gate of the campsite by a van driven by Giorgio, our guide from Etna People, along with his girlfriend Valeria, Carol and Erik and a nice couple from Singapore. Giorgio drove us through the unspoilt wilderness of the Parco dell Etna, with lots of indigenous trees and plants, and up the north side of Mount Etna, a UNESCO World Heritage Site since 2013. Etna is the highest mountain in Europe at around 3000 metres (it is, apparently, visible from the moon!) and one of the world's most active volcanoes, with eruptions occurring frequently (hopefully not today!), the latest one having been in March.

After around an hour, we stopped close to what is known as the Black Mountain and walked up to the top of the craters. We saw where the most destructive recent eruption and lava flow had destroyed and buried hotels and other buildings (it had also partially destroyed the town of Catania on the coast, many miles away from where we were) and walked along the edge of three craters from a lateral eruption. The flow of lava is comparatively slow – about 0.4kms an hour (I think Giorgio said – but there was a lot to remember!). Giorgio was an excellent guide, who made the day very comfortable and added a touch of humour to proceedings. He explained that living so close to Mount Etna (he opens his curtains in a morning to a view of the mountain) had inspired his passion for geology, which he studied at university.

Figure 140 Crater on Mount Etna, Sicily

After descending from the craters, we drove a little further and then donned our safety helmets and torches to explore a cave that had been formed by the lava flow and had been used since the 1700s as an ice-house to supply ice to Sicily.

299

Our next stop was for a very pleasant lunch, with a wine-tasting that took place amongst an enormous display of wine barrels at the Don Saro Winery, before driving to a gorge at Alcantara with the most amazing rock formations, for which, Giorgio informed us, there were various explanations, including the most plausible in his view: the 'slow-cooling causing a wider crack' option. We'd had a wonderful day and were ready for a nice cup of tea when we got back to the van in the evening!

We had been undecided whether to leave the site the next day, as we were running out of clean underwear and desperately needed to do a wash! However, we awoke to a violent thunderstorm that decided us to pack up and move on, so we said farewell to the lovely ocean noise and the cold showers (we'd begun to long for the old, but hot, showers in Pompeii!!). As we left, the sun came out and the sky was a beautiful blue; we figured the weather was definitely playing tricks on us!

As we drove to our next destination, I spotted what seemed a much shorter route, still on the national road network, so we decided to go that way. Ms Satnav had the last laugh as usual, as some of the roads there were appalling! However, it was no joke when we rounded a bend to be faced with very severe subsidence: basically half the road had disappeared! The van violently pitched one way and then the other, bumping, shaking and lurching into and, thankfully, out of the huge hole where the road should have been; it was terrifying and Tim did well to keep us upright! We checked the van over and it seemed to not have suffered too badly, but when we reached the Villa Romana del Casale, we discovered that we'd damaged the bottom of one of the back panels as we'd grounded and, it seemed, had split the rubber on one of the windows, as it was leaking (the thunderstorm had caught up with us!).

It took us a while to regain our composure, after which we commenced our visit to the Villa Romana del Casale; another absolutely stunning UNESCO site, it's a huge Roman hunting lodge dating from the 3rd century and believed to have belonged to

Marcus Aurelius Maximianus. It was buried under mud for around 700 years before its astonishing mosaics were discovered in the 1950s; they cover around 3500m² of the villa floor and are in exceptionally good condition with beautifully-coloured illustrations of hunting scenes, chariots, love scenes and scantily-clad young women. It's difficult to describe the beauty, but we were particularly amazed by the Corridor of the Great Hunt – depicting wonderful, colourful and explicit hunting scenes, with more exotic animals such as tigers, elephants, rhinos, cheetahs and lions – spanning a length of over 100 metres!

Figure 141 Villa Romana del Casale, Sicily

The thunderstorm continued to follow us along flooded roads as we left and, after a quick supermarket dash, we finally arrived at **Eurocamping Due Rocche** on the south coast. Beautifully situated, but a bit of a shanty town, with ageing shower/toilet blocks and, worst of all, more cold showers! Well, Tim had a cold shower and was very jealous to find that my shower eventually warmed up (not hot but at least warm).

We didn't want to stay more than one night, so we packed up and drove along the south coast to the Valley of the Temples, another amazing place! The sun shone as we meandered along some of the best-preserved Greek temples – that once served as a beacon for homecoming sailors – and the ruins of a walled city. The first temple we came to – the Tempio di Giove – would have been the world's largest Doric temple but, sadly, its construction was halted by war; later earthquakes, coupled with the removal of many stones for construction, mean that it is a much less impressive building today than it should have been.

The Tempio della Concordia was next up: a truly remarkable building that has become UNESCO's logo. Constructed in 430 BC, it has survived almost entirely intact, partly due to the addition of internal pillars during its conversion into a Christian basilica in the 6th century AD.

Figure 142 Valley of the Temples, Sicily

Finally, we reached the 5th century BC Tempio de Hera, perched high on the ridge top. The colonnade, as well as a large sacrificial altar, has remained largely intact, despite earthquakes.

Apparently, much of the preservation of this area is due to the efforts of an Englishman, Sir Alexander Hardcastle, who lived there during the 1920s and devoted his life to ensuring the care of these ancient monuments.

We walked along the remains of the city walls, high on the ridge, that are now dotted with the remains of tombs dating from the 3rd and 4th centuries AD, around the time of the building of the basilica.

There are other temples and mosaics on the island of Sicily, but we felt that we had seen the most amazing examples during those last few days, so decided to head back towards Messina and get the ferry back to the mainland. It was comforting to note that some new roadworks were being carried out, though unfortunately the detours resulted in us doing a few circuits of the same bit!

The rain had caught up with us once more – we couldn't seem to escape it – and it was getting late as we passed through Taormina again and past the site we'd stayed at previously (with the cold showers), deciding, instead, to stay a little further on at **La Focetta Sicula Campsite,** where we got a pitch right on the edge of the beach.

Our urgent need for clean clothes drove us straight to the washing machines and we put in two loads of washing. Unfortunately, we hadn't realised how many of our things cannot be tumble-dried (well, as was pointed out to us, everything can be tumble-dried, it's just that some things don't come out very well!), so yet again we ended up with clothes strung around the van; we could hardly move!

The rain had continued all night, so we packed up and set off towards the ferry, no thanks to Ms Satnav who took us to a ferry terminal which, it turned out, was for commercial traffic only. When we followed the instructions given by the attendant there and found the correct terminal, Ms Satnav didn't recognise it! I'm afraid we really lost faith in her altogether.

Southern Italy: Coligriano di Calabro, Alberobello and Matera – October

Arriving on mainland Italy, the sun broke through and temperatures reached 30°C as we drove along the motorway. At last, after another long-winded, confusing, roadworks diversion, we were nearing our chosen destination for the evening. Ms Satnav was telling us to turn off in around 3kms, but, with about 1km to go, we spotted a Lidl sign, so we turned in and did a quick top-up of basic items. We were astonished to find that, on leaving Lidl, she was directing us back the way we had come, finally turning down a road we had passed about 10kms previously! She obviously knew we needed to do some shopping; maybe she was on our side after all, ha ha!

Thankfully, the **Thurium Campsite**, near Coligriano di Calabro, seemed very pleasant and clean and again we were able to park overlooking the beach. Our first job was to put up a washing line to get the rest of our clothes dry. While I hung out the washing, Tim plugged us in to the electricity, but it wasn't working. A kind Dutch man nearby helped us to find a plug connection that worked, and we eventually got our evening meal!

We awoke to a beautiful morning, so decided to stay another night there and enjoy the weather. Reception had provided the required discs to operate the shower but, unfortunately, having walked about a third of a mile to get to the showers (we'd elected to park near the beach rather than near the showers/toilets!), we then realised we'd forgotten the discs, duh! Tim gallantly ran back to get them and was rewarded with the best shower he'd had for over a week. I, on the other hand, just got my face washed when the water stopped; I hadn't even got the rest of my body wet!! I stood there feeling utterly helpless and just had to get dressed and come out; very disappointing, especially as a woman was already using a shower next to me when I got in and it was still going when I got out!

After breakfasting in the sunshine, Tim decided he'd better have a good look in the van's garage (the motorhome equivalent of a car boot), as we knew that various items had moved around when we'd hit subsidence on the road. It transpired that one of our storage boxes had completely disintegrated and the reversing sensor cover had smashed; there were wires everywhere! What with dodgy showers, rough roads, unhelpful satnav directions and crazy drivers (we'd seen one driving around 50kmh, whilst smoking and texting, and our Dutch neighbour had badly cut his knee when a car pulled out in front of his bike), it seemed like they were all out to get us! But, hey, what would I write about if it had all been easy going?!

Once our tasks were completed, we went for a lovely walk along the beach, paddling in the sea on our way and finally (although we had to cross a very dodgy, rusty bridge across an estuary to get there) reached a beach bar, where we stopped for refreshments before returning.

The afternoon was spent relaxing and reading and we enjoyed another al fresco meal in the evening, though the smoke from our barbecue seemed to be determined to waft across our neighbour's van, oops! The evening was spent cleaning up, in readiness for our departure tomorrow, but we couldn't find our little hand-brush anywhere; after a while we gave up looking, in the hope that it might turn up eventually (spoiler alert, it didn't).

Our next stop was Alberobello, almost on the east coast, just above Italy's heel. We had a reasonably good journey and I'd put in the coordinates for an aire (or *aree di sosta*, 'rest area' in Italian) close to the town. The coordinates dropped us near a roundabout but luckily we noticed a campsite sign, leading us to a small site that seemed to be a bit sloping and rather full. Having noticed another campsite on the satnav screen, we decided to try that and, following directions, found ourselves on a tiny back road leading nowhere! So, we had another attempt at finding the *aree di sosta* about 1½ miles away which turned out to be the original site (**Camping Bosco Selva**) that we'd been looking for! We did find a nice, reasonably level spot in the end but nothing ever seems straightforward does it?

As the afternoon was wearing on, we quickly got parked up and set off into the centre of Alberobello, another UNESCO Heritage Site, which is famous for its huge concentration (about 1500) of Trulli houses: traditional Apulian dry stone huts with conical roofs, specific to the Itria Valley. The origins of Trulli houses date back to prehistoric times and apparently they were generally constructed as temporary field shelters and storehouses or as permanent dwellings by small proprietors or agricultural labourers. They were built using local limestone, but without mortar so that they could be dismantled in a hurry so as to avoid taxes; things don't change much do they?! The Trulli houses in Alberobello date back to the 14th century and are now the oldest existing examples.

Figure 143 Alberobello, Italy

It really is an amazing sight to see all of these strange-looking houses that make Alberobello a very pretty little town. Unfortunately, it's also become something of a tourist trap and many of the Trulli houses are now shops selling memorabilia. We had a 'trulli' wonderful time though, helped along by a cool drink in one of the bars, before making our way back (uphill all the way) to the van.

The showers on this site were actually quite pleasant (though not the cleanest we've seen) and, duly refreshed the following day, we went on our way through the mountains, arriving at our next stop: Matera, yet another UNESCO site (we've ticked a few of them off haven't we?!). Just before we reached the town, a passing car flashed at us and pointed anxiously at the van. Needless to say, we were a bit concerned and managed to pull up about a mile later to find that the bike cover had almost detached itself! We then had to find somewhere to park and, having done a couple of fruitless circuits, were thrilled to spot a park and ride park that actually had a special place for motorhomes! Even better, we only had about 10 minutes to wait for a very clean, electric mini-bus that took us right to the centre. Unfortunately, being rather high in the mountains, we ended up with a rather chilly day of sunshine and showers (hence the rather grey photo below).

Matera looks, at first sight, to be a complete jumble of rather shabby-looking houses on the side of a gorge and it does have a very ancient feel to it, as, indeed, it should, having been inhabited for around 9000 years, since the Paleolithic age. Matera is, in fact, believed to be the world's oldest town and has been used to evoke biblical scenes in various films. The natural caves (*sassi*) in the mountainside have been adapted over the years and used as dwellings, more recently with man-made frontages added. The town was very prosperous in the 17th and 18th centuries but as its population increased, living conditions worsened and unsuitable caves were used, often housing families with six or more children, living in the cramped space alongside their animals. Malaria was rife and the infant mortality rate had risen to 50% in the 1950s, when, eventually, the Italian government stepped in and compulsorily re-housed around 15000 people.

Since then Matera's history has become a source of interest; some of the caves are being restored and the town's fortunes are on the rise again, with a number of restaurants and bars available for the many tourists now visiting.

Figure 144 Cave dwellings at Matera, Italy

We had a really good look around and visited one of the cave churches, with frescoes from the 11th and 12th centuries. We also visited a typical cave-dwelling that had been furnished as it would have been when its residents were evacuated in 1956. I must say that this really gave us a feel for the cramped conditions that a family of eight would have lived in, alongside, for example, a horse, a pig, chickens, etc.

We called for a coffee and a Panini in a little café, but, about 25 minutes later, having had our coffee, Tim went to check on the progress of the Panini, only to find the poor girl hadn't even started on ours yet; I think we'd timed it badly, arriving just after a large party of German tourists. We decided to try elsewhere and found a fabulous take-away pizzeria not far away, where we got two good-sized slices of delicious, freshly baked pizza for €1 each.

Western Italy: Lido di Salerno and back to Pompeii – October

Eventually, we caught the park and ride bus back to our van, and set off on a two-hour journey (starting with Ms Satnav taking us the wrong way down a one-way street) through some beautiful mountain scenery to the west coast of Italy. The roads were very rough again, even though this was the national road network (Carole King even sang 'I feel the earth move...' as we drove along), but we were making good time... until we were diverted off the autostrada because a huge viaduct over the gorge had completely collapsed! (We don't know whether anyone was injured; there has, since then, been the dreadful collapse of a motorway bridge in northern Italy, in which a number of people sadly died.) Unfortunately the diversion wanted to take us along a route only 2.3 metres wide and we wouldn't fit! Time for me to don my luminous jacket and do some traffic directing again, while Tim backed the van up a hill and round the corner to get out of the way!! It was quite a detour before we were able to re-join the motorway further on.

We were only a few kilometres away from our intended destination for the night when Ms Satnav took us down a dead-end street. We were just in the process of turning around in a goods yard there, when another English van (and we haven't seen many of those) did exactly the same thing; turned out they were heading for the same campsite. We ended up going in convoy; our satnav showed an ACSI site further down the coast, so we all decided we'd settle for that, then, as we got nearer the coast, another site showed up on the screen, very close by, which turned out to be a pizzeria! In the end we figured we weren't far away from the original choice by then, so we had another shot at it and arrived to a lovely welcome from the staff. By then, though, it was after 7.00pm (we were just in time to see the amazing sunset over the Amalfi coast and Capri) and we didn't feel like cooking so ate in the restaurant, along with our new friends, who were from New Zealand but were currently based in Hull and had been travelling for 18 months. We had a good chat over a lovely meal (cooked by an English lady who's lived in Italy for 30 years!) and put the world to rights; we'd done such a lot of that, it ought to have improved by now.

We tumbled into bed, exhausted, only to realise that, almost next door, was a night club, just ramping up for the night – keeping us awake until gone 3.00am listening to the thud, thud of the bass – happy days!

After saying farewell to the New Zealand couple, we sat outside for breakfast in the beautiful sunshine, with the sea and sand only a few feet away from us and an amazing view of the Amalfi coastline.

We'd bought, at one of the stops along the way, a new box to replace the broken one in the boot, but it was a bit bigger and it took the rest of the morning for us to empty and re-pack the boot in order to get everything in securely and for Tim to fix the reversing sensor; always something to do it seems.

After lunch we went for a nice, relaxing, stroll along the beach. There were lots of holiday parks along the way that looked reasonably inviting from the road, but rather tatty from the beach; it seemed that nobody had thought about clearing away the mess at all!

Another very pleasant day dawned, so, after breakfast, we got the bikes down (at last!) and cycled into Salerno. There was a path (we think a footpath, but it served us as a cycle path) for about a couple of miles, but then we had to brave cycling on the roads; not the most pleasant of rides, but at least it was a dual carriageway so there was room for cars to overtake us easily! It was further than we'd anticipated getting into Salerno centre and the final stretch was along very narrow one-way streets. We ended up walking with the bikes for quite a way then stopped for some lunch overlooking the port for tourist boats. Salerno hadn't really endeared itself to us and Tourist Information Offices seem to be very few and far between (or shut!) in Italy, so we decided to continue a bit further in search of some redeeming features. Failing to find any, we cycled back (around 25kms altogether!) and spent the rest of the afternoon enjoying the sunshine (and recovering from the exertion).

In the evening we ate our meal outside and as we sat down to relax Tim's chair gave way! Thankfully, he wasn't injured, just a bit shocked, and rather annoyed as these were brand new chairs we'd bought for this trip, and the back had completely snapped!

We made an early start the next day, catching the bus from outside the campsite into Salerno (much easier than cycling, I don't know what we'd been thinking yesterday!), chatting to a couple from Sweden on the bus and as we continued our journey on a very pleasant boat trip to the picturesque town of Positano perched on the edge of the Amalfi coast. After exploring the pretty streets, we stopped for a delicious pizza in a very nice restaurant with its own bakery, then walked to the top of Positano, with its houses seeming to be stacked one on top of the other up the hillside. Another drink on our way back down kept us going before we eventually caught the boat back to Salerno, arriving just after 6pm. The last bus wasn't until 8pm so we enquired about the price of a taxi and were quoted €40! We figured we could use our money more wisely and decided to wait for the bus (at €1.20 each). Tim needed his hair cutting, so we tracked down a salon, then had a pleasant look around the surprisingly busy shops (they open about 5.00pm after their long siesta, closing around 10 pm), before getting to the bus stop about 7.45pm.

Almost immediately a bus pulled up with what appeared to be the right destination on its board but not the number 24 that we'd been advised to catch, so we asked the driver who assured us it was the right bus. We had a moment of anxiety when the number 24 bus drove past us a little while later, but thankfully we arrived safely, having passed the other number 24 again on the way; I think it was a different bus company, but it seemed a bit odd to run the buses at exactly the same time to the same place!

The next beautiful day was spent mostly relaxing; there were lots of people in the sea, but we're total wimps, so, once we'd attended to our tasks: a bit of Heath Robinson repair work on the broken chair – not perfect but hey – and a couple of loads of washing, we sat reading, snoozing and enjoying the sunshine.

Clearly news had spread overnight about my comments regarding all the litter on the beach as last night someone had come along and made a good job of clearing it all up! We left the very pleasant **Lido di Salerno Campsite** and headed for Paestum, just a few miles south of the site, but difficult to get to by public transport and too far to cycle! Paestum, I have to admit, is not somewhere I'd heard about until reading the Lonely Planet book. However, it is yet another remarkable ruined Greek city with three huge temples dating from the 6th century BC; we did wonder, though, how come these three temples are still standing, when the rest of the city is much less preserved?! Anyway, we wandered around the remains of the city which included a small amphitheatre, forum, swimming pool and a couple of sacrificial altars, amongst lots of other ruined buildings and were amazed that we were also allowed to actually enter the temples! We then visited the museum, which we thought was extremely well presented, with displays of the many artefacts that had been discovered among the ruins.

Figure 145 Temples at Paestum, Italy

As we travelled north from Paestum we passed some more 'ladies of the day', of whom there are many around this area (we even noticed an Anti Prostituzione sign as we cycled into Salerno the other day!); Tim mentioned that he thought that these were among the least attractive of the women we've seen and that's saying something! It was a bit worrying that he'd even considered whether they were attractive at all!

We arrived back in Pompeii in the early evening, and this time decided to stay at the **Spartacus Campsite**, which was still very close to the railway station, but, thankfully, more pleasant than the Zeus site we'd stayed at previously. Our reason for returning to Pompeii was that we were able to catch a train from there to Sorrento, which, after a good night's sleep, we did, arriving late the following morning.

It was another sunny day and we very much enjoyed strolling around Sorrento, which seems to have a very relaxed, friendly atmosphere, despite the hordes of tourists (mostly English it seemed) that descend on it regularly. Eventually, we found a lovely little restaurant in the fishing harbour, where diners were able to choose their fish, which was filleted and cooked at the table. We enjoyed a fabulous meal, with mixed seafood for a starter, then rock fish in a tomato sauce for the main.

Sitting in the sun later in the afternoon, we enjoyed chatting to and hearing about the adventures of a lovely young Australian couple on a three-week holiday. After a bit of people-watching with a drink later on, we caught an evening train back to the van, feeling very relaxed.

Once again, the next morning, we caught the (slightly earlier) train to Sorrento (a grand total of €2.40 each) and this time went straight down to the port for a boat to Capri that was a little more expensive at €36 each for a journey lasting the same amount of time as our journey to Sorrento! However, we were not going to let things like that spoil a good time! After we arrived in Capri, we climbed up the 921 – Phoenician – steps (phew! it felt like we should be planting a flag when we reached the top) to the Piazza Umberto: the most fashionable square in the world according to the Capri Tourist Board, where the 17th century Chiesa (church) of St Stefano chimes out the time enthusiastically. This is certainly the place to 'be seen' – at a cost – with a couple of half litres of beer costing €16, but it was a beautiful day, a very pleasant atmosphere and the view over the town of Capri was stunning.

Everyone I've spoken to regarding Capri has lauded the Grotta Azzurra or 'Blue Grotto' that, we understand, was used by Emperor Tiberius as a swimming pool way back in AD30; so we went back down on the funicular railway (hmmm, maybe we should have done that on the way up?) and asked at the ticket office for tickets to The Blue Grotto. We were told that a boat was just about to leave so we quickly paid our €18 each and hurried over to the boat, checking again that it was for The Blue Grotto.

However, when the boat headed east as we left the harbour, we realised we'd ended up on a tour of the island. Although we hadn't planned for it, it was actually a very interesting tour, passing some amazing caves and rock formations, including the Arco Naturale (often used as Capri's icon). Eventually we did reach The Blue Grotto cave, and at this point, the Italian guide, who had been pointing out places of interest on the way, seemed to be saying we had to pay extra to get a small rowing boat to visit the cave. His English was not good enough for us to be sure what it was all about, and we weren't the only ones: there were lots of indignant passengers all trying to find out what was actually going on.

Suddenly the boat began to head back towards the harbour; we think, in retrospect, that, as a lot of the passengers didn't want to visit the cave and there was likely to be a long wait, the crew had decided to head back. We were then told that, if we did want to visit the cave, we could, at no extra cost, board another boat to take us back there! We were beginning to get somewhat despondent by now, but, having started, we thought we'd finish, so boarded the other boat. After 20 minutes or so, we set off and soon reached the cave, where we sat for almost an hour, rocking violently (we were beginning to feel a bit queasy I must say), waiting for our turn to board one of the little rowing boats, only to find we had to pay yet another €14 each to do so!

We truly don't mind paying a little extra for 'tourist' things sometimes, but I must say that we felt thoroughly ripped off at this point. Our oarsman did his best to cheer us up by singing to us as he rowed us through the tiny mouth of the cave and into the grotto itself. It was, indeed, a beautiful azure blue (apparently it's the sun's reflection through the cave mouth on to the sandy floor below) and quite an experience, and we were pleased we'd been, but I do think that it was done very badly; we were not informed that there was an extra cost until we actually reached the Blue Grotto and it wasn't just us who'd not understood, all of the passengers were complaining. However, we felt that our €18 trip around the island had been much better value than some people on the second boat who'd paid €15 just to get to the Grotto and still had to pay the extra for the rowing boat!

By the time we arrived back at Capri harbour we'd spent three hours afloat and it was time to get the boat back to Sorrento – another half hour – then, finally, the train back to Pompeii. Our day had been at times pleasant, at times frustrating, and very expensive all in all (and we hadn't even had anything to eat!), a stark contrast to our visit to the Pompeii ruins that had been only €12 each.

Rome – October

Whilst packing up the next morning, Tim popped to the nearby Carrefour and almost witnessed a fatality: an idiotic driver overtook at speed a car that was waiting at the pedestrian crossing – narrowly missing the person crossing – then veered across towards the car waiting in the opposite direction, before careering off down the road, completely crazy!!

We left the very clean and pleasant Spartacus site (although the pitches were a bit tight), with its very friendly staff and headed off on a thankfully uneventful journey to **Real Camping Village,** near Rome.

We arrived in time for a late lunch and a lovely Hungarian family on the next pitch very kindly gave us a glass of Schnapps each to finish off, that Tim said had put hairs on his chest. (I was carefully monitoring mine!) We then went to have a look around the campsite, whose sports facilities were amazing: four tennis courts (and we found more later), a five-a-side football pitch with floodlights and spectator seating, a huge outdoor pool and an equally huge indoor pool, Jacuzzi, steam-room and sauna, an enormous gymnasium, sports hall with regular classes, and massage and physiotherapy sessions. It was such a beautiful afternoon that we decided to avail ourselves of some of the facilities and after a few lengths in the outdoor (unheated) pool (once Tim had eventually braved the icy waters and dived in), we tried the sauna and Jacuzzi (we decided to give the gym a miss today, didn't want to appear greedy you know). On the way back to the van, we spotted a black cat and tried to entice it across our path, but it flatly refused, hey ho! In the evening we had a lovely meal of lamb (courtesy of chef Tim), which appears to be very rare in Italy. We'd bought it from a Hyper Spar earlier, which seems a bit of a contradiction in terms, but it actually is the same Spar brand that we have in the UK.

We'd been given some information about public transport into Rome, but, having chosen this site because it was 'only one Metro stop from Vatican City', we were surprised to find we had a '10-minute bus ride' (according to the man at reception), which actually took half an hour to get to the Metro station! He'd also omitted to mention that we needed to buy a ticket in advance, so when we got to the Metro we went to the machine, only to find it was broken and we couldn't use our credit card. An official told us to try the newsagent, but they also had technical problems, so we ended up having to go in search of a bank in order to get enough cash to buy an advance ticket for the next few days.

Thankfully, we'd set off in plenty of time and still arrived at the entrance to the Vatican with time to spare before our allotted entry time, so we shared a slice of delicious pizza and a coffee whilst waiting.

Once amongst the crowds in the Vatican museums we were treated to the most astonishing display of statuary, antiquities, mosaics, tapestries, beautifully frescoed ceilings and walls beyond description, with the final pièce de résistance of course being the Sistine Chapel and its beautiful Michelangelo frescoes.

Figure 146 Vatican, Rome, Italy

Figure 147 Vatican, Rome, Italy

Eventually, after over three hours looking around the Vatican, we emerged into the sunlight and made our way towards the fast-moving queue for St Peter's basilica, also filled with many beautiful paintings, statues and other objêts d'art to see, it is impossible to do it all justice with a description. It does seem, though, that so much money is lavished on these religious buildings whilst often the people they 'serve' are poor.

Finally, footsore and weary (I know we have your sympathy), having walked almost seven miles, we made our way back on the Metro to the bus stop, except our bus didn't stop opposite where we'd alighted and we had to walk another half a mile or so to find the correct stop! On the way, we spotted a really nice shop to get some bread and noticed they had Blue Stilton cheese! However, at €49 per kilo thought we'd stick to local varieties.

We decided to try the train next morning, despite having been warned by reception staff that the timetable was 'vague'. Thankfully, a train did arrive at around the scheduled time and we arrived in the centre of Rome in a much more pleasant and stress-free way than yesterday!

Our first stop was the Colosseum, what an amazing structure! It was built in AD80 and seated 50,000 people. The noise of the crowds during a spectacle in the arena must have been heard for miles. It was apparently not named because of its own size but because of the huge Colosso di Nerone (statue of Nero) that stood nearby. The photo shows the maze of tunnels that would have been beneath the floor.

Figure 148 Colosseum, Rome, Italy

Next we crossed over to the Forum. I must say that Rome does seem to be just one big archaeological site; everywhere you look there are bits of temples, arches, statues, etc! The site of the Roman Forum was first developed in the 7th century BC (or, in Italy, AC: Ante-Christ, which just doesn't sound right does it?!) and expanded over the years to become a hub of activity, but fell into disrepair and was known as the Cow Field in the Middle Ages, when a lot of the stone and marble was plundered.

Figure 149 Forum, Rome, Italy

The majestic Palatine Hill overlooks the Forum and Colosseum and contains the ruins of luxurious palaces and villas, as well as traces of habitation going back to the 8th century BC. It is claimed that Romulus established Rome on this hill after he'd killed his twin brother Remus.

Having covered almost 11 miles by then, we headed back in the direction of the Metro and Tim checked for Pokémon (he'd found a few in the Vatican yesterday!) while we admired the little that remains of the Circo Massimo; I thought the Colosseum was big, but that place used to hold 250,000 spectators!

Finally, we spotted the Metro sign and crossed over the very busy road, only to find that we'd got to the wrong side and had to cross back again; we'd walked within yards of the correct entrance, duh. We walked back to the campsite from the train station with a couple from Stratford-on-Avon who we'd briefly spoken to the night before and who were pitched not far from us on the same

321

site. Over a bite to eat in the campsite restaurant we found we had quite a lot in common, not only in the similarity of our respective relationships but also that George, a former chef and College Principal originally from our home county of Yorkshire, had worked in many places familiar to Tim, and knew some people we both knew, whilst Jenny had worked as a nurse and had particular interest in special needs as I do.

Another trip into the city the following morning saw us walking beyond the Colosseum and Forum to the wonderfully explicit carvings of Trajan's Column and the area known as the Imperial Forums: there are four of them, which were destroyed and built on in the 1930s, but excavations have unearthed quite a lot of the remains.

Just around the corner from there is the beautiful 15th century Renaissance Palazzo Venezia – positively modern – then, a bit further on, is the amazing Pantheon. Built around 27 BC and modified by Hadrian in 125 AD, it is one of the most influential buildings in the Western world; it has the largest unreinforced concrete dome ever built and the interior is almost exactly as it was 2000 years ago, largely due to the fact that it was taken over as a place of worship (as is the case with many of these ancient buildings) and therefore well-maintained.

Figure 150 Pantheon, Rome, Italy

Back on to the streets we came across the Largo di Torre Constantino, another area with some astonishing remains of temples etc, and, in particular, the pine tree that is said to mark the spot where Julius Caesar was killed in 44 BC (it seems that

Shakespeare had used a little artistic licence in placing that event on the steps of the Senate). Not too far away, we found a lovely little restaurant off the beaten track, frequented by lots of Italians, which is always a good sign. We had a wonderful, reasonably-priced lunch: Tim had rabbit, I had stuffed aubergine, then we indulged in the home-made dessert; mine was a chocolate cake with pears, Tim chose the lemon cake and they were so light they melted in our mouths, yum!

Next on our list of Rome's must-see icons was the lovely Baroque Trevi Fountain. Predictably, it was very busy, but definitely worth seeing, although the model being photographed on the steps also seemed to be getting quite a lot of attention. Apparently an average of €3000 per day is thrown in by people making their wishes! After a little more meandering, we found another column that appeared to be a copy of Trajan's Column, with the same spiral carvings all the way up, depicting battle scenes. It turned out to be the column of Marcus Aurelius (I always said he was such a 'copy-cat') and the statue at the top was that of St Paul. A little later on, we reached the Spanish Steps: very nice, but I have to say they are just steps, albeit designed by a Spaniard and again, very busy.

We stopped at a pretty little Betty's-style café for an iced tea, then, purely by chance, stepped in through the door of the Chiesa di San Silvestro in Capito where, believe it or not, Pope Innocent II had the head of John the Baptist brought in the 12th century, and we actually saw it, though I wouldn't have recognised him!

Finally, we walked through the impressive Piazza del Popolo, laid out in the 16th century as a grand entrance to Rome's then northern gateway and played 'sardines' with lots of Italians on the Metro as we made our way back to the campsite.

George and Jenny came and joined us later in the evening and we sat outside with nibbles and a glass or two of wine; a very pleasant end to a very pleasant day.

We'd paid up until the next morning, but decided to stay another night and settle up on our way out, as we desperately needed to get some washing done. Once it was all hung out, we said goodbye to George and Jenny as they (and, it seemed, all the other vans near us) were leaving today and we headed back into Rome. We walked along the side of the (rather dirty) River Tiber and through some lovely streets and piazzas around the Jewish quarter; there is a very sad history of persecution prior to and during WWII, but the area has since made a good recovery.

As we roamed around we came across the last remains of the Temple of Apollo, alongside what appeared to be part of another huge amphitheatre! There are remains of buildings dotted all around Rome that are given little or no importance, but if they were in any other town they would be a major tourist attraction! A small diversion took us via the uninspiring Isola Tiberina as we made our way back to the train and said 'Arrivederci Roma' (good name for a song!).

When we got back the whole area we were in was filled with Dutch vans and there was just one parked around the corner, oops, I think they were meant to be in our spot! That's why everyone else had left, but the receptionist had only briefly mentioned they needed the spaces at the weekend, honest!

Florence and Siena – October

As we were cleaning up the van ready to leave in the morning, we realised the back panel had come seriously adrift again. We managed to borrow a ladder from reception and Tim climbed up and fixed it on, then the ladder came in useful while we gave the very grubby outside of the van a cursory clean.

Finally, we set off; the site was just beside the main dual carriageway, so we thought it should be straightforward, we never learn! First of all, Ms Satnav told us to turn left into the oncoming traffic on the dual carriageway, then to turn left down a road that didn't exist. We ended up going what seemed like miles before we were confident of heading in the right direction; all the more amusing then, when we pulled into a service area and she kindly informed us, "You are going the wrong way down the street"!

As we neared our destination, we spotted a Carrefour so decided to stop and stock up. We avoided the Stinco meat and the Yukki milk (no kidding!) then, when putting away our purchases, realised the back panel was hanging off again; that's why people were staring at us! Tim ended up on the roof yet again, fiddling around; I was thinking I'd have to re-name him Topol!

According to Ms Satnav we were only a few metres from our chosen site at **Antica Etruria**, on the outskirts of Florence, but we couldn't find it anywhere. After two trips up and down the same stretch, we pulled in to the side of the road and, when Google confirmed it was nearby, decided to have a walk. Just then, a security guard from the logistics company next to the site very kindly came out and waved us in, bless him, he'd obviously noticed our quandary! There was no signage though and the site was tucked away at an angle.

Well, I did say the site was next to a logistics company... seemed they never stopped, night and day. There was also a train-line at one side and the main road at the other, then, at 6am, the owner's free-range cockerel made its presence known, goodness me!

Getting showered became another adventure as the ladies' showers were out of order, so I had to use the men's. Unfortunately though, operating the shower was by coin, but the meter, on the wall outside the shower, instructed you to start the shower before putting in the coin! The shower then ran cold for the first minute of the allotted three! No time for preening and certainly not the most relaxing shower I've ever had!

Information we'd been given had said there was a bus nearby into Florence, but it seemed that it took 90 minutes and I'm sure you're not surprised we didn't relish that. A little research showed there was also a station not too far away and we saw there was a train at 10.06am; we're beginning to think these campsites get a bonus for directing people towards the local buses. By then, we only had a short time to get there, so jogged most of the 1.6kms, following Google maps to the station, only to find it wasn't running (it was Saturday, of course, so the timetable was different! If only we'd a brain between us!). The next train was over an hour away, so we went to explore and discovered a small path that cut across from our site to the station, making the entire journey only about 350 metres, so we walked back and had a cuppa before going back for the next train, with a predicted journey time of around 20 minutes.

35 minutes later, we were still on the train and, it seemed, had passed through the built-up area and were whizzing through the lovely Tuscan countryside (and without a ticket, as there was no ticket machine at the station). It turned out our train wasn't a direct one, so we had to get off at the next station and get another train back into the centre of Florence!!! Clearly, Tim had taken a liking to riding on the train, as, having seen Siena on the timetable, he then suggested we head there, 1½ hours away. We'd been deliberating about staying near Siena but, as you probably realise, getting to different sites is not always straightforward (understatement of the year I think!), so this seemed like a good compromise.

Consequently, mid-afternoon saw us on a whistle-stop tour of Siena, well, just to the fabulous 13th century Duomo really. It is a most amazing structure and really unlike any other church I've ever seen, with its exterior and *interior* stunningly constructed of white and greenish-black marble in alternating stripes. We managed to have a good look around, though I nearly lost Tim in there, as he was wearing a striped T-shirt. Pity he wasn't wearing a striped bobble hat, we could have had a Where's Timmy competition!

Figure 151 Inside Siena's Duomo, Italy

Siena was a really pleasant town but we only had time for a quick drink in the huge Piazza del Campo, with the 14th century Palazzo Communale towering over it, before speed-walking the 20 minutes back and down the 10 large escalators to the station; I hadn't realised (well, not until we were coming out of the station when we arrived) that Siena was on top of such a hill!

We noticed, though, that places seemed to be a lot cleaner, and the roads in much better condition, the further north we travelled. There is, apparently, a degree of rivalry between the wealthier north and the poorer south of Italy and southerners are still not well-regarded in the north, the opposite way around to the UK generally!

Of course, just our luck, we arrived in Florence (called Firenze in Italian) at 5.50pm and the train we needed to get back had gone at 5.47pm, so we had a drink in the piazza Santa Maria Novella, with the eponymous 13-15th century church and its green and white striped marble façade close by. Apparently, the style of the striped façade was around in Roman times and stripes have appeared throughout Western architecture ever since; they are usually reserved for important civic and sacred buildings, being most commonly associated with the medieval churches of northern and central Italy. We finally arrived back for a wonderful meal (à la Tim) of rabbit fillets with grilled courgette and aubergine and Mediterranean potatoes!

We were planning on having a more leisurely breakfast before making our way into Florence the following day, but then realised that there were very few direct trains running, it being Sunday. So we headed for the showers again; this time, Tim's stopped after only a minute and, as I'd finished, we quickly had to do a change over! Thankfully, no men came in to use the toilets during that process as I was 'barely' covered, ha ha!

We'd got the measure of the trains by then (after lots of experience of them the previous day!) and arrived in the centre of Florence just after 10.00am, where we had some breakfast in a little restaurant in the Piazza della Signoria, close to the 13th century Palazzo Vecchio – the city hall – and the 14th century Loggia dei Lanzi, an open-air gallery of Renaissance sculptures.

The Ponte Vecchio (old bridge) was, apparently, the only bridge across the Arno in Florence until 1218, but the current bridge was rebuilt after a flood in 1345. There have been shops on the Ponte Vecchio since that time; initially, there were all types of shops, including butchers and fishmongers and, later, tanners, whose industrial waste caused quite a stink. Consequently, it was decreed, in 1593, that only goldsmiths and jewellers be allowed to have their shops on the bridge in order to improve the wellbeing of people crossing the bridge. Miraculously the bridge avoided destruction in 1944 and withstood a tremendous flood in 1966.

Figure 152 My painting of the Ponte Vecchio in Florence, Italy

From there, we wandered through the shopping area to the Palazzo Pitti, built in 1457 and now used as a museum, before heading back over the bridge and up to the iconic Duomo and what a sight it is! A huge construction with a pink, white and green marble façade begun in the 13th century but not consecrated until 15th century, with, of course, the amazing cupola designed by Brunelleschi and the beautiful bell tower; the whole structure is impossible to capture in one photo!

Figure 153 Duomo, Florence, Italy

By then it was time for us to make our way back for the train (or wait another two hours) and, once back, Tim magically rustled up a roast pork dinner in the evening. We were, by this time, nearing the end of October and the days were beginning to noticeably shorten; we were still enjoying some beautiful weather, but it was taking longer to warm up in the morning and getting chilly in the evenings.

We'd hoped to go to Pisa the following day and visit the famous tower; thankfully, we'd checked beforehand and found that it, along with all the other major museums and visitor sites, closed on a Monday! Incidentally, we've noticed, in the information at various Roman archaeological sites we've visited, that the name of Italian people in the distant past was 'Italics'. Of course, it all makes sense now, it must have been the *Italics* who built the *leaning* Tower of Pisa!

As we'd already booked tickets for the Uffizi for Tuesday (it also closed on a Monday), we had a day to spare, so, after a quick wash load, we popped to the local supermarket; very reasonable prices there!

After lunch we got the train into Florence and visited the Basilica di San Lorenzo: the Medici family's (wealthy bankers in the early 15th century) parish church and mausoleum designed by Brunelleschi in 1425. The two huge bronze pulpits and some of the decoration in the sacristy were by Donatello, who is buried in the chapel and Michelangelo was commissioned to design the facade, although his design was never used. Talk about name-dropping! (Not the Teenage Mutant Ninja Turtles!)

In the museum below the church there was a room full of reliquaries of various saints; it does seem rather bizarre to have bits of bones, etc in special display cabinets.

We then came across a huge market, indoor and outdoor, with stalls everywhere, and had a good look around. Later, Tim went for a massage, while I went for a mooch around and came across yet another market – this time a French one – in the very pretty Piazza della SS Annunziata and, a little further on, a young woman singing some fantastic operatic arias in the Piazza di S Firenze, so I got myself a drink in one of the bars and sat to listen. After meeting up with Tim, we made our way back to the van.

We arrived in Florence next morning in time for a leisurely amble down to the Uffizi Gallery and began our tour around. The building alone is outstanding; the ceilings in the corridors and some of the rooms are works of art in themselves. The route around the gallery takes the visitor through 13th century paintings and sculptures right up to the 17th century and includes works by some very famous artists, such as Giotto, Botticelli, Leonardo da Vinci, Michelangelo, Rubens, Caravaggio and Titian, amongst, of course, many, many others. We stopped only briefly for a drink and a view of the city from the balcony and it took us 3½ hours to get around the gallery!

Once outside in the beautiful sunny afternoon, we had another walk around the streets and finally decided to try the much vaunted Fiorentino steak; I can assure you that it was very good indeed! The cheese board was deferred until we arrived back at the van.

We thought we'd got the measure of the showers here, but, having got myself all ready in the shower cubicle the following morning, Tim put the money in the meter outside and the adjacent shower came on!! I had to quickly swap cubicles, along with my towel, shower gel, clothes etc!

After breakfast, we popped to the local supermarket for some fresh produce then got ourselves ready to leave. However, the barrier was down and, as the owners weren't on site, we had to ring them to get them to open the gate and had to pop the money into a locked box outside the office! It was a very pleasant and clean site though, despite the crazy showers!

The site owners had very kindly given us the address of a camper supply store nearby, so that was our first port of call, and we were able to get some new plates (Tim had been having a smashing time) and some toilet fluid. Then we were on our way; sadly, Pisa would have to wait for another time, as would the Cinque Terre on the Italian Riviera that we'd heard is lovely. We hoped to return to northern Italy soon and take some time to explore some of its little villages.

At one of the roundabouts we were on, we narrowly avoided colliding with a car that pulled straight in front of us. We were then behind it, and about half a mile further on watched the young woman driver turn left, directly into the path of an oncoming car and they smashed into each other! No wonder so many vehicles in Italy have bumps and dints!

We drove through some beautiful coastal and countryside places on our route, but didn't see any other GB vehicles on the roads at all, of any variety. The locals are all obviously used to left-hand-drive vehicles and I do get some strange 'double-takes' when I put my feet up on the passenger-side dashboard!

Ms Satnav was up to her usual tricks; we complied with her request to 'continue on the A10', but she clearly wasn't sure of our route: at one time the icon was 'driving' across the sea and later was spinning around making us feel quite dizzy! Further on, she insisted we turn down an impossibly tiny road, but we rebelled, following what we thought was the correct route; she then decided we should continue along that road! So rude, no apology or anything!

By late afternoon, we found **Il Villaggio di Giuele** at Finale Ligure – an ACSI site – and were surprised to be told (by a none-too-friendly receptionist) that, as they were constructing a Christmas Village, we had to pay extra to stay on the site. To add insult to injury, the pitches we were permitted to park on, even with extra money, were too short for our van and, worst of all, had a massive drop from the road, resulting in us grounding the van again and damaging the wiring underneath! In the end, feeling very frustrated, we had to park diagonally across the pitch, with our 'back end' encroaching by quite a bit into the adjoining pitch! To be honest, we really didn't feel like caring any more!

It was, to be fair, a very nice site otherwise, with a lovely outdoor swimming pool, restaurant and shops etc, but it just felt that some of these sites are very greedy; the electric wouldn't even boil our kettle! We met another English couple, who were also rather disgruntled with the site and we saw another car and caravan come in and drive straight out again; it felt like they didn't want our business.

A gin and tonic was just what we needed, so that's exactly what we had, before tucking into a wonderful pasta Bolognese.

During the night the nearby church clock was determined to make sure we knew the time: 13 bongs at 12.30am and, at 7.00am, after continuous bonging, Tim decided it was time to get up and make our morning cup of tea!

After threatening the woman on reception that we'd ring ACSI and complain about the site not adhering to the advertised prices, she finally relented, so when we left we felt, at least, that some justice had been done.

Southern France – October to November

We drove past more beautiful towns and villages (this area was definitely on the list for another visit) and eventually crossed the French/Italian border. There had been times when we'd wondered whether we'd leave Italy unscathed, but, although we still bore the scars from some serious knocks and 'hairy' moments, we'd made it and had thoroughly enjoyed all the places we'd visited, many of which were exceptional. Generally, though, we felt that, with some notable exceptions, the southern part of Italy was definitely poorer and less welcoming than the northern area.

After a couple of hours we arrived at **Les Cigales Campsite** at Mandelieu-La-Napoule and soon got chatting to our new neighbours, Liz and Tony, who, since retiring, had spent around six years sailing to America and various other places, and a year on the French canals; they were currently on a one-year motorhome holiday. They made us feel quite staid!

Tim then spent a happy (!) half hour or so with his head in the toilet cassette aperture, I know...! Somehow the mechanism had ceased to operate, but thankfully he got it working again. Later, we had a walk down to the beach and along to the outskirts of Cannes, where we stopped for a drink before heading back. I noticed that Tim's stripy t-shirt was very versatile: having provided camouflage in the Duomo in Siena, it now allowed him to blend in with the locals there; he just needed a string of onions and a beret!

Having now arrived in France, it did seem a bit perverse that we ate at the Chinese restaurant just over the road; well, we hadn't been to a Chinese restaurant for a long time! We both chose duck (surprise, suprise!), though differently presented, then, for a dessert, we each had a banana fritter flambéed in saké, very nice.

In the morning we got the bikes down and cycled the 10kms into the centre of Cannes. We'd spotted a cycle track on our walk yesterday that we thought would take us all the way into Cannes, hah! It ended a few metres past where we'd walked! We had a look in the windows (!) of some of the very expensive shops in Cannes and meandered around the very pleasant old town of Cannes. Finally, we stood on the famous red carpet at the Cannes Film Festival for our film premiere of Barby's Adventures with Tim Tim (we wish!)!

Figure 154 Cannes, France, complete with photo-bombing fans!

We spent the next couple of days relaxing in the sun: one day, we cycled down to the beach, and the next walked down to the sea along the riverside from the campsite. It did seem a very friendly place and there was a lovely atmosphere, with families enjoying the sun, sea and sand. We were intrigued by a little river ferry and wondered why that was necessary when there seemed to be plenty of bridges; then we saw it ferrying the golfers from one side of the course to the other, aha!

Tim had a second, unplanned, shower when I turned the tap on (at his request!) and he sprayed himself thoroughly! We then said farewell to our nomadic friends and to Les Cigales Campsite: a very peaceful and friendly site, with good-sized, level pitches and hot showers with room to swing a small cat (although the cat wasn't too keen!)

We stocked up with essentials (two boxes of wine....oh and some bread and milk) at the hypermarket and this time got in the slowest queue ever, with a cashier seeming to be utterly bored with his job. Incidentally, on our previous visit we had – to save time (!) – gone through the self check-out; what a mistake that was! We ended up having to call the assistant over for just about every item!

Finally, we got on our way, eventually arriving at Domaine Saint Hilaire around 4.45pm. If you've been paying attention, you will recall that this is the house and vineyard belonging to Tim's brother Nick and his wife, Lisa at that time (although they weren't in residence at the time). As we drove into the car park at the back, there were a few overhanging branches that we pointed out to Manager, Edouard and, within minutes, 'master-of-all-trades' employee Nick Frith appeared with a ladder and a chain saw and removed every offending branch!

We'd been in contact with George and Jenny (who we met when staying near Rome; do try and keep up!) and found that they were very close by, so we'd suggested they join us for a night at the Domaine and they arrived not long after us. Tim cooked an amazing meal and we had a wonderful evening with them, exchanging stories of our respective travels and life in general.

After a leisurely breakfast we said farewell to George and Jenny, then, whilst I sorted out some washing and managed to make a start on a watercolour painting, Tim and Nick attempted a repair to the van's wayward back-corner panel. The problem was that the panel needed to be firmly held in place, but, because this was a coach-built van, on a wooden frame, it also needed to be able to adjust to the movements of the rear and side panels as we drove along. Nick, a former set-builder for Monty Python, cleverly thought of using sponges soaked in glue to achieve the desired effect.

We'd originally planned to leave the next morning, but the van repairs needed completing and some time to dry, so we decided to have a nice relaxing day (you've no idea how tiring all this travelling is, I bet you think it's easy don't you?!) and I have to say the Domaine had a very relaxed feel to it. The van was finally finished, so, after lunch, I settled down to finish my painting, though I nearly had a 'cat-astrophe' when the resident moggy decided to jump up on to my knee as I sat there with my paints, etc!

Figure 155 Painting at the Domaine, France

Spain: Figueres, Benicássim and Calonge – November

After breakfast, we got on our way, stopping briefly in Mèze, nearby, to purchase some fish soup from one of the little *coquillages* (fresh fish stalls) there. Then we set Ms Satnav and off we went. After reading Tony and Liz's blog (the people we met near Cannes), we had felt that we should perhaps have a name for our satnav. So, after much thought and deliberation, we decided to call her Sybil, partly for the alliteration of Sybil Satnav and partly because of her rather 'fawlty' nature!

After a while, we were funnelled, single-file, across the border into Spain, with very serious Guardia Civil officers checking most vehicles and/or documents. Amazingly, they waved us through; we must look honest! The Catalan word for welcome is *benvinguts*; I have to say it doesn't have the most welcoming ring to it somehow!

As we drove along (avoiding Colera like the plague!), we noticed lots of Catalan flags flying in support of their bid for independence from mainland Spain. Catalan citizens had long believed that their region put more into Spain's economy than it received but their bid for independence subsequently resulted in some of their leaders being convicted of sedition and misuse of public funds.

We soon reached **Figueres**, parking the van in a supermarket car park, which was also, officially, an aire and, after lunch, walked the mile or so to the Salvador Dalí Museum. Born in Figueres in 1904, it remained Dalí's home town until his death in 1989; he is, in fact, buried at the site of the museum. Of course, Dalí is known for his surrealist work and his somewhat eccentric behaviour, which seemingly did not please those who held his work in high esteem.

The museum building itself is quite a sight, but what a treat was in store for us inside! As well as his very imaginative works, Dalí produced some very fine pieces of art and sculpture, many of which involved his wife, Gala (what a name Gala Dalí!) and which were great to see. Naturally, though, the highlights were his very wacky and often enormous models, paintings and *trompe l'oeil* works (optical illusions), many of which have become synonymous with his name.

Figure 156 Dalí Museum, Figueres, Spain

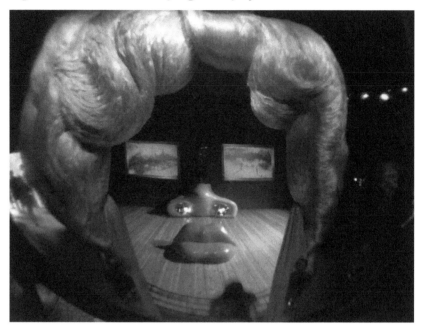

In the morning, we drank our morning cup of tea while the golden rays of the rising sun illuminated the supermarket trolleys, accompanied by the quiet tinkle of running water, as the waste from next door's motorhome ran down the car park. The French couple had a Chausson van, similar to ours, with faux (well, I assume so!) leopard-skin seat covers, and they were clearly aware they'd left their waste water plug out, as one of them came out of the van for something and made no attempt to rectify their 'error', bringing down the tone of the motorhome community and giving Chausson owners a bad name, tut tut!

On the bright side, we were able to get some fresh bread and croissants from the supermarket and fill up with the cheapest fuel we'd seen on this trip and at least it wasn't an 'erotic supermarket' of which there seem to be many in this area.... or was it?! ☺

Ms Fawlty lived up to her name and had our van icon spinning around again, as we fumbled our way out of Figueres, then, on a three-lane autopista, she warned us of a narrow road ahead!

After an hour or so, we arrived at Colònia Güell, just south of Barcelona, which was founded in 1890 by entrepreneur Eusebi Güell, when he moved his textile industry (specializing in velvet) from the centre of Barcelona. The whole town was built in the 'modernist' style, using leading architects of the time: Francesc Berengeur, Joan Rubio and, notably, Antoni Gaudí.

At the information centre, we visited the exhibition explaining the industry and providing an excellent social and cultural history commentary. We then roamed around the town admiring the architecture of some of the wonderful public and private buildings designed by Berengeur and Rubio. However, the pièce de resistance was, of course, the church, started in 1908 by Antoni Gaudí and funded by patron Eusebi Güell. Unfortunately, it was never finished (we seem to have seen a lot of unfinished projects on our travels!), partly because of WWI and, of course, Gaudí's sudden death in 1924. Mainly though, it seemed that Gaudí had, whilst designing and beginning the building of this church, been commissioned to design the Sagrada Família in Barcelona, and many of his ideas, put into use on this church, became the basis for the Sagrada Família.

Two naves were planned for the church here, but only the lower one was completed, now referred to as the crypt. You may recall that, on our first trip to Spain, we visited the Sagrada Família; we were wowed by that building and I can tell you that this church, although significantly smaller, is no less astonishing. Gaudí's use of light and space and innovative architectural techniques is fantastic, and apparently it was built almost entirely from locally-recycled materials. The site was declared a UNESCO World Heritage Site in 2005 and well worth the visit.

Figure 157 Gaudí's Crypt, Colònia Güell, Spain

It was only about a half hour's drive from there to our stop for the night: **El Garrofer Campsite**, just south of Sitges, a site we actually stayed on when we visited Barcelona last year. We returned mainly because it was a good stop-off point and, more importantly, it was still open at this time of year; many sites close for the winter in September or early October.

The memories of our previous visit to El Garrofer Campsite came flooding back in the morning, when we saw that the birds had decorated the back of the van and the bike cover with some beautiful artistic splashes!

Just as we were leaving we met the couple that we'd parked next to for a week earlier this year at El Campello (near Alicante)! What a small motorhoming world it is sometimes!

It was approaching lunchtime as we were travelling along, and we were on the lookout for a pleasant place to stop, but by 2.00pm we still hadn't seen anywhere, so reluctantly settled for a litter-festooned piece of land adjacent to a garage, alongside a couple of lorries. Typically, about two miles further along, we came across a lovely little parking area, right on the edge of the beach! Such is life!

We passed Jordiland (why aye man we did) and Platja Miami (Miami Beach), before reaching the Taj Mahal in Benicàssim, amazing, all in one afternoon! Interestingly, we also noticed a sign for Pinguins Burguer: that's a new one on me!

We drove past the entrance to our campsite as we needed fuel, but on the way back Sybil announced, "You are going the wrong way down this road," and we definitely weren't! Eventually, we arrived at **Bonterra Park**, which I'm sure you must remember was where we got our most amazing standing ovation, earlier this year! We planned to stay there for the next three weeks, which was something of an experiment for us as we'd never stayed anywhere for a prolonged period. However, there was little likelihood of us becoming bored during that time, as there were lots of activities on site and we were very pleased that our friends Colin and Sue, who we met in Seville on our very first trip (I do hope you're keeping up!), had already arrived from their home in Spain to spend a few days there with us.

We'd booked an off-site restaurant for the evening, but on arriving at the campsite, we found that the band we'd met on our previous trip was playing that evening. Consequently, we changed our plans and listened to them as we ate at the restaurant: the food was very good and excellent value at €12.50 for a three-course meal, including half a bottle of wine per person!

Afterwards, we sat outside and whiled away the rest of the evening with a little more alcohol than perhaps we should; for some reason the van was spinning around again and this time it wasn't the icon on the satnav screen!

Another beautiful day dawned, so, after a lovely al fresco breakfast, we all went for a walk along the Via Verde, finally stopping for refreshments (non-alcoholic!) at a lovely little bar/ restaurant, before walking back.

In the evening, we decided to use another of our disposable barbecues to cook some steaks for us all. Colin loaned us a couple of blocks of wood (which he occasionally used to jack up the van when stationary) to rest the barbecue on, on top of our table and he and Sue provided wine, chips and salad to accompany the steak.

After the meal, we retired inside Colin and Sue's van as the wind was gusting, but, after a while, a very kind German man from across the way knocked on the door to alert us to our own little bonfire! Fanned by the wind, the barbecue had set the wood alight and had begun to burn the table too! Eek! Ironically, today was 5th November: we must have been sub-consciously missing bonfire night; thank goodness it didn't turn into a bigger display! Colin was going to need another two blocks of wood for his van and, thankfully, that was the last of our disposable barbecues (and sadly the table!)

Site workmen were carrying out some maintenance on the trees, so we decided to sample the coffee at the bar where it was a little quieter and we weren't breathing in diesel fumes from the machinery. I must say, though, that their maintenance process was very efficient: the falling leaves were beginning to make the site somewhat untidy so they denuded the trees, with the added bonus of letting the winter sun shine through (the leaves would, of course, have provided welcome cover during hot summer days). We did notice that the Germans and Dutch parked close to us seemed to be much more scrupulous than us about clearing up the leaves on their pitches!

After a quiet, relaxing afternoon (amongst the leaves!), we spent a pleasant hour or so with Colin and Sue in the evening.

In the early afternoon we went for our meal (that had been originally planned for Saturday evening) at La Llar (apparently Catalan for 'the call') restaurant, not far away. Needless to say, Tim and I were virtually multi-lingual by then – well, we could order two beers in six languages – but re-arranging the meal seemed like it might be more than we could safely handle, so we'd asked one of the helpful, multi-lingual, receptionists to re-schedule for 2.00pm today. The meal was typically Spanish and very nice, but the restaurant lacked a bit of atmosphere as we were almost the only people eating there (only two other individuals). Tim and I shared a starter of cured fish (thank goodness, we wouldn't have wanted them to be ill!) and for his main, Tim had a stew of rabbit and snails (each to his own!); I did sample one of the snails, which was actually okay!

On the way back we called in at one of the Asian *bricolage* (DIY) stores that was, as usual, stocked with lots of useful things! We bought a new dustpan and brush (we were at a loss as to where ours went, it must have been bristling with excitement for an adventure on its own!), a set of bolts to fix Tim's broken chair and a 'tennis racquet' with electrified strings for swatting insects.

We stopped off at the campsite bar, where a few musicians were having a 'jam' session, then finished the day off with a few nibbles and drinks in our van in the evening and exchanged stories of our travels; Colin and Sue had been travelling on and off for about 12 years and had driven around Morocco and the USA, amongst other places. We definitely felt quite unadventurous!

In the morning, Tim popped to the supermarket, which was literally just across the road from the site, for some croissants. It was really nice not having to think about stocking up with shopping and all the angst that accompanies it (where, how, when, can we park the van....), we could just get what we needed at any time! However, whilst there, he met the couple that we had first met in a motorway services area, then bumped into again here at Bonterra Park in the spring! They were about to leave today though, so we had a brief chat with them in the morning and said farewell, until the next chance encounter!

We also said goodbye to Colin and Sue later in the morning, then sat out in the sunshine and, armed with our new 'racquets', invited some of the local insects to come and play tennis, they seemed to get a real buzz out of it!

In the evening a German van arrived on the pitch that Colin and Sue had vacated and we had great fun watching them setting up, it seemed as if they were novice campers (we were seasoned travellers of course!) and they levelled up the van and got all their mats down etc, then repeated the process three times! We were amazed when they moved again in the morning, this time to the pitch opposite for some reason!

Today was my turn for a massage at the site, while Tim walked into town for a haircut, after which we both walked back into town to have a look around the market where I bought some fantastic trainers for €6! (Which, incidentally, lasted me for ages; very good value.)

After lunch and a couple of hours in the glorious sunshine, the late afternoon chill (around 4pm today) drove us indoors; interestingly, though, there was a good hour more daylight there than in Italy, darkness falling around 6.00pm in Spain at that time of year. Consolation was at hand, however, listening to the band playing in the bar during the happy hour (or two), followed by fish and chips that, considering we were in Spain, weren't bad at all!

We got the bikes down after breakfast and cycled along the excellent cycle route to El Castellón, around 15kms each way. Once there, we parked the bikes and had a wander around the shops, very good market hall and pleasant plazas there; sadly, pretty much everything of historic interest had been destroyed in various wars over the ages. Thankfully, my new, cheap trainers were very comfortable, as we covered around five miles on foot, but we found a nice little place to have some tapas and a glass of wine. We felt as if we stood out like 'sore thumbs' in our t-shirts and shorts though, as all the locals were wearing their winter coats; clearly our blood hadn't thinned that much while we'd been away!

We noticed a hoarding advertising Cemento Cola; now there's an interesting new flavour and I reckon it would definitely make you feel quite full up! (It's actually fast-drying cement!)

As temperatures were even hotter – around 23° in the shade – the next day, we decided to make the most of it and sat out in the sun, reading and generally watching the world go by. In the afternoon we stocked up for the weekend at the supermarket (they don't open on Sundays) and bumped into Tony and Liz, the adventurous round-the-world (almost) sailors we'd parked next to in Cannes a couple of weeks ago. They'd just arrived and were planning to stay for a few days. After that, we ventured up to the boules court and played our first-ever game of boules and I won! Amazing, must have been beginner's luck as I'm not known for my sporting skills!

In the evening, we enjoyed a meal in the bar/restaurant whilst listening to the Spanish singer and watching the various dancers (trying to pick up a few tips).

Another beautiful day dawned and we sat outside to enjoy our smoked salmon and scrambled egg breakfast, accompanied by a little champagne, well, why not?! (I don't want to hear...) Then we walked about half a mile down to the beach to soak up the sunshine again and I did another pastel sketch, while Tim read.

Figure 158 Pastel sketch, Benicàssim, Spain

The wind was very strong during the night (still troubled by the garlic) and we awoke to find bits of our outdoor furniture had blown on to other people's pitches, so we hastily retrieved it. We'd decided to visit Peñiscola today; you may remember we called there briefly earlier this year but didn't explore it and we'd since been told it was worth a visit. I was interested to know what exactly the word means; apparently it is a local evolution of the Latin *peninsula* and when I looked up its two parts in the dictionary, I found that the Spanish word *cola* means 'tail' (it's often used for our word 'queue' and is probably where we get our word 'colon' from); the word *peñis* (looking that up in the dictionary strangely took me back to my developing years!) is related to *peñon* (remember the cliff in Calpé?), meaning 'rock' (I'm making no suggestions as to what connection that might have to any similar English words). No surprise then that the old town of Peñiscola is on an outcrop of rock, connected to the mainland by a thin strip of land. Some further research had indicated that the trains there were fairly infrequent and at varying prices: the 9.30am train cost €3.50 each, whereas the later trains were €14 each!

Consequently, we set the alarm and arrived at Benicarlò-Peñiscola station at around 10.15am, feeling pleased with ourselves that, for at least the outward journey, we'd saved a few pounds. Our joy was short-lived, however, when, being unable to see any signs as to how to get to Peñiscola old town, we were informed, by a well-meaning Spanish man, that it was 'very far' and we would need a taxi! The taxi set us back €17 but at least dropped us outside the Tourist Information Office. You won't be surprised to hear that our first question to the extremely friendly lady there was, "Will we be able to get a bus back to the station?" She gave us some very helpful information and we set off to explore the 67 metre-high rocky crag, often referred to as the Gibraltar of Valencia, topped by a 14th century castle.

Figure 159 Castle at Peñiscola, Spain

We really enjoyed looking around the castle, built by the Knights Templar between 1294 and 1307 on the remains of an Arab Citadel. From 1411 to 1423 it was the home of the exiled Pope Benedict XIII (Pedro de Luna); he had been appointed Pope during the time of a split in the Catholic Church – referred to as the Western Schism – when the people of Rome rioted, insisting on an Italian Pope, and Benedict was abandoned by 17 of his Cardinals. At the start of his term of office, Benedict was recognised as Pope by seven countries, including France, Scotland and Portugal and he continued his rivalry with the subsequently elected Pope until his death, as he had been the last living cardinal created by Gregory XI, the last Supreme Pontiff. He was clearly a learnèd man and his rooms at the castle contained many shelves of books and some beautiful illuminated manuscripts that he had created.

The old town of Peñiscola is very pretty, with beautiful views over the sea; it has been used for numerous film sets – such as El

Cid – and TV series, eg Game of Thrones. It also hosts an annual comedy film festival in September and whilst we were there, some filming was taking place in part of the castle. Unfortunately, at that time of year, most of the little cafés and restaurants were closed and the wind that had bothered us in the morning hadn't let up and, of course, was particularly strong when we were on the top of the castle ramparts!

We decided to get the bus (€1.50 each) to the centre of Benicarló (the adjacent town), in the hope of finding a nice little spot there for some lunch. We'd thought Peñiscola was quiet, but Benicarló was positively deserted! Finally, we found a little Spanish café where we had some soup and I ordered fish that I'd imagined coming with a nice salad or vegetables, but no, it was just a plate of little fried fish! Anyway, it was very pleasant and we lingered over the meal and a coffee, before walking back to the station for our train; yes, if we'd only realised in the morning, we could have saved ourselves the taxi fare and walked into town! We live and learn!

After spending a quiet day, on which our only outing was a walk along the lovely promenade, admiring again the once palatial villas that were the playground of the elite in the early 20th century, the following day was the appointed time for my second massage (I'd booked three sessions on a special offer!). Meanwhile, Tim cycled into El Castellón again as he needed to get himself a new shirt, and in the afternoon we joined Tony and Liz for happy hour in the bar, before having a bit of a practice with some of the music for our gig tomorrow evening.

Next morning we walked into the town of Benicàssim and had a browse around the market again. Having stopped for a coffee to soak up the lovely atmosphere in the town, we nearly gave up as the waitress seemed determined not to notice us in the corner!

The afternoon saw us get down to a bit more rehearsing, before setting up the equipment during happy hour, then we just had time to get changed and back down to the bar for our concert in the evening. The place was filled to capacity and we started with a couple of songs for Remembrance Day, before launching into our set, which went on for 2½ hours! We were exhausted, but they were a great crowd with lots of people up dancing and we received some very complimentary comments afterwards.

After we'd got all the equipment packed away again the following morning, Tony and Liz popped around to let us have some photos from last night. Later, we got the key for the chalet that my daughter Kate and her partner, James, were to occupy when they arrived that evening, and went to the supermarket across the road to get some essential supplies in for them: naturally some wine, beer and, of course, some tea and milk too! We also went to the Asian store and got a couple of towels for them, as they were not automatically provided with the chalet and from there cost only as much as it would be to hire them!

After meeting Kate and James at the railway station, Tim used his best Spanish to ring for a taxi, only to find that the driver who turned up was English and had been told to pick up some foreigners!

We ate in the campsite restaurant in the evening courtesy of the management, in thanks for our performance the previous evening and they brought out a cake to celebrate Kate's 30th birthday (earlier in November, but you have to make the most of these events don't you?).

Figure 160 Kate's birthday cake, Bonterra Park, Spain

We had a leisurely walk into town the following morning, then along to the start of the Via Verde, where we had a birthday lunch (see comment above!) on the terrace at El Palasiet restaurant, with a beautiful view over the bay of Benicàssim.

Figure 161 Bay at Benicàssim, Spain

After a wonderful meal, Tim and I needed to retreat for a quick fix on a cup of tea, while Kate and James continued the celebrations through happy hour, and they were definitely very happy when we rejoined them later to singalong with the evening entertainment.

We embarked on another leisurely walk into town in the morning and this time noticed that a band was setting up at one of the little bars, so we sat with a couple of drinks while we listened to them; they were a really excellent bluesy-type band, with a fantastic Amy Winehouse-style singer. After a late lunch at a little restaurant not far from the campsite we relaxed in the evening with a few very good games of Rummikub, that Kate won. Unfortunately, something Tim had consumed (liquid or otherwise?) made him start hiccupping and he continued throughout the night!

After a not-so refreshing sleep for Tim, Kate and James hired bikes from the campsite and we all cycled along the Via Verde, stopping off at a few scenic points along the way to Oropesa del Mar. Naturally, we needed a drink, so we stopped at a little bar, overlooking the lovely beach and had a few delicious tapas too! One item on the menu there had us puzzled though: Mussels to the Sailor's Blouse! We hadn't a clue what that meant!

By the time we got back, Tim was suffering from his lack of sleep last night, so he went for a snooze, while the rest of us went to a beach bar and relaxed on the comfy sofas at the edge of the sand, mmmm. In the evening, chef Tim prepared his special meatballs and they were very nice!

We cycled the opposite way the following day and headed along the excellent cycle paths beside the coast all the way to the marina at El Castellón. We'd planned to have a few tapas again, but there were so many lovely restaurants on the front and the menu del día was only €12 each for three courses plus bread and wine or beer so, of course, we couldn't resist – well, it would have cost us more than that to have ordered a couple of tapas – and the food was delicious! I was getting a bit worried that I would need a new set of clothes to fit into soon!

Another cuppa was needed when we got back, before we settled down for another Rummikub session that Kate won again!

The next morning, Tim and I had some washing and a few other jobs to do to get ready for our impending departure, so while we got on with those, Kate and James went down to the beach for a bit of relaxation. We met up with them later on, and enjoyed the rest of the beautiful sunshine on the comfy sofas at the beach bar again.

In the evening, Tim cooked a delicious salmon pasta dish at Kate and James's chalet, but had under-estimated the strength of the Italian chilli oil we'd bought. We all were breathing flames as we played Rummikub again (it's a great game but a bit addictive!).

Another morning's wash-load was out on the line before we all walked into town and sampled a Spanish breakfast of tostadas with tomato pulp in one of the popular little street cafés, then had a quick meander around Benicàssim's market and back to the beach for a couple of hours. As it was our last day together, we thought we'd treat ourselves (as I'm sure you've noticed, we'd been positively frugal these last few days) to the menu del día at one of the villas that, as mentioned previously, had been the place to be seen around 100 years ago; it had been beautifully restored and was now a restaurant on the promenade.

Figure 162 Villa on the Promenade, Benicàssim, Spain

Kate and James went along to enjoy the happy hour again, while we went and packed everything up in the van, ready for an early start the next day. We managed a last few games of Rummikub before having a reasonably early night.

We were up at what felt like the middle of the night and after a quick cup of tea we tip-toed around, removing the electricity cable, reversing off the levellers and securing everything inside the van (we had to put a five-litre box of wine in the oven as we needed the space for Kate and James's suitcases, hoping that we'd remember to remove it before switching the oven on!). By the time we'd driven up to the top of the site to empty the waste water, it was around 6.45am and we were reprimanded by a site official for making a noise before 7.00am; we pleaded insanity and were let off with a caution eventually, but we couldn't wait around and picked up Kate and James, with their suitcases, at about 6.55am, then beat a hasty retreat as soon as the gates opened at 7.00am, before we were in any more trouble! I must say, though, that we'd enjoyed our stay at Bonterra Park. Despite it being a very large campsite, we find it very relaxing and the facilities are excellent; its popularity is evident, as it was almost full. Many people stay there over the winter months – and who can blame them when the pleasant weather is so dependable – and the town has retained its Spanish feel, despite being a tourist destination.

Our early departure had been necessary as Kate and James had to be at Barcelona airport for around 9.30am for their flight home; thankfully, there were no traffic problems and Sybil got us there just in time – despite her dropping off a couple of times (must have been the early start!) – although I think we possibly exceeded one or two motorhome speed limits on the way (shhh!) Once we'd said our goodbyes, we headed for an aire at Blanes, around 45 minutes away, but it was a very uninspiring place, so we just had a bit of lunch and set off again, this time to **Camping Internacional De Calonge**, on the east coast about 40kms below Palamós. Once we'd parked up, we got the chairs out for an hour or so then went for a walk down to the beach. What a beautiful place it was, with some lovely little coves, crystal clear water and a walk along the cliffs, with steps carved into the rocks; we decided to explore further tomorrow.

The campsite, too, was very spacious, clean and pleasant, but very much perched on the side of a hill, so it was quite a work-out going up to the toilet and shower blocks! We noticed a picture on the shower/toilet block doors of a little 'Scottie' dog, with a cross through it – so I guess that meant that labradors, poodles, etc could go in – wonder what the Scottie dogs had done that was so wrong!! We also noticed, later in the evening when the lights were on, that you could see very clearly into the toilet cubicles through the clear glass windows at eye-level! I made a mental note to bear that in mind on my next visit to the loo!

Well, we could tell we'd travelled North already, the temperature was decidedly lower than we'd been used to and we donned trousers and jumpers for the first time for some time. Sadly, the grey sky provided a shower of rain mid-morning, so we grudgingly paid the €6 for 24 hours of internet connection for one device (we have since learned how to use a phone as a hub to provide internet access on the laptops), so that we could research sites for the rest of our journey and book our channel tunnel crossing.

By then, the rain had cleared so we decided to explore the coastal path; it really is a beautiful coastline and the path meandered for about three-quarters of a mile along the coast around lots of pretty coves and fantastic rock formations.

Figure 163 A beautiful cove, near Palamós, Spain

We reached a point where I was a bit concerned we might end up having an impromptu swim, so, rather than risk it, we took the path that climbed slightly upwards, becoming a cliff-side walk for another three-quarters of a mile or so, and as we descended into St Antoni de Calonge, a beautiful stretch of golden beach was visible all the way to Palamós. We hadn't had any lunch and the walk had given us a bit of an appetite; however, the cafés along the edge of the beach were all deserted and Tim was beginning to think he'd have to eat me, when (thankfully, but I think you'd have realised as the book would have ended abruptly!) we spotted a little row of bars and cafés, where we had some lovely tapas and a drink before heading back, this time at a much faster pace as it was beginning to feel decidedly chilly!

Another cool morning followed, but the sun was shining, so we donned our shoes and set off for the coastal walk again, this time in the opposite direction. The coastal path wound up and down lots of steps and over rocks for around 2½ miles, via one beautiful cove after another, before we reached the town of Platja d'Aro – Catalan for 'golden beach' – which might give you a clue as to what was awaiting us after we rounded the edge of the last cove (we reckon that on the two walks we must have passed through at least 30 of these fabulous little coves); this was definitely an area where we'd like to spend a bit more time when the weather is warmer!

A drink at one of the bars at the edge of the beach was sufficient refreshment before we wandered back along the path to the campsite, where Tim conjured up steak and chips for our evening meal.

We set the alarm so that we could have an early start as we had a long way to travel the next day. Our plan was to set off from the site around 8.00am, pick up some bread at the nearest town (there weren't any shops close to the campsite) then stop somewhere for a late breakfast. Unfortunately, we were thwarted at the first hurdle as we hadn't realised that the site office didn't open until 9.00am, then, to make matters worse, the receptionists didn't turn up till around 10 past! We finally got set off around 9.25am and, despite Sybil flashing red with anger and declaring that we were going the wrong way up a one-way street, eventually reached the Mercadona a few miles up the road. We topped up our supplies and bought some croissants that we ate in the van, parked at the side of the road, very romantic!

Sybil was quite cross with us and seemed determined to add around 50kms to our journey in order to get us to follow her preferred route, but we resisted and she finally gave in. We passed through some lovely countryside, with beautiful trees in their autumn colours, enhanced by some welcome sunshine. After we'd passed Els Angels (!), Sybil decided to further punish us by taking us around the outskirts of a town (following a huge, slow wagon) on a very bumpy road, and it seemed that the only reason was an eight tonne limit through the town (and we were well below that weight!).

Back to France and Home – November

We'd been a bit concerned as Sybil was suggesting that the distance we had to cover was much more than we'd expected, but then I realised I'd put in the wrong coordinates, oops! Thankfully, they'd been for a site further along the correct road, so we hadn't gone out of our way. The temperature was dropping drastically though, from 14° as we left the site, down to 7° as we headed north through the mountains into southern France.

We arrived at **Camping La Cascade**, near St Rome de Tarn, just before dusk and were the only campers on the site! But blimey, we'd thought the last place was on a hill, this one was on a very steep, terraced, valley side and, on the trek to the very clean facilities, we nearly needed oxygen! A lovely casserole in the evening renewed our energy levels!

We awoke to sub-zero temperatures and a covering of frost, brrr! We donned several layers of clothing and I cruelly made Tim walk down to the river, so I could see the gorgeous reflections in this beautiful valley of the River Tarn; after that, the walk up to the pretty little town of St Rome de Tarn at the top of the valley for a fresh baguette, definitely warmed us up.

Figure 164 St Rome de Tarn, France

Finally, we set off, passing under the famous Millau viaduct – that keen readers may recall we crossed on our travels earlier this year – and filled up with fuel at Millau. Once again, we ignored Sybil at first – she was very keen to get us to the motorway by the most tortuous route – and a combination of map reading and following signs saved us around 30kms! We'd still not seen any British lorries on the roads: lots from Hungary, Bulgaria, Poland and Slovakia, as well as from Spain and France of course, but none from Britain.

Our journey took us across the mountain ranges again, this time up to over 1100 metres high through light snow, as temperatures rose no higher than 3°. I know, I knew it was cold at home, but have pity on us poor travellers! On our way we passed the Viaduc de Garabit, a railway bridge constructed between 1882 and 1884 by Gustave Eiffel (no prizes for guessing one of his other famous constructions) across the River Truyere; it is an impressive structure at 565m long, with its main arch having a 165m span. Eventually, we arrived at **Camping Le Clos Auroy** mid-afternoon and had a walk up into the little town of Orcet, another very pleasant, typical French town, before battening the hatches for the evening.

After breakfast we walked up into the town for some bread then set off again, eventually stopping for lunch at a roadside service area. I was just in the process of opening a can of tomato soup (you see, I do cook sometimes!), when suddenly Tim shot past me, exclaiming something like, "Oh dear me, I appear to have omitted to apply the handbrake" (or words to that effect!), as we watched the grass verge whizzing past! He reached the offending handbrake just in time to prevent an unwanted out-of-control excursion across the busy area. Phew!

You may recall that we stopped at **Jouy le Potier** on our way down to Spain earlier this year (you don't? Really, do pay attention!), and this was the little village we headed for today. We'd enjoyed a meal at the Logis there on our previous visit, so decided to make it our last stop on this trip and went there in the evening. The Taiwanese (but French speaking, with very little English) co-owner (her husband is the chef) greeted us with the same enthusiasm we'd received previously – one of the reasons we'd returned – and we enjoyed a lovely meal of venison. A large cat was ambling between the diners in the restaurant and we asked the Taiwanese lady (in French) if the cat was hers. Her embarrassed, giggling response, whilst repeating emphatically, "Non, non" and making 'pregnant tummy' gestures puzzled us considerably! She then said it was the house cat and walked away, still giggling; we were not sure what that was all about; maybe there is some French saying that we're unaware of!

We'd tried various ways of asking Sybil to take us to the Tunnel Sous la Manche (Channel Tunnel) and with each attempt she came back with a total distance of around 550kms, which was much more than we'd expected, so we set our alarm and were on our way by 7.30am, calling for some fuel for our mammoth journey. Confirming our belief that we were roughly in the middle of France, we passed the Aire du Centre de la France (very precise!) after a little way, and shortly afterwards stopped to pick up some coffee and something for breakfast, in order to save time; it cost us almost €15 for two very mediocre coffees and two similarly mediocre sandwiches.

Eventually, we reached Paris, but didn't realise in time that Sybil was taking us on the inner ring road, aaagh! Traffic was horrendous and she scolded us yet again for going 'the wrong way', this time on a four-lane motorway that she'd sent us on! We did get a glimpse of the Seine, the Eiffel Tower and the Sacré Coeur as we passed but it ended up taking us well over an hour before we were able to move at any kind of speed again and by now the prospect of reaching the tunnel in time for our crossing was becoming a bleak one.

We finally saw a British lorry as we headed north away from Paris and eventually began to see signs for Calais; we were puzzled to note that the distance given was around 120kms less than Sybil was declaring we had to travel. We hardly dared to believe it, but couldn't imagine how the signs could be so far out, so we relaxed a little bit, but not completely, just in case! The temperature was still hovering around 3° and the skies were leaden, as we drove through a sleet shower, but we were a bit alarmed when we saw a sign for Isbergues!

As we got nearer to Calais it became apparent that we didn't need to worry about the extra 120kms, but we were intrigued as to where Sybil was going to take us! We reached the tunnel in good time and even managed to catch a slightly earlier train than planned. Amazingly, whilst travelling under the Channel, with the engine turned off, Sybil stayed on, tracking our progress; I swear she'd taken on a life of her own! When we reached the English end, we couldn't stop laughing when Sybil then told us to board the ferry to go back to Calais; that's why she'd calculated it as further than it was!

So, at last, we'd arrived safely – although somewhat battered and bruised – in the freezing temperatures in England! We'd travelled almost 6000 miles and had lots of adventures: some fun, some scary, but all very memorable and exciting!

As I've said, we are both fascinated by language and have enjoyed experiencing the numerous languages and language variations that we have come across; I've tried to share some of those with you and hope you have found it interesting too. Looking back over our three trips, we have been so lucky to visit such amazing places, of which I hope I've given a flavour throughout. Good luck with any travels that you may have, we hope that you enjoy them as much as we continue to do!

Watch out for more of Barby's Adventures with Tim Tim!

Happy Travelling!

Campsites and Aires

Country	Region	Nearest Town/City	Campsite/Aire	Page
England	Yorkshire	Robin Hood's Bay	The Flask Holiday Park	3
France	Centre	Jouy le Potier	Aire	145/361
	Centre	Mezerey	Aire	6
	Centre	Orcet	Camping Le Clos Auroy	361
	North east	Chalons en Champagne	Camping de Chalons en Champagne	269
	North east	Metz	Camping Municipal Metz	129
	North west	Le Mans	Pont Romain Campsite	257
	North west	Rouen	Campsite Les Terrasses	260
	North west	Rouen	Camping de l'Aubette	261
	North west	Vannes	Flower Camping	247
	South	St Rome de Tarn	Camping La Cascade	359
	South coast	Mandelieu-La-Napoule	Les Cigales Campsite	335
	South west	Agde	La Pepiniere Camping	111
	South west	Cap D'Agde	Mer et Soleil Camping	76
	South west	Carcassonne	Camping de la Cité	92
	South west	Lourdes	D'Arrouach Camping	94
	South west	Narbonne	La Nautique Camping	107
	South west	Toulouse	Le Rupe Camping	107

Country	Region	Nearest Town/City	Campsite/Aire	Page
	South west	Villeneuve lès Béziers	Les Berges du Canal Camping	115
	West coast	Île De Ré	La Tour des Prises Campsite	240
	West coast	La Rochelle	Camping Beaulieu	243
	West coast	Lacanau Ocean	Les Grands Pins Campsite	238
	West coast	Mimizan Plage	Club Marina Campsite	236
	West coast	Moliets Plage	Saint Martin Campsite	232
Holland		Amsterdam	Amsterdam City Camping, aire	130
		Den Haag	Stad Den Haag, Camping	132
		Schiedam	Aire	138
Italy	Centre	Campobasso	Dominick Ferrante Aire	280
	Centre	Florence	Antica Etruria Campsite	326
	North	Lake Garda	Bella Italia Campsite	271
	North east	Fano	Aire	279
	North east	Venice	Serenissima Campsite	274
	North west	Finale Ligure	Il Villaggio di Giuele	334
	Sicily	Licata	Eurocamping Due Rocche	301
	Sicily	Near Taormina	Camping Lido Paradiso	293
	Sicily	Sant'Alessio	La Focetta Sicula	303
	South	Benevento	Sannio Camper Aire	282

Country	Region	Nearest Town/City	Campsite/Aire	Page
	South	Coligriano di Calabro	Thurium Campsite	304
	South east	Alberobello	Camping Bosco Selva	305
	South west	Rosarno	Villaggio Camping Mimosa	292
	West	Pompeii	Camp Site Zeus	283
	West	Pompeii	Spartacus Campsite	313
	West	Rome	Real Camping Village	316
	West	Salerno	Lido di Salerno Campsite	312
Portugal	Centre	Monchique	Camping Vale da Carrasquiera	207
	North west	Aveiro	Costa Nova do Prado Campsite	222
	North west	Lisbon	Lisboa Camping	217
	North west	Porto	Campsite Orbitur Angeiras	223
	South	Silves	Algarve Motorhome Park, aire	204
	South coast	Alvor	Camping Alvor	209
	South coast	Lagos	Turiscampo Yelloh Village Campsite	210
	South coast	Manta Rota	Aire	202
Spain	East coast	Benicàssim	Bonterra Park Campsite	151/343
	East coast	Benidorm	Camping Benidorm, Campsite	30
	East coast	Calpé	Camping La Merced, Campsite	31
	East coast	Dénia	Los Patos, Campsite	41
	East coast	El Campello	El Jardin Campsite	158

Country	Region	Nearest Town/City	Campsite/Aire	Page
	East coast	Peñiscola	Camping Vizmar	151
	East coast	Valencia	Valencia Camper Park, aire	47
	North coast	San Sebastian	Area de Bereo, aire	7
	North coast	San Sebastian	Camping Igelda	98
	North east	Figueres	Aire	339
	North east coast	Calonge	Camping Internacional De Calonge	356
	North east coast	Palamós	Empord Area, aire	149
	North east coast	Saint Pere Pescador, Roses	Aquarius Camping	71
	North east coast	Sitges near Barcelona	El Garrofer, Campsite	60/342
	North east coast	Tarragona	Las Palmeras, Campsite	50
	North west	León	Aire	224
	North west	Potes	Camping La Viorna	227
	South	Córdoba	El Brillante Campsite – now closed	172
	South	Granada	Fuente del Lobo, Campsite	21
	South	Granada	Reina Isabel Campsite	167
	South	Ronda	El Sur, Campsite	16
	South	Seville	Area de Autocaravanas de Sevilla, aire	9
	South coast	Casares	Area de Casares	14
	South coast	Estepona	Camping Parque Tropical, Campsite	20
	South coast	Nerja	Nerja Camping	180

Country	Region	Nearest Town/City	Campsite/Aire	Page
	South east coast	Almería	La Garrofa Campsite	179
	South east coast	Cartagena	Area Autocaravanas Cartagena, aire	26
	South west coast	Cádiz	Las Dunas Campsite	196
	West	Cáceres	Aire	7
Switzerland		Luzern	Campingplatz Gerbe Campsite	270
		Ticino	Acquarossa Campsite	271

Helpful Information

I thought a little information might be helpful for some of you, but feel free to ignore this section if you're a seasoned camper! We had considered hiring a van first to see how we got on, but the cost seemed to us to be prohibitive, especially when there are so many 'extras' that are needed. Obviously vans come in innumerable different sizes, models and styles and everyone has their own view as to which is best. A campervan is usually a van conversion/smaller van, whereas a motorhome is generally coach-built with more seating and sleeping space. Some motorhomes are the length of a 53-seater coach and even have extra panels at the sides to provide yet more space within! Clearly, there are benefits and drawbacks to each of these: the smaller vehicles are, of course, much easier to manoeuvre, especially on some of the back roads in Europe, but, obviously, have less internal space. The larger the vehicle, the more restrictions there are in terms of where you can go and where you can park (and how much fuel you use), but the facilities inside are more luxurious. Then, of course, there are caravans, the main benefit of which is that you have a car to travel in once you've parked up, but setting up with a caravan is more time-consuming.

In our opinion (such as it is), if you want to travel to one or two places and stay at each for a fairly long period, get a caravan; otherwise, a campervan or motorhome – small or large – makes more sense. We chose a Chausson 718 EB: a 7.5 metre-long, right-hand-drive, French-made van, with a fixed rear bed; the habitation door was on the driver's side, which, as most of our travelling was to be in Europe, was great. We loved it and it seemed to tick all of our boxes at that time.

Floor plan of the Chausson van

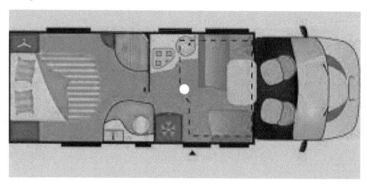

Another consideration is what you'd like to get from your travels: you may wish to spend just a couple of short breaks each year in the vehicle, or you may wish to travel constantly for several months or more; you may wish to be more independent (and thrifty?) and perhaps use aires (see below), or you may prefer the safety and facilities of large campsites; you may wish to keep away from tourist areas, or to see as many well-known tourist destinations as possible. Cost, of course, also has to be taken into account: not only of the original purchase, but of the cost of travel (including tolls that can be exorbitant on some of the roads in Europe) and site fees. Again, everyone, quite rightly, has their own opinion.

If you're unfamiliar with the camping world, let me very briefly explain a little about the difference between aires and campsites. A campsite is usually a fairly large site (although there are plenty of lovely, comparatively smaller, ones), normally comfortably accommodating many campervans/motorhomes, as well as caravans and often with chalets or static caravans for hire. A small site may just have essential facilities, but many sites have bars, cafés/restaurants, shop, children's play area, swimming pool, etc, as well as service points, and will cost, depending on the time of year, anything from around £14 to over £50 per night (in our experience on these trips) for two people. An aire (French for 'area'; they are known by different names in different countries), however, can vary considerably between a piece of rough ground in a village, or a car park in a city centre, for example – that may or may not have a service point and no, or few, electric hook-ups (EHUs in camping parlance) – to a huge tarmac area, well-lit and with numerous service points, electricity, Wi-Fi, shower and toilet blocks etc. An aire may accommodate anything from two or three motorhomes to 100 (or maybe more!), that may be squeezed in so tightly you can barely open the door, or with lots of space and lovely views. Many of the aires are free, or have a nominal charge, the expectation being that visitors using the aire will patronise shops and services and so help the local economy, but some aires do charge higher fees.

Electricity supplies (if they exist) on aires and campsites also vary considerably. In the UK, most sites provide at least 10A, but many in Europe may be as low as 3A. Bearing in mind that a hairdryer, for example, uses 6.5A, and a kettle 8.7A, you can imagine that you need to be careful to check the ampage provided before switching on too many appliances (and remember that your fridge may also be using the electricity). If you overload the system it will trip out and although on most sites it is possible to re-set it yourself, there are a few where you're required to ask a staff member to re-set it for you, which doesn't always go down too well!

There are also many clubs and societies that will give you off-season discounts if you stay at their sites. The main ones that we used are: The Caravan and Motorhome Club, The Camping and Caravanning Club and ACSI. There is also a scheme in France called France Passion (Spain has a similar scheme) that provides details of vineyards, farms, etc, on which camping for a limited time (usually one or two nights) is free; again with the hope that campers will purchase wine, cider or whatever the establishment produces. In addition, there is a huge choice of books providing information about various sites, aires, etc, a good source of which is www.vicarious-shop.com

List of Figures

Lightning Source UK Ltd.
Milton Keynes UK
UKHW050027141022
410407UK00011B/93